SOTHIS PRESS

Sothis Press aims to completely reimagine the public domain book with an emphasis on universal access to captivatingly designed print editions. We believe that technology will enable every single book ever published to be perpetually accessible in beautiful print form. Sothis is beauty in ubiquity.

www.sothis.press
1 Waterhouse Square, London, ECIN 2ST

London of the Future

Aston Webb

SOTHIS PRESS

ISBN 978-1-0365-2444-9

This edition is published by
Sothis Press © 2023. The company
is registered in England and Wales.
The Company Number is 14900389.

London society.

LONDON OF THE FUTURE

By THE LONDON SOCIETY

UNDER THE EDITORSHIP OF

SIR ASTON WEBB, K.C.V.O., C.B., P.R.A.

E. P. DUTTON AND COMPANY

681 FIFTH AVENUE, NEW YORK

FOREWORD

In accepting the invitation to write a few introductory words to the interesting volume which has been compiled by those who have the welfare of The London Society so greatly at heart, I should like, as President of the Society, to bear testimony to the thoroughness of the work which has been done since the spring of 1912, when the first meeting took place. Month by month since its inauguration the Society has gone steadily ahead. Even during those anxious times when our thoughts were always directed to the other side of the Channel and to lands far more distant, the work was carried on steadily by those who were unable to take an active part in the great events which were happening. Now that Peace is once more with us, even although there are many troubles and anxieties to be overcome, the Society is able greatly to extend its usefulness, and there are many subjects of great public interest which are under consideration by the Council.

This volume, the production of which has been a labour of love to the eminent men who have contributed the articles on such a variety of subjects, is now laid before the public with an earnest hope that it may be well received and that it may be the means of some of the suggestions contained in the book being carried out to the great advantage of London.

Plymouth

CONTENTS

LONDON OF THE FUTURE

ILLUSTRATIONS

LONDON OF THE FUTURE

LONDON OF THE FUTURE

PLANS AND DIAGRAMS

LONDON OF THE FUTURE

INTRODUCTION

SIR ASTON WEBB, K.C.V.O., C.B., P.R.A.

CHAPTER I

INTRODUCTION

WITH A SHORT ACCOUNT OF THE LONDON SOCIETY

THE production of this book has come about in more or less an accidental way, and is due almost entirely to the untiring exertions and enthusiasm of members of The London Society, who have given their time and special knowledge in individual chapters to the different problems with which London is faced, and have suggested their possible solution. The writers of each article may be considered as experts in their subject, and it is hoped that as a result some general idea may be gained by the reader of what, in the opinion of The London Society, are some of the many pressing needs of London. On the other hand, though it will be found that there is a general agreement amongst the authors of the various chapters, it must be understood that there has been no endeavour to make the views expressed therein those of The London Society as a whole, for it will be evident that it would be impossible, in the first place, to obtain such adherence, and, secondly, that even had this been possible it would have tended to dullness and monotony if the conclusions of each writer had been fixed beforehand.

As a result, each writer has had a free hand and is responsible for the opinions he has expressed; but on the other hand it is thought that there will not be found much with which the Society as a whole is not in accord.

There will no doubt be some readers who are unfamiliar with the objects, aim and work of The London Society, and it may therefore be useful briefly to state them here.

First and foremost, the object of The London Society is to interest Londoners in London, and by doing so secure their active co-operation in influencing public opinion so as to impress the authorities (including the Imperial Government) with the importance of taking a large view of London as a whole, at the same time recognizing that while it is obviously impossible to carry out all that is required at one and the same time, nevertheless, that they may see the importance of securing that what is done shall be part of one great scheme, and so give a unity and completeness to London improvements of the future which has been denied to her in the past.

This in itself may seem an ambitious programme for any independent society to undertake, especially a society with no executive power and very limited funds. But there is a power greater than office or money which can and does influence such high matters, viz. the power of public opinion; and difficult as it may be in so vast a city to create a public opinion, even though it is in the public's own interest, yet when once this has been done, all will become possible. The London Society is proud to have amongst its members many of the most influential Englishmen on such matters, and it is confident that they will in time make their influence felt.

There is another power which the Society possesses and which it believes in, and that is the power of suggestion—and here again the Society is fortunate in having amongst its members those who have so ably contributed to this book, who by position and education are fully qualified to make illuminating suggestions.

In support of this power of suggestion one may point to Gwynn's *Suggested Improvements in Westminster*, published in 1766, or to the sketch plans prepared for the improvements of Paris in the early part of the nineteenth century, to see the influence of these suggestions on the improvements in those cities, as subsequently carried out.

Another aim of The London Society is the jealous preservation of all that is old and beautiful in London as far as is possible. It appears necessary to emphasize this, as it seems by some to be thought that it is the desire and aim of the Society to reconstruct London, and to turn it into another Paris, sweeping away any parts of old London that may come in its way. Nothing could be further from the Society's object, or, it might be added, within its power, even if it wished to do so.

With these objects and aims in view, The London Society was

formally inaugurated on February 9, 1912, at a meeting held at the Galleries of the Royal Society of British Artists. Subsequently the Earl of Plymouth accepted the position of President of The London Society, a position he has since held to the great advantage of the Society. A little later, on January 13, 1913, a meeting was held at the Mansion House under the presidency of the Lord Mayor, when Earl Curzon of Kedleston delivered an address and aptly described the objects of the Society to be "to make London beautiful where it is not so already, and to keep it beautiful where it already is."

Lord Curzon further uttered two words of caution to the Society which have ever since been borne in mind, first, that while "the plans of the Society should not be lacking in imagination or idealism, they should, if they are to be effective, be business propositions," and, secondly, that the Society should avoid speculative, impracticable and impossible finance.

No society could have a better send-off than this inspiring address by Lord Curzon; it was subsequently printed in full by the Society, and also appeared as an article in the February number, 1913, of the *Nineteenth Century*.

The Society being thus formed and a Council and Executive Committee appointed, offices were secured at 27 Abingdon Street, Westminster, with Mr. Percy Lovell as Secretary, and later Miss Crum as Assistant Secretary, the annual subscription being fixed at one guinea, life membership being compounded for by a payment of ten guineas.

Sub-committees were appointed to consider the treatment of the south side of the Thames, the Charing Cross improvements and the important matter of London's arterial roads and transport.

In the year following the formation of the Society the membership quickly increased, and the Society rapidly got to work, taking part in the controversy regarding the entrance to the Mall from Charing Cross, which resulted in an agreement being come to between the Office of Works, the L.C.C. and the Westminster City Council, though unfortunately the outbreak of war has so far delayed its execution.

The Society also joined in a deputation to the Prime Minister, which was sympathetically received by Mr. Asquith, asking him to appoint an authority to lay down the main lines and improvements to the arterial roads of London that were so urgently required. The Prime Minister suggested that in the first instance a series of conferences should be held with the local authorities concerned and the lines of the roads agreed upon, and that this being done, the deputation should come to him again.

The suggested conferences were held, The London Society taking part in them, and the lines of roads were practically agreed upon when we again referred to the Prime Minister; but the war had broken out, the Prime Minister was unable to see us, and we were referred to the then President of the Local Government Board, who in his turn referred us to Sir George Gibb, but the war perforce absorbing all attention, nothing further was done at the time.

Since the conclusion of peace, however, a Ministry of Transport has been formed with a department dealing with roads, and apparently endowed with much the same powers as were suggested by the Society, and thus the aim of the Society in this important matter appears to have been gained.

A series of lectures and dinners were also commenced in this year 1913, at which papers were read and addresses delivered on matters affecting London, and were largely attended.

A quarterly *Journal* [1] was also started, when in August of the second year of the Society's existence the catastrophe of the Great War broke out; most of the Society's activities had perforce to be laid aside, and it says much for so young a stripling that The London Society survived the shock.

But while the regular activities of the Society had to be abandoned, the Committee met and decided that the most useful work they could be engaged upon during the war would be the production of a map of Greater London within a 15-mile radius, brought up to date, and showing on one complete map the great arterial roads and bypasses as drawn up by the Traffic Branch of the Board of Trade and agreed with the local authorities, together with certain additions proposed by the Society, including their proposals with regard to additional parks, parkways, open spaces and waterside reservations around the Metropolis. This scheme had the further advantage of giving employment in the preparation of the map to a certain number of architects and surveyors, brought to

[1] The issue of the Journal has now been increased to monthly.

distress through the war and unfit for military service, though unfortunately at only very moderate salaries.

The idea was at once taken up, and a special committee appointed, each member of which undertook the supervision of a particular area, and with the help of the Prince of Wales's Fund, the Artists' General Benevolent Institution, The Architects' Benevolent Society, and private donations, a sum of something like £1,000 was collected and expended entirely in salaries, the supervision being given voluntarily. The plan took some three years to execute, and was brought up to date with the assistance of the Ordnance Survey Authorities. Messrs. Stanford kindly undertook the publication of the plan, and it has been most excellently reproduced by them.

It was first exhibited at King's College by kind permission of the University authorities in April 1919, and again at the first dinner of the Society after the war, when the Earl of Crewe was the principal guest, and it is now permanently exhibited at the London Museum.

An activity which was thrust upon the Society during the war arose through the action of the South-Eastern Railway Company applying to Parliament in 1916 for powers to strengthen the existing railway bridge at Charing Cross. It was obvious that, if this were done, any proposal for removing the bridge would be rendered much more difficult. The London Society felt compelled to oppose the Bill before the House of Lords Committee, as was also done by the L.C.C., the Port of London, the Gas Companies, and the Royal Institute of British Architects, The London Society being empowered to appear before the Committee by special instructions from the House of Lords. In the event the Bill was passed by the House of Lords but thrown out in the Commons.

In the following year the Bill was again introduced by the South-Eastern Railway Company, this time in the Commons, who reversed their previous decision and passed the Bill. The House of Lords again referred it to a Select Committee, when The London Society and the R.I.B.A. were forsaken by their previous companions, and appeared before the Lords Committee alone, with Mr. Honoratus Lloyd, K.C., as their counsel. The Committee finally passed the Bill, but added some very important conditions, principal among them being one debarring the Company from doing any work to the bridge above high-water level for a space of three years, in order to give the authorities concerned time to prepare a scheme, and in addition declining to sanction any enlargement of the station without a further application to Parliament; and since that time nothing has been done by the Company at Charing Cross.

At the moment the Society is seeking an opportunity to lay the matter before the Prime Minister, with a view to the Government's support for the removal of the present station to the southern side, the construction of a fine road bridge in place of the existing unsightly railway bridge, and the erection of a national memorial on the site of the present station. In the meantime the Society is considering the details of this scheme, together with further improvements in the centre of London, which could not be shown sufficiently in detail on the development plan already described, but which it is proposed to publish later as "the heart of London development plan."

It has been necessary to go somewhat into detail regarding the work done by the Society, both in connection with the development plan and the Charing Cross bridge removal, as, in spite of all the publicity that has been given to both these matters, the public seem still to know little of what The London Society has been doing.

During the war the membership of the Society naturally suffered, though new and influential members kept coming in, with the result that at the end of 1918 the subscription list stood at a slightly higher level than at the end of 1913, while at the end of 1919 it was nearly half as much again, and has since largely increased—a very encouraging result.

Having introduced The London Society, the parent of this volume, a short introduction to the various proposals contained in the articles may be of use.

It will be seen that the articles deal with both the æsthetic and the practical side of London's requirements of the future; in many cases both sides are treated in the same chapter.

Mr. Raffles Davison has written a paper on *The Opportunities of London* full of suggestions, cheery hopefulness, and much practical wisdom. Above all, he urges Londoners to persevere in well-doing, to continue their interest in spite of delay and disappointment, remembering that such improvements as are proposed cannot be achieved in a lifetime, but while one generation may sow it will probably fall to another to reap. Mr. Davison rapidly reviews the opportunities of London, which unfortunately largely consist in removing the eyesores already perpetrated by the railway companies, such as their bridges across the river and roads, their stations and sidings.

The Dean of St. Paul's has lately suggested the blowing up of Charing Cross Bridge as our National War Memorial. It would be a good beginning. But we must do more than that. We must construct as well as destroy; and Mr. Davison, while suggesting what should be done, is at the same time not unmindful of the difficulties to be faced and grappled with. He deals with the approaches of London Bridge and the Southwark Cathedral—an immensely important subject in itself—and the treatment of the river's Surrey side. These are not ideal dreams, but practical questions which will have to be settled sooner or later and should be seriously considered now.

The London Museum has hardly received the recognition it deserves for the work it is doing for London, but it might perhaps do still more by looking forward as well as back. The Road Plan of The London Society is already on its walls, and already some of the roads are being carried out. But how attractive a large model would be of the centre of London with its opportunities of improvement clearly shown. It should be on a large scale, with a gallery round from which one could look down on it and see the opportunities of London realized, the river embanked on both sides, its new bridges and approaches, railway tracks converted into highways, sites for great new buildings provided, etc. The London Society would no doubt assist in the preparation of the model and its execution, while others would help with their pockets.

But to return to Mr. Davison's essay. He suggests once more the creation of a responsible controlling and directing power in touch with the needs of London and the public authorities who have to supply them, and there can be little doubt this is required. In the meantime, it is for The London Society (and any others who will help), by suggestions explained by maps and books and illustrations at dinners and lectures to "keep the mind aglow," feeling sure there is, as Mr. Davison says, deep down in our national character something that will respond to the realization of the great opportunities of London. Mr. Raffles Davison has himself done much work at The London Society to forward this realization.

In the chapter on *Roads, Streets and Traffic of London*, by Colonel Hellard, the war has already advanced matters more rapidly than could have been anticipated when the Society was engaged on the development of the London plan. A Ministry of Transport has been created, and great things are expected and hoped from it. It was feared in the first instance that the interests of the railways might unduly overshadow the interests of the roads, but recent events have so strikingly shown the importance of good road communication that it seems hardly possible that this vital means of transport should in the future be overlooked.

Colonel Hellard, the author of this chapter on roads, was Superintendent of the Traffic Branch of the Board of Trade, and himself prepared the scheme for the arterial roads which was submitted to the various local authorities and included, with certain minor alterations and additions, in the Society's development plan.

A road development plan for London sinks into insignificance by the side of a road development plan for the whole of the United Kingdom, yet this is what is required, and required immediately. No doubt every city and town of the country would willingly assist by preparing a road plan of its district, and in doing so create an interest locally in the requirements; for schemes prepared solely by a large official staff in London cannot possibly meet local needs and interests, and must inevitably leave the public in ignorance of what is proposed, and therefore without interest in the subject. The urgency of this matter of roads is greatly increased through the needs of the great housing schemes now being hurried forward throughout the country. The sites of large villages, in some cases almost towns, are being rapidly selected with what must be very imperfect information as to the probable future means of access and transport to the adjoining towns, where the demand for labour will be greatest, and so the new roads will have to follow the sites of the houses and not the houses the roads, which should be in convenient proximity to the houses.

How much of the scheme when settled will be carried out by the Government from Imperial funds and how much by local authorities has yet to be seen, but it is hoped that the main arterial roads, at any rate, may be taken over by the Imperial Government and maintained by them, and thus for the first time since the Romans our main roads will be under one control and maintained by one central authority.

The Society may congratulate itself that for the last seven years it has never ceased to do what it could by deputations, lectures and plans to bring this pressing matter of main roads before the Government, and may fairly feel a sense of satisfaction that the Government has now taken a step which, if rightly used, should remove a great reproach.

Local authorities must also be awakened to the fact that in addition to the welfare of their own ratepayers, which is naturally their first and great concern, the welfare of the general good must also be considered by them, and that they may most properly be asked to consent to the construction of main routes through their area, though there may be no apparent or immediate benefit to their particular city or borough; for it may be taken for granted that what tends to the prosperity of the country generally tends also to the prosperity of the individual cities and boroughs. The careful reader of Colonel Hellard's paper will see the lamentable mistakes that have been made in connection with our roads, even during the last hundred years, often on the mistaken conclusion that the railways would supplant the roads, whereas at the end of that time it is found that the roads, with the improved modes of transport, are for suburban and local traffic the more important of the two.

This naturally brings us to railways, and the chapter by Mr. H. J. Leaning on the subject. Mr. Leaning has for years given attention to this subject, and, with the technical assistance of acknowledged railway experts, has prepared a very thorough survey of the whole position; and here again the war has added urgency and brought about a complete change in the problem, which will have to be taken up on a vast scale by the Ministry of Transport, and the Society hopes Mr. Leaning's suggestions for London may be of use.

The railways cry out for a great scheme of unification and intercommunication, for they, like the roads, have grown up without a plan and without any large prevision of outlook, but rather, in the words of the Traffic Commission, in the individual interests of the competing companies.

We English are a liberty-loving people and presumably, therefore, object to schemes, but we have suffered in almost every department of our public life through this idiosyncrasy.

In dealing with railways The London Society must regretfully record how little they have done for the beauty of London, or indeed of any cities or towns through which they pass. Indeed, it is rather a matter of joke with them that their bridges, their stations and their sidings are useful but not ornamental. London has suffered almost without a murmur untold indignities in this respect, and our splendid river has been spanned by structures of indescribable ugliness.

Ruskin raised his voice against the defilement by railways of the country-side, but it must be admitted that nature has come to the rescue of the companies in the country and clothed their railway banks and cuttings with beauty and a flora and entomology all their own; while the long, level tracks and the sweeping curves form grateful and graceful features in an undulating landscape.

While nature has thus covered up to a great extent the sins of the companies in the country, it is possible science may come to the rescue in the towns and show the railways how they may, like the doctors, bury their mistakes by placing their lines and stations underground, and it is hoped that the Transport Ministry may in due course see to this being done.

It is electric traction that has made the mere mention of this possible, and though electrification is rapidly being applied to suburban traffic, yet there are no doubt difficulties at present with the main line trains; still, there can be little doubt that these will in due course be overcome, and we shall see all lines disappear into the earth at a radius of some 15 miles from Charing Cross, and the stations and bridges go with them, while the old railway tracks may become highways; though this is anticipating, and perhaps outrunning Lord Curzon's caution.

The question of the reduction of the London termini will be found fully dealt with by Mr. Leaning, together with the suggested abolition of central termini for suburban traffic and the elimination of passengers' luggage.

The most difficult of all problems, that of goods, has lately been grappled with, and the proposal of a central clearing station for goods has been adversely reported upon by a committee especially appointed to consider it; but for parcels and personal luggage up to 1 cwt. it is suggested that the present pneumatic tube system might

THE PROBLEM OF CENTRAL LONDON VIEWED FROM THE AIR.

THE SMOKE PROBLEM.

(Two problems that must be solved in the future.)

To face p 24.

be extended and utilized. The whole chapter will be found full of research, suggestion and application.

During the war a third means of transport was developed by leaps and bounds, viz. *Aviation*, and the paper by Lord Montagu, an acknowledged authority, brings the matter up to date, though no one can say what developments still await it. At present one of the difficulties for London is the provision of an adequate and centrally situated aerodrome, some forty or fifty acres in extent, which we are told is required. The provision of this will indeed tax the ingenuity of those responsible for the amenities and beauty of London, and one must hope in the meantime, by invention and skill, the requirements may be reduced to smaller dimension; but, however this may be, there can be no doubt commercial aviation has come to stay, and whatever its subsequent requirements, they will have to be met. Lord Montagu predicts a great development in the transport of mails to different places by aircraft. If so, a certain relief would be automatically given to roads and rails, and any considerable increase for passenger and commercial purposes should give a corresponding relief to London's roads and streets.

In connection with roads and railways, we come to *The Bridges of London*, ably and scholastically treated by Sir Reginald Blomfield. He points out that four of these bridges—London, Waterloo, Westminster and Vauxhall—are of good design, while one—Waterloo Bridge—is very good. The remaining bridges are not worthy to cross the Thames. Several of them are already insufficient to take the traffic and will have to be replaced, let us hope, with worthier structures, and if the railways can be put under the water and the south side embanked, there will still be some hope for the Thames.

Sir Reginald Blomfield does not even mention the iron railway bridges across the Thames, of which there are four. All of them carry the South-Eastern and Chatham Railway across the river, and one carries the London, Brighton and South Coast Railway in addition. None are worthy to remain a moment longer than absolutely necessary, while Charing Cross Bridge is not worthy to remain at all: firstly, it is only just able to carry its present restricted traffic and will soon become unable to do that; secondly, it is extremely unsightly; and thirdly, it takes the place of a road bridge which is urgently needed, and it is perhaps this last point that will appeal most to the public.

The distance between Westminster and Waterloo Bridges is 1,200 yards on the north side and 820 yards on the south, a greater distance on the northern bank than exists between any other of the Metropolitan bridges, and nearly double those of Paris. Thousands arriving at Waterloo Station and wishing to drive to the neighbourhood of Charing Cross have to go round either by Westminster or Waterloo Bridges daily, and the same with those wishing to reach Waterloo from Charing Cross, while the poor little foot-bridge at Charing Cross is greatly congested at times, and Waterloo Bridge is already so overcrowded that it will have to be widened or rebuilt unless some relief can be afforded by a road bridge at Charing Cross. The position and level of the bridge is a matter still under discussion, but the first point is to get the authorities to take the matter up seriously and make a bridge at Charing Cross as worthy a memorial of the Great War at the beginning of this century as Waterloo Bridge is a worthy memorial of the great war at the beginning of the last century.

A great " Place " there should be at either end, with memorials to those who have fallen. The miserable and inadequate Charing Cross Station would, of course, go, and one be erected on the other side, if required, which is doubtful. The measures taken by the Society to prevent any unnecessary difficulties being placed in the way of the execution of this great scheme have already been referred to in a previous part of this Introduction, but time is slipping away and will not recur.

Another chapter that deals with a subject closely affecting Charing Cross and the traffic of London is that on *The Channel Tunnel*, by Sir Arthur Fell, one of the foremost supporters of the scheme. This is another subject the war has brought into prominence, and is believed by many to be nearing a decision, though the Cabinet still hesitates between two opinions. Sir Arthur Fell points out that this tunnel, if constructed, is going greatly to affect London, and " to hold out possibilities of a new and great future for London." It would, of course, at once render the present Charing Cross Bridge and Station quite impossible, and the author of this chapter, it will be seen, contemplates a great Empire Station over the water on the Surrey side. His proposals fit in entirely with the views so long urged and expressed by The London Society with regard to the improvements at Charing Cross, so that, should the experts decide that the making of the tunnel would in no way jeopardize our national safety, we must all hope that Sir Arthur Fell's aspirations may be fulfilled, and that at the same time a great Metropolitan improvement, long advocated by The London Society, may be carried out.

Yet another chapter directly affecting the Thames and London traffic is contributed by Mr. Paul Waterhouse, under the title ***The Surrey Side.***

Comparisons are often made, are indeed made by Sir Arthur Fell in his chapter, between the condition of the south side of the Seine in Paris and the south side of the Thames in London: the former prosperous and beautiful, possessing some of the finest public buildings in Paris, the latter derelict and almost deserted, yet through it is the most direct route from Westminster to London Bridge. One reason, no doubt, for this is that while the Seine is a comparatively narrow river that seems to connect the one side with the other, the Thames is of such a noble width that it seems rather to separate them.

Great things are expected from the Council's excellent example of placing the new County Hall on that side, and it is rumoured that the Government will some time follow suit with some of their buildings. There is one thing we must regret in connection with the County Hall, and that is that the Embankment roadway could not have been kept open to the public as it is in front of St. Thomas's Hospital. The mere erection of public buildings on the south side is not enough. What is wanted, and has long been wanted, as pointed out by Mr. Waterhouse, is a riverside roadway and embankment similar to that provided on the north side, and the cost of which would probably be largely met by the value of the reclaimed land. Whether this be so or not, it is an improvement long delayed and long overdue, and one to which the L.C.C. should forthwith set their hand. What the defunct Board of Works carried out with so much magnificence should surely not be impossible for the L.C.C. on a much restricted length.

Mr. Paul Waterhouse, as the chairman of the Committee of The London Society, which has this particular question in hand, has given much time and study to it, and besides the Embankment, considers in his chapter the much-debated question of a Temple or St. Paul's Bridge, together with the traffic problem on the Surrey side, which up to the present, with its singular difficulties and opportunities, has been left almost entirely to chance. But Mr. Waterhouse points out a better way, suggesting a position for the new station with easy communication with the City and the East End, and a lay-out of streets which he believes would " plant hope and the chance of prosperity in the very heart of a derelict region which has never yet enjoyed the opportunities which its close proximity to London proper deserves." But Mr. Waterhouse must be left to tell his own story, though he modestly says he anticipates his views will be at variance with the views of many in The London Society. Even if they are, Mr. Waterhouse's views are always well considered and worthy of every consideration, and lead us to think.

The chapter by Professor Adshead, Professor of Town Planning at the London University, deals with *Central London*, perhaps the most difficult because it is the most costly of all areas in which to carry out improvements, and yet this is the area in which improvements are most urgently required.

The congestion is greatest in the City and in the dock area, but all the main arteries through Central London require either widening or relief roads. This congestion, as Professor Adshead points out, has been brought about not only by the increase of population, but also by the change of habits of the population. As the means of transport increases, the centre is required less and less for residential purposes and more and more for business and pleasure. The traffic from the Docks increases, and has long outstripped all existing accommodation. The war has left us with a legacy of overcrowding in almost every department of town life, housing, railways, buses and tubes, streets, docks and roads ; and Professor Adshead has much to say and many suggestions to make to which the City and Municipal Authorities will do well to take heed.

The Port of London and its Future is dealt with by the Chairman of the Port of London Authority, Viscount Devonport, than whom no one is so well able to speak of the progress and future of this vital spot of the Empire's prosperity, for Lord Devonport has been at the head of affairs of the Port of London Authority ever since its formation, except for a short time during the war, when he patriotically undertook the Food Control.

The Authority has only been formed some ten years, but Lord Devonport is already able to point to new dock construction, new cold storage accommodation, fine office accommodation and the commencement of a great housing scheme. As time goes on, The London Society hopes that the Authority will take even a wider view, and insist on the improvement of approaches and the increase of the present inadequate warehouse accommodation in the neighbourhood to which Professor Adshead refers; and in the meantime The London Society can congratulate London on having a public Authority which is doing a great work in a part of London little known and little visited, yet this centre is vital not only to the welfare of London but to the whole of the Empire, for to this centre the produce of the Empire mainly flows.

The dock area is included in what is generally termed the *East End*, and on this subject The London Society has again been specially fortunate in having a chapter from the pen of the Right Reverend H. L. Paget, D.D., for ten years Bishop of Stepney and now Bishop of Chester. Dr. Paget throws a fascination and romance over this neighbourhood that will delight no less than perhaps surprise many of our readers, and shows us how the loss of the great weaving industry has brought desolation, and an invasion of aliens has brought a change over a whole district which should, as the Bishop says, have been the last place in the whole world to have been allowed to become monotonous and down at heel.

When the Bishop comes to the future of London, he almost regretfully says that the reconstruction of this part is long overdue, and hopes when it comes it will recognize the suggestions and indications that come from the character and tradition of the place itself.

But the Bishop goes further and explains with great detail and charm the lines on which this reconstruction should proceed and the special requirements that have to be met. And then, in Part III, he describes the small trades still carried on there, and their thankless and ungrateful tasks, although, he says, they are amongst the most quick-witted people in the world, and pleads for a very gradual and careful reconstruction, with the presence of a noble river always in view.

And then, in Part IV, the Bishop touches on the all-important and difficult question of the alien races, who in this part of London are rapidly outnumbering and replacing our own.

A more sympathetic and suggestive paper on East London cannot be imagined, and The London Society must always be grateful to Dr. Paget for the time and thought he has given to it.

Mr. Raymond Unwin, out of his great experience, gives us a fascinating chapter on the momentous and stupendous subject of *The Development of London*, a subject that requires the wide outlook of the statesman and the technical knowledge of the architect and the engineer. And Mr. Unwin's first requirement is for a scheme, a broad scheme, capable of endless adjustment in detail, like Mr. Ebenezer Howard's plan for a garden city, which he has happily lived to see carried out.

But who is to prepare this scheme? Mr. Unwin suggests an authority appointed for the purpose. If so, it should consist of a few of the wisest heads and with the widest vision possible. It need not be worked out in great detail, but must contain an idea capable of being translated into a practical scheme. Mr. Unwin throws out many illuminating suggestions. Like Mr. Niven, he pleads for a green belt at least a mile wide round London, and garden cities as separate units outside it. He suggests this, apart from the health point of view, as a means of putting a stop to the continuous growth of an already overgrown and unwieldy city. He would have certain areas allocated for residences, others for shopping areas, factories and so on. He suggests means should be taken to ensure the easy transit of workers to and from their work, and points out that with the present congestion people who have left the City to live find it difficult to get to the City to work. As authors of other chapters have suggested, he would have the railways through London electrified and placed underground, and such places as Covent Garden, with its huge road transport, removed elsewhere, where all the necessary facilities can be provided.

Mr. Unwin then goes into the interesting possibility of allotting land for divers purposes if the land around the City were in one ownership, as at Letchworth, and its effect upon its value, and on this subject Mr. Unwin must be left to tell his own story. It has been thought out with much thoroughness, and striking examples are given, and he sums up with the conclusion that wise town-planning regulations, while they will alter the apportionment of land values, will cause more increase than reduction.

Mr. Davidge, in his interesting and exhaustive chapter on *The*

Housing of London, begins with the axiom that good travelling is the key to good housing, and once again urges the necessity for the proper placing of community centres by some central guiding authority and scheme or plan.

Interesting diagrams are given, showing density of population not only in London itself, but also in the fringes, and he then proceeds to investigate the causes of recent development—the leasehold system, the lack of transit, and the lack of co-ordination by municipal authorities. The question of cottage and flat is considered, and by diagram it is shown that the incidence of local rates is highest where people are poorest, and the remedy suggested is the broadening of the rating area. The necessity of an improved standard of housing is insisted upon—and not only in the houses themselves but in the playgrounds and open spaces around them—and finally the consideration of the essentials of the home brings a very interesting chapter to a close.

No one could be better fitted to deal with the subject of *The Government of London* than Mr. W. E. Riley, late architect to the L.C.C. and author of this chapter.

Mr. Riley begins by an exhaustive description of the present government of London, the number of the authorities, their various functions and the mode of their election, and, in considering how far the present organization of such an immense system can be improved, points out that, unlike the representatives at St. Stephen's, their services are given free, although a high standard of general knowledge is obviously required, and that fully three years is necessary to get even an elementary knowledge of the important public work required.

If London is extended to Greater London, Mr. Riley shares the view that seems to be very rapidly gaining ground, that in the end the detail must be delegated to local authorities, with a great co-ordinating central body with parliamentary duties, and looked upon as a career of itself and not merely as a stepping-stone to St. Stephen's.

This chapter will give some idea of the enormous, complicated and responsible duties at present thrown upon the authorities charged with the government of London, duties made none the lighter by the number of authorities and the haphazard and disjointed way in which they have from time to time been set up.

Mr. Niven deals eloquently with *The Parks and Open Spaces of London* and the value they are to the health and well-being of a crowded city like London. He points out that though London is at first sight well provided with open spaces, they are ill distributed, and urges the importance of an uninterrupted space right round London, which he thinks might even yet be obtained, together with a civic park for each borough. This may not be obtainable, and a glance at the Society's development plan shows how much is still possible, and in the unbuilt areas round London, where land can still be had at almost agricultural values, it behoves the local authorities to see to it while there is yet time. Mr. Niven has many suggestions for the improvement of our parks and open spaces and the construction of boulevards and promenades, which in themselves would form breathing spaces and opportunities for exercise and recreation. He pleads for an extended use of the squares now closed and deserted, and we all know how Leicester Square and Lincoln's Inn Fields—to quote two very different examples—have been opened with nothing but good to all concerned. Further, Mr. Niven urges an extended use of roof gardens when the Smoke Abatement Society has done its work.

Another great open space he deals with is the Thames, with its tributary streams, and lastly the canals, which are now nearly derelict, though commissions have sat and committees have reported on them as a very useful subsidiary branch of transport, but so far nothing has been done.

Lord Meath's name in connection with open spaces and the best interests of London is too well known to need any introduction. He is also an active spirit in the Empire movement, and in the chapter on *London as the Heart of the Empire* he urges that in the changed conditions produced by the war London should become not only the capital of England but the capital of the Empire. He would have resident representatives of the Dominions co-opted on to the governing bodies of the City Corporation and the London County Council, so that all parts of the British Empire may feel they have a governing interest in their great Empire. Lord Meath therefore advises that no effort should be spared to make London worthy of its larger significance. He advocates the making of a continuous avenue uniting all the parks and gardens round London and the conversion of the Euston Road into a ring, as at Vienna and Cologne.

WATERMEADS, MITCHAM.

(These views are part of the Riverside Reservations shown on the Development Plan prepared by The London Society.)

To face p. 32

He further proceeds to point out that while there are numberless streets that can be removed without loss, care must be taken to preserve all those interesting historic and homely features we love and which give to London its greatest attraction. Lord Meath compares the proportion of open space per acre to the population in London, Paris and Berlin, to the great advantage of London, and advocates still further extensions of open spaces such as we should expect from one who, as Chairman of the Metropolitan Public Gardens Association, has done so much pioneer work in increasing the public pleasure grounds of London.

It is mainly owing to the late Sir William Richmond that any improvement in the condition of the London atmosphere is due. Sir William refers in his chapter on *The Smoke Plague of London* to the various efforts made from time to time by the Government and Local Authorities to abate the nuisance with little result. Even the London County Council, who succeeded in 1891 in applying the smoke abatement provisions of the Public Health Act, 1875, to the Metropolis, failed to make these provisions effective, and in these circumstances Sir William Richmond formed in 1899 the Coal Smoke Abatement Society as an independent body determined to see that any existing laws there were should be obeyed.

Sir William gives an interesting account of the Society's activities and efforts, which have certainly resulted in a considerable improvement in the air, and a debt of gratitude is due to him and his Society for these efforts. In 1914 the Local Government Board appointed a Departmental Committee on Smoke Abatement, on which the writer of these notes sat for a short time ; but its proceedings were interrupted by the war, and it has only lately resumed its sittings under Lord Newton's chairmanship. There can be no doubt that the removal of the hideous veil of dirt and grime, which lowers our vitality, obscures all our buildings and monuments, and very often the City itself, is one of the first necessities for the beautification of London. During the coal strike in the spring of this year (1921) it was noticeable that the London atmosphere was appreciably cleared, and in this direction the solution of the problem may be near at hand, for we are told that the increased use of oil, electricity and gas will do much to abolish the smoke plague of London.

Sir William Richmond is a great loss, and a successor is sorely needed to continue the crusade. Who will volunteer ?

LONDON OF THE FUTURE

This series of short chapters or essays is appropriately concluded by a chapter by Lord Crewe, than whom no one has taken a keener or more beneficial interest in the welfare of London and Londoners and in the preservation and increase of its amenities. Lord Crewe points out the value to London of its past history, not only in its buildings but also in the memories of the great men who in succeeding generations have lived in it. Some of them he mentions in a few graceful touches, and concludes with the same moral as Lord Curzon's at the first meeting of The London Society, that in designing great London improvements we ought to revere, and so far as is possible conserve, what is left of London of the past.

It only remains to thank once more, on behalf of The London Society, all who have contributed to this book, and to express the hope that it may have some influence in solving the many very pressing problems with which the future of London is surrounded.

ASTON WEBB,
Chairman of Council.

March 1921.

THE OPPORTUNITIES OF LONDON

T. RAFFLES DAVISON, Hon. A.R.I.B.A.

CHAPTER II

THE OPPORTUNITIES OF LONDON

THE chief object of this book on London is, I assume, to quicken the thought and stir the imagination of its citizens and all those who take a genuine interest in the well-being and aspect of the capital of the Empire. So far as the things suggested are desirable and possible, they will answer their purpose if they help in any material way towards the forethought and enterprise which are imperatively demanded in the continuous evolution of a great city. The problem is one compounded of many issues, for whilst the economic results are of vast importance, so also are the ideals of beauty and dignity which are necessary to be kept before us. One of the most urgent and difficult aspects of the problem, too, lies in the continual changes and developments which are bound to accompany the progress of invention and enterprise. The gradual but certain alterations in modes of transport alone, forced into great significance by recent events, involve constant thought and preparation, and the time must surely come when certain limits will have to be fixed against the terrible congestion which threatens the well-being and life of modern cities. Having said this much, it may perhaps be easier to enlist the sympathies of our readers: unless our own imagination can be fully roused as to the possibilities which lie ahead of us, we shall never be able to deal adequately with the problem of London.

A consideration of the opportunities for the improvement and development of London leads to the conclusion that the point of view from which they may be regarded must be very fully taken into account. It is obvious that many things which might be done to dignify and beautify would be impracticable in view of the needful balance to be drawn between considerations of art and utility.

It is desirable that proper economical and practical needs should have weight as well as the great importance of giving expression to the ideals of beauty and dignity which are essential to the vast congregation of buildings, squares, parks and streets which indicate the wants of a great population. The discussion which has been evoked by the proposition for a new road bridge at Charing Cross shows how complicated and varied are the influences for and against city development. In the very forefront of all schemes for the improvement of the Thames environment on the north and south sides comes the railway question. Once remove the railway difficulties and the task of improvement is lightened to an enormous degree. The blemishes over our fine river and about its banks are owing largely to what were once considered necessities, but should now be regarded as difficulties to be overcome. Once imagine Charing Cross, Cannon Street and St. Paul's Stations removed, alluring chances of great improvements present themselves, as a set-off against which it might be claimed that almost insuperable obstacles are presented. The point of view from which city improvements can be regarded varies so greatly that it is almost impossible to foresee the extent and character of the opposition which will be offered. We can understand much of it, such as the financial difficulties, and the questions of trade, transport and private interests, but the visionary or the idealist (who is said to be the only really practical person in the world) has to insist that the practical issues involved must also be considered as well as those visions of beautification which form the crown and flower of all things.

It is in the hope of inspiring to some extent the ambitions of London citizens for a finer and more beautiful city that certain improvements are suggested; if they are worth paying the price of cost and effort, they will surely be carried through, but if not, they may at least suggest something which may be as good, or better. It is one of the penalties attending all enthusiastic efforts for any given ideals that those who persist in them may be set down as dogmatic or unreasonable.

Briefly put, the great need of the time is for adequately designed schemes for better transport facilities—fine roads, definite plans for city beautification, and control as to the location of certain classes of buildings. Beyond this we need a paramount authori-

A GREAT OPPORTUNITY : CHARING CROSS BRIDGE.

To face p. 88.

tative body, with full powers for the enforcement of the designed improvements.

The splendid opportunities which the future holds for London can never be fully realized without the express wish and demand of its citizens. It is impossible to believe that the inertia which exists can be overcome by the already overworked official staffs. To realize these opportunities we must have a large vision, a great ideal, and a strong determination for the best.

There is so much more in the right development of London than the making of fine streets and buildings that the heart of the problem is only reached by studying the economic side of it. If we do not put the right kind of buildings and markets in the right places, we not only spoil the general amenity but we increase the difficulties of transport. The best places for factories, for warehouses, for wholesale trade establishments, for new or extended Government Departments, for hospitals, schools, churches, etc., are not now to be considered in the light of former days, when anything was allowed to be put anywhere. Now that great central railway stations and hospitals are out of favour, the planning of towns is largely affected. We are thus driven to an order of procedure in dealing with city planning something like the following:

1. The first thing to be settled is the most desirable locality for every different class of building, and the aim will be to approximate as nearly as may be to the ideal.
2. The next thing is to devise the best possible means of transport to and from the various parts of a city so that the largest numbers may be best conveyed to their objectives.
3. The final aim will be how to effect the above objects in the most practical, convenient and beautiful way.

It is apparent enough that you cannot hope to bring an old city up to the highest standard of requirements under the above heads, but after all London has to exist, and carry on its life as a great modern city. The many difficulties which are raised by an old-established order of things in the pathway of improvement are not at first apparent, but the creation of vested interests is alone a serious matter, and raises financial difficulties which are often insuperable. On the other hand, judiciously planned improvements produce new values of a very important kind. This may be fully illustrated by considering what would happen if a new Charing Cross Bridge was built, starting from a little above the present level of the Embankment. The increased value of such buildings as the National Liberal Club, the Hôtel Metropole and Hôtel Cecil, with an outlook over a continuous line of Embankment Gardens instead of the dismal block caused by the present bridge and station, would surely be very considerable. Besides this, all the ground now covered by the present road access to Charing Cross Station would become an asset of exceptional value. The new street from the Embankment up to the Strand would contain some of the finest business sites in the West End, whilst the whole effect of spaciousness and dignity about Charing Cross would be worthy of a great civic centre.

We have only to imagine aboveground railways into London replaced by an underground service to see at once how some of the worst eyesores in London would disappear and more valuable areas of building land be set free. The bridges crossing the roadways at London Bridge, those crossing the lower end of Queen Victoria Street and Ludgate Hill, and the most absurd one of all at Charing Cross would go, and tunnel-like coverings over fine roadways would be things of the past, whilst cheerful spaces and fine road vistas would be opened up. Can we doubt that this is only a question of time?

During many discussions in the last seven or eight years it has been made increasingly clear that the only way to grapple effectively with the problem is to approach it from various standpoints and concentrate the attention of committees on different areas. Amongst the divisions of the whole was the development of the possibilities of improvement for the river area, with more especial reference to the south side of the Thames, and a South Side Committee was formed to deal with it. This South Side Committee of The London Society sat at frequent intervals, commencing its work with the urgently needed improvement of traffic over the river at Charing Cross. It was soon made clear that though it was very desirable to have a new bridge at Charing Cross and a fine new southern embankment, the whole subject of the London railway service loomed largely in the foreground of all satisfactory developments. It was felt that whilst the present arrangement of railway service continued, no fully satisfactory treatment of the river and its adjacent area could possibly be obtained. The awkward arrangement and crossing of railways at London Bridge, the in-and-out service to Cannon Street and the linking up of northern and southern services appeared to be impossible of acceptance as continuing factors for the future. This, of course, involves a consideration of the financial interests of the various companies and the efficient service for public needs, and unless these important matters can be satisfactorily solved it is futile to attempt laying down schemes of fine boulevards, new buildings and adequate bridges. It would have been an education for anyone interested in the future of London to have joined in the considerations which came before this South Side Committee. It was some time before the many points which were involved in the matter came to be realized in their full importance, and it was felt that the relative values would never be satisfactorily settled without the provision of some controlling authority, which should deal with the problem as a whole and impartially with the varying and possibly conflicting interests.

It would be a delightful task to set forth an ideal treatment for the banks and environment of the fine river which divides London into north and south areas, and as it is the ideal which should govern and inspire the practical, it would have been well if this had been attempted, so that the public might be able to judge how fine it could be, and then to demand as near an approach to the ideal as is practicable. The carrying out of the Channel Tunnel, which seems nearer now than ever before, largely affects the matter, and adds both to the ultimate possibilities of great design and the difficulties of solution.

If we briefly name our opportunities, it is enough to show how great they are. To begin with London Bridge, it is obvious that the approaches both on the north and south side present visions to the idealist of surpassing value, where we find horrible combinations of railway bridges crossing the roadways and mean and awkwardly placed stations. Contrast these with the splendid possibilities of opening up Southwark Cathedral to the river front and the creation of a noble approach to the City which would be possible at the north end of London Bridge. Suppose that the Fishmongers' Hall and the new buildings to be erected on the balancing site on the east side could be finished in harmony with a worthy street leading up to a fine civic centre, where now the poor statue of King William stands in front of a haphazard rounded corner of ordinary commercial buildings. These are points which appeal most strongly to the idealist.

Then if we consider the possibility of doing away with the ugly Cannon Street Station and its railway bridge, how fine would be the opening up of the view, and what increase to the value of the adjoining property! Further west we have the Southwark Bridge being improved, and a projected scheme for a St. Paul's Bridge to end on the south side—only some 300 feet apart from the other! At Blackfriars the road bridge is spoilt by the hideous South-Eastern and Chatham railway bridge close alongside it, and then at Charing Cross we have the eyesore of Charing Cross railway bridge, breaking into a stretch of one of the finest riverside gardens in the world, which should surely have a clear unbroken prospect from Waterloo to Westminster. In view of the possibilities, this is perhaps the most appalling mischance along the whole river.

Those who desire a new road bridge at Charing Cross and the removal of the station to the other side of the river appear to be in a great majority, but to some of these the importance of a cross-river road starting from the level of the Strand is a pre-eminent factor, while to others the direct access from the Embankment to the new bridge and the continuity of the gardens from Waterloo to Westminster are of far greater importance. This is not the place to discuss rival schemes, but if the imagination of the public can be stirred by the great possibilities which lie before us, it may well be left to further detailed discussion to arrive at the best result. At all events, it is claimed that a low-level bridge is a possibility and that the schemes suggested are the result of practical and detailed consideration. After the years of obstruction offered to the Embankment by the obnoxious railway bridge, it is a worthy aim to remove it for ever. The slight raising of the Embankment level to form a starting-off point for the new road bridge would prove no difficulty either from a practical or artistic point of view, and nowhere need there be a road gradient of more than 1 in 50.

The Victoria Embankment is one of the achievements of the Victorian era of which we may well be proud, and to create another embankment on the south side of equal quality would at once transform the Thames into one of the finest waterways in the world. The idea of a transcontinental railway reaching a magnificent railway terminal on the south side of the river, and approached direct from Trafalgar Square over an Imperial Way and bridge and through a King Edward's Place in the southern embankment, should surely stir the desires of all who would see London take its place as a capital city worthy of the Empire. It has been argued that a War Memorial should not be wholly a utilitarian affair, but a worthy memorial would assuredly be one which would add to the city grandeur, combined with the public usefulness of such a scheme as this.

Fine thoroughfares of approach to London from the outside are sadly lacking. It is curious that we should find one of our best in the Mile End Road in the East End! We have nothing comparable to the great road from Charlottenburg into Berlin. Yet the possibilities lie before us.

It has often been stated that idealists bring forward costly and impossible schemes for towns, that they urge the creation of vistas, squares, fine roadways and open spaces which are too burdensome for realization. If all the suggested improvements had to be put in hand within a limited period, we might well call them impossible, but if we want a noble city these sort of things are sheer necessities, to be obtained as soon as is economically possible. In some cases our roadways are actually too wide, and if the streams of traffic were kept in well ordered lines space might often be saved; the principle of gyratory traffic could be more frequently developed. A fine city needs fine vistas, important centres should have some cohesion of architectural effect, circuses and squares ought not to be surrounded by haphazard collections of buildings; our pavements are generally too narrow, street signs and advertisements are too much out of control, whilst all sorts of ugliness are permitted in the uppermost levels and skylines of buildings.

Every time some great new building is projected, the question of its site should not be left to be settled chiefly or entirely on practical grounds—the governing body of a great city should hardly encourage the establishment of warehouses in a street like Kingsway or pickle and jam factories anywhere in the best parts of the city. When a fine site is wanted for a new Opera House or a

University, should it not be of great moment to the community that it should be provided in such a place that the city effect may be ennobled and beautified ? Large buildings are now being projected, and their location should be one of our serious considerations. If we examine the different proposals for creating changes and improvements in certain specific places or areas, we find that the objects of the various designers vary greatly, and that no uniformity of agreement as to what is desirable can be arrived at amongst those whose outlook is so different; yet this is a serious obstacle to success.

The length of a single lifetime is so short that the efforts of individuals go very little way to influence the life of a city. It is quite certain that a body like The London Society cannot afford to live only in the present. Those who are now devoting their thoughts and energy to furthering its aims are only preparing the ground for others who will follow, and no isolated efforts, however splendid they may be, will go for much unless the citizens of London and their governing bodies will continue from one generation to another to pursue great ideals with persistent courage. Little indeed does the average citizen realize how great are the visions and how deep are the disappointments which some amongst us see and feel as the opportunities of London rise before us and disappear. We have lost opportunities at the London Bridge approaches, in the final treatment of the Mall approach, in the adequate setting of fine buildings on the Embankment, in the worthy treatment of several great new thoroughfares, in the creation of beautiful vistas in and about our beautiful river—in a thousand ways we have not done what we ought to have done, and left undone so much that we might. Our city is still untidy, our streets congested, our love of money supreme, and still across the south side of the River Thames lie the muddy banks of derelict London!

What are we to think of the long perspective of opportunities which crowd into mind, of the opportunities lost, or neglected, or still possible, for the creation of a better and more beautiful London ? Is it not obvious that those whose thoughts have been led in this direction should desire to give some expression to them as the importance of the subject continually grows and presses for more definite and practical consideration ? Though the subject bristles with difficulties, which seem to increase the more it is considered,

A LOST OPPORTUNITY: HOW WE ALLOWED THE WELL-DESIGNED APPROACHES TO LONDON BRIDGE TO BE SPOILED.

To face p. 44.

the interest and fascination also increase with every step we take. It is by no means a new subject, and it has occupied the thoughts of able minds for many years past.

If the finest imaginable schemes were displayed to-day for the improvement of London, it would not follow that we should be a whit nearer great improvements, for the machinery for turning them into possibilities is lacking. Our only real hope lies in the creation of a responsible controlling and directing power which shall be urged into action by the determined desire and enlightened opinion of the public. Very interesting are the designs put forward by able men, but where ideals differ so widely, who shall decide? The provision of light and air to the greatest amount would be the foremost feature in the ideals of many who care little in comparison for the impressiveness of ponderous buildings: our beautiful wide waterway would never be encroached upon in any future they devise, no streets like tunnels or darkening piles would be tolerated by them. To some folk the ponderosity of Berlin makes a strong appeal, to others the lightness and grace of Paris, but let us hope that those who have some say in the further improvement of London will find a way to give us all the dignity which should be expected in a great city without undue sacrifice of that picturesque quality which is natural to our race and without any sacrifice whatsoever of our heritage of light and air in river, roads, parks and squares. Some at least amongst us must go on seeing visions and dreaming dreams in face of all the hard facts which progress and enterprise constantly bring before us. Is it too much to hope that deep down in our national character there is something which will respond to the appeal which is now being made to realize the great opportunities for the creation of a greater and more beautiful city?

ROADS, STREETS AND TRAFFIC OF LONDON

COLONEL R. C. HELLARD, C.B.

CHAPTER III

ROADS, STREETS AND TRAFFIC OF LONDON

THE system of main roads in Greater London has been gradually built up in a somewhat haphazard way, based on the six main roads that date from the time of the Romans, represented to-day by:

Edgware Road	.. Leading to St. Albans	.. Watling Street.
Kingsland Road	.. Leading to Cambridge	.. Ermine Street.
Romford Road	.. Leading to Colchester	.. —
Dover Road ..	.. ..	.. Watling Street.
Clapham Road	.. Leading to Leatherhead and Worthing	.. Staine Street.
Basingstoke Road	.. ..	.. —

There are nineteen main roads radiating from the County of London, which develop into twenty-three further out as they approach the boundaries of Greater London. None of these roads can be said to be of really adequate width throughout for the traffic they are called on to carry.

Paris, with less than half the population of London, has forty-two main roads radiating from the city into the surrounding country, and of these twelve are more than 100 feet wide.

So long ago as 1809, in the days of the mail coaches, attention was being directed to the insufficient widths of the main roads leading out of London, and some form of central control was then contemplated; but the subsequent introduction of railways, which drew the traffic from the roads, did away with all chance of their improvement at that time, and allowed the control of the roads to once more drift back into the hands of the various local administrations, with the result that the road system of to-day is very much as it stood more than a hundred years ago.

NECESSITY FOR IMPROVEMENT.

Now that the introduction of motor transport has for some

years been attracting the traffic from the railways back to the roads, the urgency of improvement as regards both capacity and control has become acute, but to attain success there are two things absolutely essential, apart from financial considerations:

1. A general scheme to which all projects should conform.
2. Co-operation among all the authorities, owners, and agencies concerned.

For some years past the local authorities and the general public have taken more interest in the roads and streets of the Metropolis and have shown a greater desire to effect improvements than the Government of recent years has ever exhibited. The Government expressed its sympathy from time to time, to a limited extent, by the appointment of the 1905 Royal Commission and by the prosecution of inquiries in other forms; but in the long run it left the question exactly where it stood before, and until recently did nothing further to bring about some definite result. It must be admitted that it appointed a Road Board in 1909, but expectant London was even more disappointed with that body than by the former deplorable lack of action on the part of the Government.

COMPLEX NATURE OF THE PROBLEM.

London is the largest and most important of the densely inhabited areas in the world, and is the capital of the Empire, yet its highly complex system of government entails difficulties not ordinarily met with. The County of London, with an area of 116·9 square miles, contains 27 boroughs, besides the cities of London and Westminster; and the outside ring which completes the Metropolitan Police area an additional 575·94 square miles, comprising a further 9 boroughs, 65 urban districts, and portions of 13 rural districts situated in five different counties. Within this large area of 692·84 square miles, with its population of 7,250,000, the London County Council is the principal central authority; but its jurisdiction, which does not extend beyond the London County boundary, is not supreme, as all the cities and boroughs in the county have a voice in these matters, while the outside administrative units are all equally independent and self-assertive.

ROADS, STREETS AND TRAFFIC

STEPS TOWARDS A SOLUTION OF THE PROBLEM.

The Arterial Roads Conferences which met between 1914 and 1916 showed that practically all the local authorities concerned took a keen interest in the subject, and arrived at a wonderful degree of unanimity as to what is absolutely necessary and as to the urgency of the matter; but no definite steps with a view to carrying out any of the approved schemes were taken at that time, and there seemed no likelihood of this consummation without some central authority to provide the initiative.

The establishment of a London and Home Counties Authority was considered by a joint committee of The London Society and of the Town Planning Institute, and a Bill was drafted to give effect to this proposal. It was not intended to supersede or interfere with the existing authorities, but to co-ordinate their efforts and deal with the larger questions of development, housing, and transport throughout the extended area of the Metropolis. The Bill, however, was not proceeded with, as it was hoped that other action would be taken at once as regards the roads, whereon the housing schemes, which are of such pressing importance, must be based.

A Select Committee on Transport, with Mr. H. Wilson-Fox as chairman, was appointed on August 6, 1918, but, unfortunately, owing to the close of the session, its work was not completed, and its reports were therefore only of a preliminary nature.

Another Select Committee on Transport (Metropolitan Area), with Mr. W. Kennedy Jones as chairman, was appointed on May 29, 1919. It attributed the demoralization of traffic in Greater London to the absence of a Supreme Traffic Authority possessing executive powers to control, co-ordinate and safeguard public interests; and it recommended the immediate creation of a Supreme Traffic Board for Greater London, with executive power covering the Metropolitan Police area. No immediate action, however, was taken in this direction pending the passing of the Transport Bill then before the House.

MINISTRY OF TRANSPORT.

The Royal Assent was given to the Transport Bill in August 1919. The powers conferred on the Ministry under that Act are not altogether sufficient to meet some of the problems to be dealt with, but the appointment by the Ministry of an Advisory Committee on London Traffic, presided over by Mr. W. Kennedy Jones, gives great hope that there will be no further delay in taking such steps as are possible, under existing powers, to relieve the present congestion, and that the necessity for the immediate improvement of traffic facilities in and around London in its various aspects will be energetically pressed forward with a view to such further legislation being initiated at an early date as may be found necessary to meet the situation.

INCREASED COST OF DELAY.

It is most unfortunate that so much valuable time has been lost already; and, as a consequence, where fifteen or twenty years ago many improvements could have been made in the growing sections of the immediate outskirts for very little, they will to-day cost from five to ten times as much to carry out. As regards the construction of new roads and the widening and improvement of old ones, the policy of leaving each generation to deal with its own problems as they arise is unnatural and unsound, where with ordinary foresight such problems need never have arisen had the previous generation realized its proper responsibilities in the matter. To make provision merely for to-day's requirements is therefore not sufficient. We should look well ahead and provide for the future. In this connection, Liverpool has set an example that might well be followed by London.

The time lost daily by millions of people through insufficient road accommodation represents a loss of money which, though impossible to estimate with accuracy, must be very large; and yet we have been content to allow delay due to congestion of traffic in the streets to go on increasing year by year without any serious attempt to deal with it. It has been stated that the cost of transport in London is 30 per cent. higher than in any other large town, and therefore the cost of this inaction is so heavy that it would seem to be the cheaper course in the long run to take the matter up energetically at once, and recognize that the money thus laid out for the public benefit is really a most excellent investment, calculated to save millions of pounds in the future.

ROADS, STREETS AND TRAFFIC

GROWING IMPORTANCE OF THE ROADS.

A census taken on April 26, 1911, showed that while the residential population of the City was under 20,000—mostly caretakers—the day population at work in the City was over 360,000, exclusive of the 1,077,000 persons who merely entered the City on that day between 7 a.m. and 7 p.m. Of the journeys made by this vast migratory population in various public vehicles in 1909, 40 per cent. were made by rail and 60 per cent. by road; but in 1913 only 32 per cent. were made by rail, with an increase by road to 68 per cent., while the total number of journeys per head of the population of London during this period increased by over 30 per cent.

The growing importance of the roads is further emphasized by the rapidity with which motors have been substituted for horse vehicles. Among passenger vehicles enumerated in 1914 only 4 per cent. were horse-drawn; and this change was rapidly extending to the commercial world, for whereas in 1911 94 per cent. of the trade vehicles were horse-drawn, in 1914 they were reduced to 85 per cent. Moreover, the number of vehicles enumerated each year on most of the roads leading out of London showed a marked increase, amounting as a total to 19 per cent. in 1914 over 1911. It is of interest to note that the greatest increase occurred in the zone lying between the 6- and 9-mile radius from St. Paul's, the figures being:

Within 3-mile radius	10 per cent.
From 3 to 6 miles radius	20 „
From 6 to 9 miles radius	33 „
Beyond the 9-mile radius..	19 „

Due, however, to the shorter length of the motor vehicle, its greater pace and flexibility, which all go to lessen the period of its road occupation, the coefficient of obstruction for each class of vehicle is reduced, and therefore the volume of traffic does not increase at quite the same rate as the number of vehicles so long as this transfer from horse to motor is in progress. The traffic census taken each year from 1911 to 1914 showed that this coefficient of the average vehicle during that period was thus gradually reduced by about 6 per cent., and that it was greatest in the centre zone, with a very marked fall as the distance from St. Paul's increased, amounting to as much as 18 per cent. in the outer zone beyond the 9-mile radius.

NATURE OF THE TRAFFIC AND HOW DISTRIBUTED.

The nature of the traffic in the east of London differs very materially from that in the west. The census of 1912 showed that commercial vehicles largely predominated in the north-east, forming as much as 65 per cent. of the traffic, while in the south-west only 41 per cent. were trade vehicles, the coefficients of obstruction of the average vehicle in these cases being respectively 5·1 and 3·2.

Of the daily traffic on the bridges in 1914, Westminster, London and Blackfriars Bridges carried the largest number of vehicles: 18,671, 18,387 and 17,550 respectively; but due to inadequate width, Tower Bridge is the most congested, with Waterloo and London Bridges next in order of density. London Bridge, however, should experience some relief when the reconstruction of Southwark Bridge is complete and the bridge reopened for traffic.

Within the radius of 3 miles from St. Paul's it may be said that all the streets which carry through traffic are congested. Apart from the bridges and some few well-known centres, such as the Mansion House, Hyde Park Corner, etc., where the enumeration of vehicles presents very great difficulties and is not of the same practical utility, the points in order where the greatest volume of traffic has been noted are: Holborn, near Gray's Inn; Piccadilly, by the Ritz Hotel; Kennington Park Road; London Road, Walworth; Commercial Road East; Whitechapel Road; Bishopsgate; and Oxford Street, west of the Circus. The points in order at which the greatest congestion occurs are: London Road, Walworth; Old Street; Peckham High Street; Camberwell Road; Kingsland Road, near Stamford Street; and Gray's Inn Road.

Beyond the 3-mile radius, Canning Town Bridge carries the largest volume of traffic, and is the most congested point, with London Road, Deptford, next, and Bow Bridge to follow. At a distance of some 5 to 7 miles from St. Paul's, traffic on the main roads is still great at such points as Shepherd's Bush, Hammersmith, Putney (where the congestion is serious), Tooting Graveney, Streatham, and along the Cambridge, Colchester and Southend Roads.

Nearer the 9-mile radius and beyond, the volume of traffic continues to be considerable on the various main roads to Oxford, Bath and Basingstoke, Brighton, Colchester, Cambridge, and along the Great North Road, with points of very serious congestion at Brentford and Croydon. There are also many other points where danger and occasional congestion arise, either from the inadequate capacity of the roadway or from some sharp turn or crossing of another road, where relief or improvement is urgently needed.

TRAFFIC OBSTRUCTIONS.

Generally speaking, the principal defect in the present road system is the inadequate width of the streets and the haphazard plan on which they are laid out, whereby many lengths of good wide roads lead nowhere, and in consequence do not carry their proper proportion of traffic. The nature of the road surface affects traffic considerably, but as a rule, until quite recently, there has not been much to complain of in the Metropolis on this score. The several dangerous crossings and corners, which entail much police control, may be difficult if not impossible to eliminate, but the same cannot be said of the various obstacles in the streets, many of which could be easily mitigated, if not removed altogether.

These obstacles may be divided into two classes:

(1) Fixed or permanent.
(2) Movable or temporary.

Generally speaking, the first is within the jurisdiction of the County and Local Authorities, and includes lavatories, refuges, centre standards, clock-towers, statues, etc., some of which might be removed with advantage, notably centre standards where apart from refuges; while the second class, which is subject to police regulation and traffic control, includes processions, tram and bus termini, street markets and stalls, standing vehicles, etc. Many of these temporary obstructions become at times practically continuous, and are the more difficult to deal with. At the termini a frequent tram or bus service entails in some cases a permanent obstruction. Even standing vehicles may be so numerous or so persistent in their occupation of the street as to be practically permanent, e.g. St. Paul's Churchyard, the Strand near Arundel

Street, etc.; and it would seem desirable in future that plans for the erection of new premises should not be passed unless provision is made for loading and unloading vans clear of the street, where the business in view entails extensive operations of this nature. Repairs to tram tracks and stopping places of trams and buses, particularly where associated with centre standards or refuges or with standing vehicles, create serious obstacles in streets of not more than 32 feet roadway. With wider roadways, many of these objects that at present create obstruction would not have the same detrimental effect on traffic.

At one time preparations were being made for a census of street obstructions of all kinds, but the war put an end to the investigations. This would be one of the first operations to undertake with a view to their removal or mitigation, and would help to show the importance of constructing all main roads of greater width than has hitherto been considered necessary. It is in this connection that sufficient foresight has never been exercised.

GENERAL LINES OF IMPROVEMENT.

Whatever standards of width may be aimed at for the various classes of streets and roads from the purely utilitarian point of view, there is another aspect which should not be overlooked. We have many examples in foreign cities of the way in which the main approaches to a city should be treated, which might well be followed in the case of London, with a view to investing our main roads with some degree of dignity and to rendering them pleasant as well as useful to the thousands who traverse them. In laying out new roads, at any rate, additional land might, as a rule, be easily acquired without undue expense for the purpose of ornamental planting; and some control should be exercised over the frontages of these main approaches, to prevent their being disfigured by squalid and unsightly erections. With this object, prominent sites should be reserved for public monuments and for important buildings of some architectural pretensions.

The widening of an existing road in built-up areas is in most cases a very expensive undertaking; and, while the work is in progress, the interference with traffic and the inconvenience to adjoining premises is very serious. Finally, when the work is completed, although somewhat wider than before, there is still only the

LONDON'S TRAFFIC TROUBLES.

(Two views in Brentford High Street.)

To face p. 56.

one road. The alternative of a relief road, where a suitable route can be found, has many advantages. It is less costly and admits of more generous treatment; no one is seriously inconvenienced during the progress of the work, and in the end there are two roads to carry the traffic instead of one.

Authority to prescribe building-lines on all the main radiating roads would be of the greatest advantage, particularly in the suburbs, in that it would arrest the growth of further obstructions and would help to lessen the difficulty and expense of widening. The Cambridge Road presents a very good example of the benefit that might accrue from the adoption of such a measure, where at each of the villages through which it passes the road is far too narrow. Opportunity could then be taken of setting back the building-line to the new frontage as sales occur, or as leases of the unimportant premises fall in, before they are replaced by a more elaborate class of building on the original frontage, when all hope of improvement would vanish.

There is more traffic moving in a general east and west direction across London than there is north and south, and therefore, of the two main avenues that were recommended in 1905, that to provide for the passage of east and west traffic is the more important; and in dealing with the proposed new roads, an east and west route will be suggested. Generally speaking, however, it is fairly hopeless at this stage to carry out extensive widenings and improvements in Central London, owing to the prohibitive cost. The best chance of relieving the congested central streets seems to lie in the improvement of some circular route whereby traffic may find its way from one point of the compass to another by passing round London without having to penetrate the central area. This remedy is all the easier for motor traffic, where an extra mile or two along a clear route saves time compared with a congested street, where its pace is necessarily reduced to that of the slowest-moving vehicle.

PRINCIPAL MAIN ROADS AND THEIR IMPROVEMENT.

The roads leading to Dover, Brighton, Portsmouth, Basingstoke, Bath, Oxford and Coventry, the Great North Road, and those leading north-east to Norwich and Colchester, are of more particular national importance, owing to their being through routes from the Metropolis to the principal districts and large towns of Great Britain, and no opportunity should be lost of bringing these roads up to a proper standard. The more congested sections should be relieved by supplementary roads where possible and access to them improved. But while this must be regarded as absolutely indispensable, the improvement and expansion of the other main roads are highly desirable in the interest of general development and should not be neglected.

At Brentford it has been decided to eliminate the congestion by a relief road, for which an Act of Parliament was passed in 1914, to enable a road, 80 feet wide and rather over 5 miles in length, to be constructed, commencing at the Chiswick High Road near Gunnersbury, leading north of Brentford Station, and joining the Bath Road beyond Hounslow. The procedure adopted in this case is not ideal, and the estimated cost, which is high accordingly, should not be accepted as any guide to cost in future projects. Moreover, as more than half the traffic through Hounslow at present passes on to the Basingstoke Road, the scheme is incomplete without an extension is carried to it beyond the Bath Road.

At Croydon the construction of a relief road, rather over 4 miles in length, has been agreed upon, but its width is limited to 60 feet, which would seem altogether inadequate for such a route as the Brighton Road, in view of the difficulties that have arisen all round London from want of foresight in the past as regards the capacity of main roads. This is all the more to be deplored as additional width could be reserved for a great part of its length at the present moment for little more than the cost of the land; whereas in a short time development is pretty sure to block in the road, situated as it is close to a large town, when any subsequent improvement would be hopeless. Moreover, the outlets at both ends of this road, as at present arranged, will be decidedly inconvenient. The direction of a main road should be obvious, and the sharp turns involved in this case will, it is feared, very much interfere with the purpose for which the road is required.

A scheme for the widening of Putney Bridge to 74 feet, which would provide for a 51-foot roadway and two footways of 11 feet 6 inches each, has been under consideration by the London County

Council, but under recent conditions the matter had to be dropped temporarily.

The recent widening of the bridge at Kingston-on-Thames to 55 feet and the improvement of the approaches has already relieved the congestion that it suffered from previously.

SUPPLEMENTARY ROADS ABSOLUTELY NECESSARY.

Two of the principal supplementary roads that have been approved by the Local Government Board Conferences are the Eastern Avenue and the Western Avenue, which, when connected with each other along the line of the Marylebone and Euston Roads, will supply the place of the main east and west avenue recommended in 1905.

The line of the Eastern Avenue from the City Road passes across Hackney Marsh, through Leyton and Wanstead, and continues north of Ilford and Romford to join the Colchester Road at Gallows Corner, about half a mile beyond Gidea Park. Crossing the roads to Waltham Abbey, Norwich and Chipping Ongar as it does, it improves the access to all these roads, which is badly needed. Its chief function, however, is to relieve the Colchester Road, the course of which is much congested at Bow Bridge and Stratford High Street, and at Ilford Bridge and in Romford. Between Wanstead and Romford the line selected lies across open ground and presents no difficulty, provided the route can be kept open.

The line recommended for the Western Avenue commences at the junction of Silchester Road with Latimer Road, and passes under the West London Railway to Wood Lane. From this point there is open ground to the south of Wormwood Scrubs, and after crossing the Great Western Railway near Acton Station and a small built-up area alongside Willesden Lane, the route lies across open country till it reaches the ridge of high ground north of Uxbridge, where some engineering works are called for to enable the road to descend to the level of the Oxford Road, which it joins about a mile beyond Uxbridge. Besides relieving the present Uxbridge Road, which carries considerable traffic, this road will open up a very large area of ground suitable for development, to which at present there is no direct access. Continued eastwards into the Harrow Road, north of Paddington Station, and following the line of the Marylebone, Euston, Pentonville and City Roads, it would join the Eastern Avenue and form a great East and West Avenue, which would relieve the congested streets lying to the south in Central London.

Commencing at the Chiswick High Road, about 600 yards east of Kew Bridge, the North Circular Road is recommended to follow Gunnersbury Lane and over Ealing Common into Hanger Lane. At Park Royal Station the line takes a north-easterly direction, keeping more or less to the valley of the Brent, and after crossing the Harrow and Edgware Roads would join the Regent's Park Road near Mutton Brook. From this point existing roads can be made use of as far as the eastern end of Bowes Road, and again through Edmonton to Angel Road Station, where, after crossing the River Lea, the road takes a general south-easterly direction towards West Ham, the Docks and the free ferry, besides giving access to Ilford and the Colchester Road. Such a road would facilitate the intercommunication between all the main roads that it crosses, and enable traffic to pass from south-west to north-east of London without entering the crowded central streets.

In South London it seems possible to provide for a circular route at comparatively small expense, much nearer in to the centre. From Clapham Common it would follow a series of existing roads, with short lengths of new road at intervals to straighten and improve the line, past Tulse Hill, Dulwich and Lordship Lane Stations to Catford. Continuing along Brownhill and St. Mildred's Roads, a length of new road across open ground to Well Hall would effect a very important junction with the road to Woolwich, and thus provide good connection between the west and south-west of London with Woolwich and the free ferry across the Thames into Essex.

A new road to Chertsey is recommended to leave the Chiswick High Road by Chiswick Lane and Burlington Lane, across the London and South-Western Railway, and over the Thames by a new bridge to join the Lower Richmond Road at New Lane. Another new bridge across the Thames near the existing railway bridge, to relieve the present Richmond Bridge, would carry this new road to St. Margaret's, and on through the urban districts of Twickenham and Hanworth, past Sunbury Station and Shepperton Green, to Chertsey Bridge. This road would open up a very large area for development, and would materially shorten the distance to Woking, Bisley and Aldershot.

Another important new road that should be constructed in the near future is the new Cambridge Road, which from the London County Council estate at White Hart Lane runs north over ground still undeveloped, lying between the Enfield Road and the existing Cambridge Road. Keeping to the west of Waltham Cross and Cheshunt, this road would join the present main road at Turnford. While neither the Enfield nor the Cambridge Road is even now of sufficient capacity throughout, population on both sides has been increasing steadily for some years past, and in a few years buildings will have spread across the intervening space between these roads, and the line now proposed will be blocked unless the land can be earmarked for this new road, which would relieve both these roads, and obviate the necessity for some of the more expensive widenings and improvements along the existing routes.

At present the New Cross Road is the only outlet for the traffic proceeding from Central London to either of the roads to Dover, Maidstone or Tonbridge; and this length of about 600 yards is seriously congested at times accordingly. To relieve this situation, a new road should be constructed, leaving the Old Kent Road near Albany Road, crossing the Grand Surrey Canal and Peckham High Street to Peckham Rye, and on by Catford to join the Tonbridge Road.

In connection with the Thames-side housing and development schemes now in contemplation, a new road is urgently required to relieve the existing Barking Road and to improve the access to the Southend Road. It should leave the Beckton Road near the West Ham boundary, cross the Northern Outfall Sewer, the River Roding and the Midland Railway, to join the road to Tilbury and Southend about a mile beyond Barking. At the same time a new approach is required to the Victoria and Albert Docks and to the North Woolwich Road, being so arranged as to avoid Canning Town Bridge and the adjoining bridge over the Great Eastern Railway, and thus relieve the present congestion on these bridges. This road should also avoid the Victoria Dock Road and eliminate the Whitegates level crossing and the existing single-track swing-bridge over the entrance to the Tidal Basin, which are causes of very serious delay and inconvenience on the present route.

OTHER NEW ROADS SUGGESTED.

Many other new roads are necessary to facilitate the free movement of traffic and to relieve congested sections on existing main roads. A bye-pass road to avoid the dangerous market area in Kingston is not a very serious undertaking, and at the same time a more extended bye-pass for Kingston and Surbiton, which would also be a valuable development road, should leave the Portsmouth Road at Kingston Vale and, following the line of the Beverley Brook, should pass through New Malden and Tolworth, and rejoin the Portsmouth Road at Littleworth Common. A bye-pass for Sutton is also desirable, for the area adjoining Sutton railway station is becoming more congested each year as the population increases, and the possibility of relief is gradually disappearing as vacant ground is taken up for building.

A bye-pass on the Tonbridge Road would relieve a congested area in Bromley and leave that town to carry on its business undisturbed by the through traffic, which has no occasion or desire to stop there *en route*. A relief road for Eltham would greatly facilitate movement along the Maidstone Road, and another for Sidcup would help in this direction. Many other connections are wanted to facilitate intercommunication between various main roads and to provide alternative means of access to them from more distant areas. Some of these may perhaps be considered to be of local interest rather than of general public utility, but even local projects of this nature, if well considered, are certain to be of benefit to adjoining districts, and are generally worthy of encouragement.

Although not of the same prime importance as the roads already specified, a Zone Road to encircle London at a distance of some 12 to 14 miles from the centre would be a very desirable addition to the road system. The line proposed for this road, which would be over 75 miles in length, follows considerable stretches of existing roads—for some part suburban, but in other parts traversing pleasant country, particularly in the south and west—connected by comparatively inexpensive sections of new road over open ground.

PROGRESS OF THE WORK.

By the courtesy of the Ministry of Transport we are able to

bring this article right up to date and to append the following notes on the progress of the Greater London Arterial Road Programme, all of which schemes, it should be noted, are shown on The London Society's map.

The urgent need of providing employment for ex-Service men this past winter brought to the fore the question of road works, and the Government accordingly decided to promote, through the Ministry of Transport, the construction of arterial roads by offering to share the cost with the County Councils and other Local Authorities concerned. To expedite the work the Unemployment (Relief Works) Act was passed, enabling land to be acquired, where urgently needed for road-making, at seven days' notice.

The Government's proposals for Greater London have been accepted by the Counties of Essex, London and Middlesex for a certain number of arterial roads, of which the following particulars may be quoted:

(1) In the South-East we have the Eltham Bye-pass, nearly three miles long, enabling London–Maidstone traffic to avoid the congestion and abrupt angles of Eltham High Street. A continuation northwards of the Bye-pass (Kidbrooke Park Extension) affords a useful connection towards Greenwich and Woolwich.

(2) The Shooters Hill Bye-pass, four miles long, branching off from the Dover road at Blackheath to avoid the steep 250-foot climb over Shooters Hill, and proceeding on comparatively easy gradients to rejoin the Dover road at Welling.

(3) The South Circular Road through Woolwich, forming part of an invaluable project for enabling traffic to skirt the Metropolis instead of needlessly penetrating the congested heart of London.

(4) The North Circular Road through Willesden, Hendon, Southgate, Edmonton, Walthamstow and Leyton, etc., performing for the North side of London the same service as the South Circular Road for the other half of the Metropolis.

(5) The Western Avenue through Hammersmith and Acton, to be continued some day, it may be hoped, through Ealing and Greenford to join the Oxford Road just beyond

Uxbridge. Town-planning resolutions passed by the Local Authorities concerned will, at any rate, keep the line of route clear.

(6) The Eastern Avenue across the Lea Marshes in Hackney and Leyton, providing a much-needed crossing-place over the Lea Valley between the Bow Road and the Lea Bridge Road.

(7) The New Cambridge Road through Tottenham, Edmonton and Enfield, in process of construction by the Middlesex County Council. No definite provision has, however, yet been made for the extension northwards through Hertfordshire to rejoin the old Cambridge Road at Cheshunt.

In addition to these works already in hand, it may be mentioned that negotiations are far advanced for the construction of the eight-mile section of the Eastern Avenue extending from the Red Bridge over the River Roding through Ilford and Romford to the junction with the London–Colchester Road at a point east of Romford.

Another scheme, the execution of which is very near at hand, is the Barking Bye-pass connecting Canning Town with the London–Tilbury Road, thus affording the means for traffic to escape congestion, abrupt corners and level crossings which render Barking a bugbear to motorists.

Two schemes should also be mentioned which were already in progress before the unemployment crisis arose last winter, viz. the Croydon Bye-pass, which forms a conspicuous feature in the view from the London–Brighton Railway near Purley, and the Brentford Bye-pass, which has been in the hands of the contractors for many months past. It seems not unlikely that arrangements will be made very shortly for an extension of the Brentford Bye-pass south-westwards to connect the Bath Road with the Basingstoke Road.

TOWN PLANNING SCHEMES.

By co-operation between local authorities, landowners and others concerned, the various Town Planning Schemes under consideration all round London afford an opportunity of helping the construction and improvement of many of these roads which may never recur, and of which full advantage should be taken at once.

IN CHISWICK.

THE HALL, STAPLE INN.

(Two of London's quiet corners.)

To face p. 64.

This is of the greatest importance, if the Road Scheme, which has been approved after very careful consideration by all the local authorities, is ever to be carried out. Encircling London so completely as they do, these town planning and housing schemes may block every possible outlet for any new road unless they conform to the general road plan. Moreover, housing schemes would fail altogether in their object if direct access by road is not available to enable inhabitants to reach their work. On the other hand, under careful guidance, slums in the interior may be swept away and the areas thus cleared devoted to more important commercial and other purposes, while the inhabitants are moved to healthier quarters on the outskirts, where fresh air and pleasant surroundings may do so much for the welfare of succeeding generations.

PARKS AND OPEN SPACES.

In considering the important question of providing clear routes of adequate capacity for the traffic of London, and in selecting the lines for new streets and so forth, we should not overlook the desirability of saving any of the old landmarks which have not already disappeared under the ruthless guise of improvement, and of leaving undisturbed the quiet nooks and corners, of which there are many, even in Central London, known perhaps only to comparatively few, where it is still possible to wander apart from the surrounding noise and bustle of the Metropolis.

While, too, it is desirable to provide easy access to them, the large parks themselves and the open spaces that go to form the playgrounds of London should not only remain untouched as far as possible, but further large areas should be earmarked as open spaces in advance of development. In the north-west it is proposed that ground should be reserved for a large public park of over 2,000 acres at Stanmore, to include the Aldenham Reservoir and its beautiful surroundings. In the north-east another large area of Hainault Forest might be reserved for the benefit more especially of the vast population that is steadily growing up to the south of it. Although the south-west is already fairly well provided for with Wimbledon Common and the parks at Kew, Richmond and Hampton, a considerable woodland area might with advantage be reserved at Stoke d'Abernon, which, with Esher, Ashstead and Epsom Commons, would make up a further large open space in the far south-west. In the south-east also, Joyden's Wood is proposed as a public park for Bexley and Crayford, and another large area immediately south-east of Croydon is suggested as a Croham Hurst and Addington public park.

Waterside reservations along the many streams would not only preserve various beauty spots, but would also secure for the public very large additional areas of open space, which in most cases are not at all suitable for the erection of dwellings. Such areas would otherwise only be utilized as private gardens, or possibly be dealt with as many streams have been already, by being run underground in culverts. Where a main road lies alongside one of such waterside reservations, as in the case of the Brent, a great opportunity is presented of making good use of such features.

LONDON
RAILWAY RECONSTRUCTION

H. J. LEANING, F.S.I.

CHAPTER IV

LONDON RAILWAY RECONSTRUCTION

URGENCY OF PROBLEM.

AMONG the many vital subjects demanding attention to-day for the purpose of economizing the national resources and increasing the trading possibilities of the country, none would yield such immediate and so great results as that of welding our London railway systems into one consistent whole.

The frequent charges of inefficiency made against the present arrangements do not reflect so much upon the management as upon the necessity for better intercommunication between the various districts, and also for more rapid services in the central area.

CHANGED CONDITIONS.

The conditions have so much altered since the lines were constructed that the old arrangements are no longer suitable. The distribution of the population has been shown by the last census to be changing rapidly, the population of the Outer Ring having nearly doubled itself in twenty years from 1891 to 1911. The same period has witnessed the electrification of the tramways and the advent of motor omnibuses. The combined effect of these factors has been to decrease the short suburban traffic on the railways and to increase the long suburban traffic.

Simultaneously we find a vast increase in the number of passengers carried by the local railways, viz. 180,026,117 in 1891 and 436,498,785 in 1911, an increase of 142 per cent. The latter figure is due to the opening of the tube railways, beginning with the City and South London line in 1890 and followed by the Waterloo and City in 1899, Central London in 1900, Great Northern and City in 1904, Bakerloo in 1906 and Piccadilly in 1907.

The heavy traffic on the tubes might have been expected to cause a heavy diminution of the traffic on the roads, but the only indication of this to be seen is in 1909, when the number of omnibus passengers decreased from 340,000,000 to 311,000,000, about 8½ per cent. All the indications are to the effect that the greater travelling facilities there are provided the greater are the number of journeys per head of population.

As evidence of this we find that whereas according to the last census returns the population increased between 1891 and 1911 by 29 per cent., the number of railway passengers on local lines increased by 142 per cent.

In the same period, however, the number of road passengers by tram and bus increased by 242 per cent.

GENERAL PLAN LONG OVERDUE.

From these figures it can be seen that both roads and railways are becoming taxed to their utmost capacity and that it is necessary to relieve both of them by some special measures as soon as possible.

They cannot be dealt with separately, as the railway plan undoubtedly governs the road plan. Now, it has been insisted by almost every Parliamentary Committee since 1863 that one general comprehensive plan for the railways of London has become a paramount necessity.

No such scheme, however, has been prepared, although in 1905, after the Traffic Commission Report, Sir Herbert Jekyll contemplated the preparation of one and got a staff together for that purpose, but the political situation did not favour the project and it collapsed. The individual railway companies could hardly be expected to do such a thing themselves, as if they did they would be liable to attack by every company whose interests were unfavourably affected.

CAUSES OF FAILURE OF PRESENT SYSTEM.

The Report of the Traffic Commission sums up the situation thus:

The defects of the system as it exists are very largely due to the manner in which the connecting lines have been laid out and to the deficiency of adequate means of terminal distribution caused by the exclusion of railways from the central area. Some of the defects are the outcome of the disadvantages of separate ownership, which must always be accepted if it is desired to secure the correlative advantages of competition.

Each connection has been made and each line laid out in the individual interests of the competing companies, without much regard to the interests and needs of the railway system of London taken as a whole.

COMPETITION NO LONGER CONSISTENT WITH EFFICIENCY.

Since then the Departmental Committee of 1911 has gone further, and finds that both the railways and the public would gain by "a properly regulated extension of co-operation rather than by a revival of competition." It is now realized that the competition which existed during the age of construction is not suitable to the age of operation. In the latter it has been checked largely by amalgamation and rendered nugatory by the Railway Rates Act, 1894.

It has therefore defeated itself, and the considered opinion of those most competent to judge is to the effect that central control is the only escape from the present system and that the best form of it would be that of a *permanent* Board of Control *independent* of Parliament.

There is no doubt that to secure continuity of policy and management there must be permanent officials of high executive ability. Such men must be independent of politics and not liable to dismissal on changes of Government.

UNITY OF OWNERSHIP DESIRABLE.

Even with such control, however, the unity of ownership of all means of communication seems desirable, because it would enable the Government to develop and improve those means of transit most required and to abandon those which are obsolete or unremunerative. This is absolutely necessary for reasons of economy and efficiency. Unity of management is not so indispensable. After a careful regrouping of our systems it would be quite feasible for the present companies to operate the lines subject to the central control of a permanent State Department. This is politics, but it is also political economy, for the alternative course of restoring the lines to their former owners would involve many years of arbitration and many millions in compensation.

THE SOCIETY'S SCHEME.

The London Society, by reason of its freedom from political

ties or vested interests, is in my opinion specially qualified to undertake the preparation of a scheme, more especially because it is able to take a wide survey and to treat the problem as a whole without incurring any charges of partiality or motive. We have therefore, while fully conscious of our want of special knowledge of the subject, studied the problem in all its bearings from the best available sources of information. We have taken the best expert advice, and have concentrated our minds upon the attainment of a unified system of lines out of the existing chaotic arrangement.

One of the recommendations of the Select Committee of 1920 on London Traffic was the preparation of a comprehensive plan showing the possible future developments of all the various means of locomotion in London. The abandonment of these recommendations and the proposed disbandment of the Ministry of Transport leaves this work unaccomplished. It is hoped, however, that the new authority which must be established will carry out a recommendation so obviously desirable.

OBJECTS KEPT IN VIEW.

We have in our scheme disregarded all questions of ownership, and have not hesitated to alter routes or workings wherever the interests of the whole seemed to demand it, the main object being to secure a maximum of convenience at a minimum initial cost. When this has been achieved, we are confident that the result in working will show very substantial savings in the annual cost of operation, upkeep, etc., and also greatly increased surpluses in the receipts, owing to the immense improvement in facilities for travelling.

GREAT ECONOMIES MADE POSSIBLE.

As evidence of the savings we may mention:

1. The abolition of the many wasteful double approaches to the Central Area now working, such as from Bromley, Epsom, Richmond, etc.

These are now maintained as feeders to rival systems and are not necessary for public convenience.

2. The avoidance of vast outlays in widening main line approaches to London and in extending termini which would soon become necessary if the present system were adhered to.

Many other economies, such as Clearing House charges, fuller use of rolling stock, cost of advertising, rates, etc., could be effected by unification and co-operation.

THE FUNCTION OF TUBES.

It is now fourteen years since the last tube was constructed, and many argue that owing to the heavy cost and low dividends no more will be made. As a means of connecting the outlying systems of railways with each other through the central area, however, they are a vital necessity.

Hitherto they have not been so used, but in our opinion that is their chief function, as only by their use can such connections be made.

An essential feature of our proposals is the elimination of all central termini for suburban trains. This is a principle almost generally accepted, as it is the surest method for avoiding congestion. It involves necessarily through connections, and these must be provided whether they pay or not.

There are certain factors about tube construction in London which make it more expensive than it need be. Owing to the prohibition of the Crown Lands Authorities, no tubes may be constructed under parks. The result is that lines have to wind round them and direct access is not always possible.

This difficulty ought to be removed, as the damage done to the parks is merely technical.

Also the stations, which in Paris and New York are under the street, in London involve expensive site purchases and expensive buildings. This in some cases is due to narrowness of streets, but not in all cases, and proper co-operation between the authorities would permit the railway station to be under the street or under the squares or open spaces.

RECOUPMENT.

Incidentally, we have indicated several new districts around

London which possess great advantages from their natural situation, but which, owing to insufficient means of access, are undeveloped.

These include such places as Sydenham in the south and Finchley and Kingsbury in the north, together with other undiscovered tracts in the west. It is suggested that the acquisition of large areas of land in these localities by the Transport Authority would secure for it the profits resulting from their own development, and this would provide a large part of the initial cost.

INCREASED RECEIPTS.

When we come to consider annual charges, we find that increased facilities always increase traffic. For instance, general electrification not only tends to increase the population of the places so served (compare Wimbledon, from 20,000 in 1889 to 58,000 in 1910 = 190 per cent., with Sutton, from 14,000 in 1891 to 20,500 in 1910 = 26½ per cent.), but also in even greater proportion it increases the use of the railway, the number of passengers from Wimbledon having increased during the period cited by 394 per cent., whereas those from Sutton only increased by 93 per cent. (*Board of Trade Report*, 1910).

ALTERNATIVE EXPENDITURE ON STREETS.

But in addition to these advantages, and far exceeding them, there is a most important factor which is not usually fully considered. If the tubes now in existence had not been provided, what would have been the sum required to be spent from public funds in road and street widenings and repairs? Undoubtedly a sum very much exceeding that now proposed to be spent on arterial roads. All this, and far more for future needs, should stand to the credit of any such scheme as that now described.

Let us suppose that the Central London Railway had not been constructed. What would have been the effect upon Oxford Street and the route generally?

This line carries an average of 40,000,000 passengers annually. This traffic is distributed unequally through the day, but during busy hours is at the rate of 28 trains each way per hour (*Board of Trade Report*, 1910). Assuming each train to carry an average of two hundred passengers, we get 11,200 passengers, equivalent to 330 buses per hour.

On the length between Tottenham Court Road and the Bank we find that before the line was made in 1895 there ran 306 buses both ways per hour. After the line had been open some years we find the number stationary (308 in 1908), but it fell to 206 in 1910. Without the line, the number would have been 536 per hour. Yet we see that the delays at crossings even in 1905 varied from nearly three hours at Princes' Street to six hours five minutes at Cornhill in a day of twelve hours. With the number of buses nearly doubled, the block might have been insurmountable.

DISLOCATION DURING ALTERATION.

In making the proposed changes there would necessarily be considerable dislocation of traffic. We propose at a later date, and when the scheme here presented has stood the test of criticism, to offer some suggestions as to the stages by which it would be carried out with the minimum of inconvenience.

USE OF EXISTING LINES.

Since the construction of the existing lines, many of them have been superseded. In some cases they can by new connections become again vital parts of the system. Others cannot be profitably included, but it is doubtful whether it would be sound policy to destroy them, except for Town Planning reasons where they interfere with the development of a district, as they can still be used for coal and goods distribution or as alternative routes.

ELECTRIFICATION.

Electrical operation of railways seems to be a part of the latest transport programme, but it must be remembered that it is a very different problem when applied to main lines when compared with its application to suburban lines, owing to the varied services required on the former.

Now, although the experts tell us that during the rush hours of the day it is more expensive to carry the same number of passengers by electricity than by steam, nevertheless, as electricity gives a greater frequency of trains, and as the central systems must always be directly connected with tubes, there is no alternative, and possibly national generating stations may, by reducing the cost, overcome this objection.

No doubt the suburban services will be fully electrified before the main lines are dealt with.

A difficulty occurs with regard to this which is due to the fact that the main line services in the summer are frequently compelled to run carriages normally used for suburban trains for their extra seaside traffic and race specials, chiefly because of their greater seating capacity.

The electrification of suburban lines only might demand the provision of a good deal of spare stock to meet this demand.

This seasonal traffic usually is, however, a cause of serious dislocation of both main line and suburban traffic, and we think there is a good deal to be said for dealing with it quite separately. We shall refer to this later.

We have in our survey divided the subject into sections, viz. Trunk Lines, Suburban Lines, Goods Traffic, Coal Traffic, and Parcels Traffic.

I. TRUNK LINES

One of the principal causes of the present confusion at the termini is undoubtedly the inclusion of suburban traffic with the long-distance traffic. It is proposed that this should be separated, and that the termini should be relieved of it as much as possible.

This would enable us—

1. To reduce the number of main termini.
2. To avoid the further enlargements and widening of approaches which would be required under present arrangements.

The public interest does not call for as many termini as now exist. In our opinion, nine of the present fifteen stations might be removed or altered in their use without any loss to public convenience.

St. Pancras, Cannon Street, Charing Cross and Holborn Viaduct might be removed altogether, and Marylebone, St. Paul's, Fenchurch Street and London Bridge, Victoria and King's Cross might profitably be converted to either suburban or goods stations.

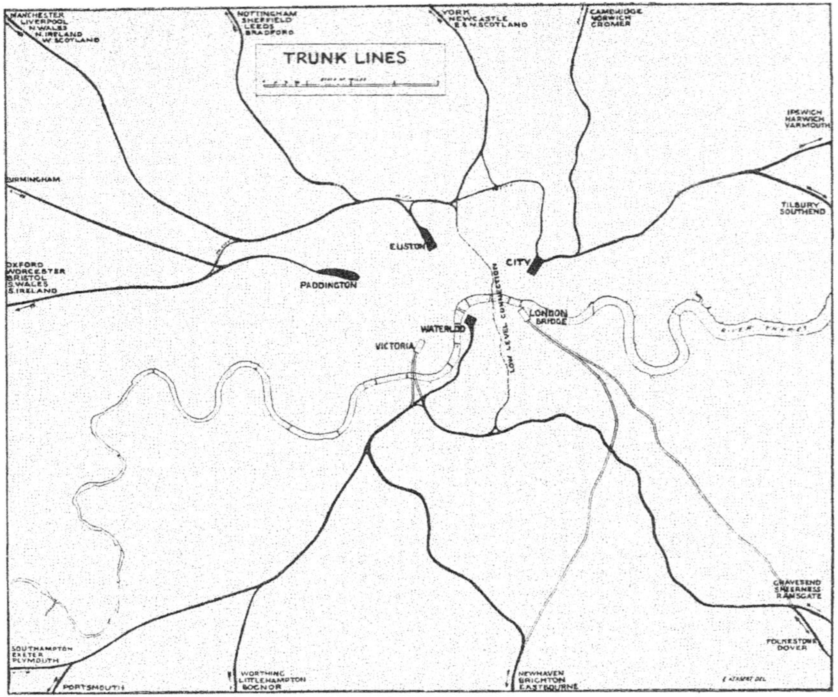

SUGGESTIONS FOR DEALING WITH TRUNK LINES.

(Drawing prepared by H. J. Leaning, F.S.I., and Ernest Herbert.)

To face p. 76.

On the south side, Waterloo Station, which is capable of great extension if necessary, and which is situated at the end of the proposed new road bridge at Charing Cross leading to the principal hotels and public resorts of London, would be quite capable of receiving all the long-distance trains from the Southern Counties and also the Continental trains. This would make the proposed new Memorial Road Bridge at Charing Cross the main Continental approach to London.

Such drastic proposals need, of course, powerful justification before one could expect them to be considered. They would only be effected gradually, and each would be treated on its merits. Let us consider each proposed surrender separately.

CANNON STREET.

The case for the removal of this station is very strong.

In the first place, the improved London Bridge Station would be sufficient to cope with every requirement, and secondly, when the new connection proposed at Deptford for taking all passengers on these lines who wish to reach City or central stations via East London Railway to Metropolitan stations is completed, the necessity for Cannon Street disappears. The number of trains running daily into this station in 1913 was 6 long-distance and 129 suburban. The corresponding figures for Fenchurch Street were 11 and 239 respectively, or approximately double.

The station was closed for two years between 11 and 4.30 daily, and all day on Sundays, and the maintenance of such an expensive station, with its wide-span roof and the costly bridge repairs, and the well-known difficulty of working it, seem to us conclusive arguments in favour. of its abolition.

FENCHURCH STREET.

This station is an obsolete structure, and there is no reason why its long-distance passengers should not go into Liverpool Street. There is a scheme which has strong support in Stepney for the removal of the viaduct from Stepney to Fenchurch Street and the construction of an underground line connected to the Metropolitan at Mark Lane. This could not, of course, be done unless the Metropolitan were enlarged to carry the extra traffic.

The scheme accords fully with the general principle advocated later for dealing with suburban traffic.

KING'S CROSS AND ST. PANCRAS.

The Midland and North-Western and Great Northern traffic under new conditions could be concentrated at Euston by making short connections as shown on the plan. King's Cross could then be treated as a local station and St. Pancras could cease to be more than a hotel.

The present bottleneck on the Midland prevents any further expansion, and King's Cross, because of its tunnels, is in the same position.

HOLBORN.

Holborn Viaduct and St. Paul's, when transformed into underground stations on the new through line to Farringdon Street, would become local stations.

MARYLEBONE.

In December 1913 the number of trains running into Marylebone station daily was 54 suburban and 16 long-distance. Paddington and Bishop's Road together had 62 and 80 respectively.

Many of the latter are Great Central trains, and if the whole of the Great Central trains ran into Paddington, the total load would be 212 trains daily, or rather less than half the number dealt with at Victoria.

The proximity of the two stations to one another, their present joint use, the greater exchange facilities at Paddington and the congestion at Bishop's Road goods station, all combine to show that there is a strong case for the removal of the latter to Marylebone and for transferring the passenger traffic from Marylebone to an enlarged Paddington.

CHARING CROSS.

The views of the Society as to this station and its bridge are sufficiently well known to make it unnecessary to recapitulate all the arguments for its removal. It is inadequate to-day, and could not be extended to make it adequate for future needs, so that, apart from æsthetic reasons, it could not always remain.

The question as to its removal to the south side is involved with that of the general rearrangement of the southern lines and that of the main Continental approach.

These changes, which could only be effected gradually, would, when completed, effect an enormous annual saving in maintenance and staffing, and would by greater concentration add to the convenience of the services and considerably relieve the streets around the abandoned stations.

II. SUBURBAN LINES.

The suburban services divide themselves into short services up to 10 miles out and long services beyond that distance.

The short services would be operated electrically, with stops at all stations, and these are the services which it is proposed to connect to the existing central system.

The long services are mostly slow until they reach the 10-mile radius, when they become express. These would have to be maintained, as during rush hours they are necessary to cope with the peak-load traffic. This is just the kind of traffic which is more economically run with steam, and it is proposed that these should for some time continue to run into the main termini.

As an illustration of this mixed traffic, the Great Northern suburban traffic is so divided, part running into King's Cross and part running, by way of the connection at King's Cross, to the Metropolitan to Moorgate Street. There is a steady through connection all day from the suburbs to Moorgate Street, but the rush hour traffic is largely dealt with by trains terminating at King's Cross. The 1913 *Report of the London Traffic Branch* (*Board of Trade*) gives the following numbers of trains arriving in London up to 10.30 a.m.: King's Cross 44 and Moorgate Street 33. It is not thought that even when electrified the whole of the rush hour traffic could be entirely dealt with at Moorgate Street. King's Cross takes the non-stop traffic and Moorgate Street the distributed service, and the result is satisfactory.

We propose to apply this principle to all the other lines, except that, instead of stopping at Moorgate Street, the trains would continue through to some place just the other side of London, the northern systems interlocking with the south, the east with the west, and vice versa.

If this method be not adopted, we shall in the near future have to provide further widenings and further enlargements of termini.

If it be adopted, the trains which now run back nearly empty would go on distributing, and would be likely to pick up more passengers from the central stations for the suburban return journey, and the termini, being relieved of the purely local trains, could be reduced in use and at some future time amalgamated in the manner proposed.

THE BEGINNING OF THE CHANGE.

The proposal here made has been gradually evolving itself ever since the connections on the G.N.R. and Midland were made with the Metropolitan.

It was followed long after by the tubes from Finsbury Park to City and West End, and then by the line from Watford connecting with the Bakerloo. We have merely pursued this development to its logical conclusion.

By the methods described we hope to secure: (1) electric communication between every part of London and every other part; (2) better and more regular suburban services.

The conditions necessary to secure these results are:

1. The abolition of central termini for suburban traffic.
2. The elimination of passengers' luggage.

In all cases where electric traction has been adopted it has fully justified itself, and uniformity can only be obtained by its general adoption.

Rapid services cannot be run when luggage is permitted. Special arrangements for dealing with it are proposed later.

Central suburban termini create unnecessary congestion, and they involve changes which cannot of course be avoided altogether at transfer stations, but they can be reduced to a minimum by through services. Very few passengers arrive at present termini who do not continue their journey to some other point.

The accompanying plan shows the manner in which it is suggested that the traffic from the main lines should be diverted to the local lines, woven into the central system.

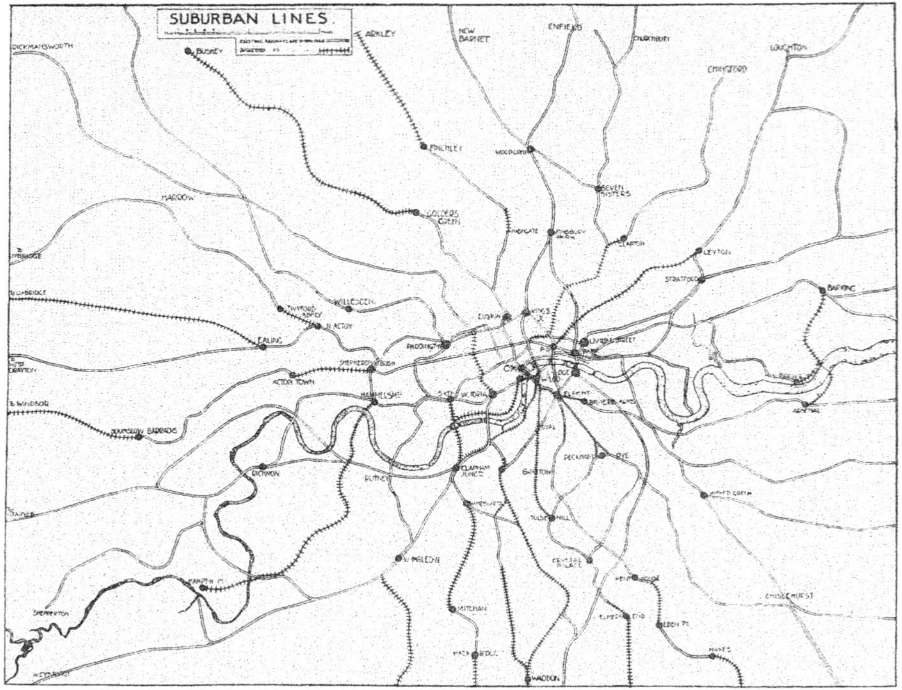

SUGGESTIONS FOR DEALING WITH SUBURBAN LINES.

(Drawing prepared by H. J. Leaning, F.S.I., and Ernest Herbert.)

To face p. 80.

In this way not only are those lines relieved, but, by acting as feeders to the local lines, they would secure to them a sufficient volume of traffic to justify the expense of their construction.

The present system of tubes has been made in a haphazard way and is incomplete and unrelated in its parts, and although now united, the connections are makeshifts and the transfer stations inadequate.

The directions of the lines shown on the plan have been settled after very careful consideration, using existing lines wherever possible, and everywhere aiming at radial directions.

Such lines as the North London to Richmond and other similar indirect services become redundant as soon as the new lines are made.

Certain alterations in direction of existing lines are therefore proposed. These are:

1. The separation of the two original lines, Hammersmith to Holborn and Finsbury Park to Holborn (now merged into the Piccadilly line). The former is shown to be continued in a north-easterly direction to Clapton, through a district very badly served at present, and the latter is continued via Aldwych under the river to Waterloo and on to Tulse Hill and Croydon. The former is extended south-west to Hampton Court.
2. The line from Euston to Clapham Common, which it is now proposed to enlarge from 8 feet 6 inches to 11 feet diameter, is cut in two, and that part of it which runs from Euston to Old Street is continued to join the Hampstead and Golder's Green line, giving access to the City from those districts. The part from Old Street to Clapham is continued to Purley and northwards connected to the Great Northern and City line; instead of the proposed enlargement of the old tube all the way, it is suggested that the enlarging should stop at the Bank and a new line be made, which would serve as an express line from the City to Clapham and Purley, the old line acting as the slow one from the City to Clapham.
3. A new line is shown from Baker Street to Victoria and continued under the river to Croydon.

4. The Waterloo and City line is extended in both directions, one way under present main South-Western line as far as Clapham Junction, to collect the local services, and the other way through the City.

INNER CIRCLE.

The treatment of the Metropolitan District lines is a matter requiring much deliberation. They have developed into the kind of rapid transit lines such as we are now aiming at, but by the number of their branches the pressure put upon the central lengths of line from South Kensington to Mansion House and Farringdon Street to Praed Street is so great as to make it urgently necessary that their capacity should be increased.

These lines, constructed in 1866 through the heart of London, could not be so constructed to-day, on grounds of cost, but they are a most valuable asset in dealing with Central London traffic, and should in our opinion be used to their utmost capacity.

Now, it is proposed to connect some of the suburban lines at Liverpool Street, Fenchurch Street, Victoria and King's Cross with these lines in order to carry these lines through London without termini.

EXPRESS LINES.

To do this it would be imperative that the capacity of these lines should be increased. At the first and last of these stations the connection exists, and at the other two it could easily be made by sinking some of the present platforms of the termini.

The new traffic would, however, interfere seriously with the existing traffic, and especially with the Inner Circle, and it is therefore proposed that a new line should be made all round the Inner Circle under the present lines, which would take the new traffic and act as express lines for the present traffic where necessary. The descent to the lower lines would be by flying junctions at points where there is room to make them, and some of the stations would have to be of two stories.

Other express lines proposed are:

1. Finchley Road, via Baker Street, along new line to Piccadilly Circus;

2. Camden Town to Waterloo;
3. Queen's Road to Bank;
4. Bank to Clapham Common,

and others as circumstances may dictate.

For short distances and the relief of highly congested points the Americans are adopting the moving platform graded in four speeds from three to twelve miles an hour. These are very efficient, but take a great width for double track, and I venture to think that the ingenious method of traction known as the Adkins-Lewis system is cheaper and more fool-proof and efficient. It might well be used as an auxiliary to the present Inner Circle or on some new routes, such as that proposed from Victoria to Marble Arch or Piccadilly to City.

INCREASED COST OF NEW CONSTRUCTION.

Owing to the great increase in cost of construction it will be many years before new tubes to the extent shown on the plan can be constructed; as an alternative, the existing suburban lines will have to be electrified and as far as possible linked up with the general system.

ALTERED WORKING HOURS.

It is possible that changes in the business habits of the people, such as working in two shifts (an expedient adopted last year in several City offices to meet the shortage of accommodation in offices), would have the effect of postponing many of the proposals here made.

III. GOODS TRAFFIC

DEFECTS.

The goods problem is not less puzzling than that of passengers. The Traffic Commission Report avoided it altogether, on the ground that the streets were not unduly used for goods distribution; but even supposing this were so, no one would contend that the present services were satisfactory. The delays are notorious, the cost of freight (due to the complicated systems) is far too high, and there is universal discontent.

As soon as the effects of the dock extension are felt the congestion and delays will increase, and it will become imperative that some measures shall be taken to satisfy the growing needs of the trading community.

REMEDIES PROPOSED.

During the past ten years the railway community has been bombarded with proposals for a Central Goods Clearing House (which it is claimed would solve the whole difficulty), and for a proposed initial cost of £14,000,000 would save £40,000,000 annually. An essential feature is the automatic sorting of the goods. Working models of this machinery have been prepared, and it is generally admitted that in itself, and for certain restricted purposes, it should have decided labour-saving effect upon the new arrangements. For this reason the Select Committee on Transport recently authorized the promoters to raise £100,000 for the purpose of erecting an installation of the machinery for actual use. So much for the machinery. In our opinion, had it been put forward on its merits it would probably have been adopted for sectional distribution long ago, but unfortunately its use was always advocated in connection with a Central Clearing House scheme in Clerkenwell, and that is a proposition which does not commend itself either to the railway companies or the Board of Trade or the traders. It is impossible to discuss it fully here. It has received most ample consideration in every quarter, and apart from the many serious objections on other grounds, expert opinion generally is against centralization either for goods or passengers. The whole tendency is in the opposite direction. Since the formation of the great goods station at Camden Town, for instance, much of the traffic which used to go there now goes through to Poplar, Blackwall and the Docks, or direct to the many local goods stations in all parts of London.

Similarly, the traffic formerly distributed from Bishop's Road and Old Oak Stations on G.W.R. now goes direct to Lambeth.

In order to prevent congestion of trucks in the central area, all trucks not fully loaded or specially consigned to a central station are arrested at one of the main sorting sidings and thence, wherever possible, are sent round instead of through London.

If this were not done the central goods stations and sidings would have to be greatly enlarged and the approaches to them widened. Fifty years hence the accumulation thus caused would become unworkable, and the streets, already overcrowded, would be worked up to the limits of their capacity. At the same time, while the distribution is becoming more direct, there is a pronounced tendency for factories for various reasons to move into the outer area. Once begun, this is likely to continue, and it is a further argument against centralization.

While therefore retaining the present arrangements, we venture to make certain suggestions for improvements which, in our opinion, would expedite and cheapen the working of the goods traffic of London, and would at the same time provide for the inevitable increase for many years to come.

Goods traffic is of many kinds, the principal varieties being—

Minerals and coal.
Bulk merchandise.
Miscellaneous goods—parcels.
Perishable articles—fish, fruit, vegetables, meat, etc.

With regard to coal, the main difficulty is fluctuating demand. There is also that of orders for particular varieties too small to fill a truck. A little time after a sudden change of weather to cold, the sidings become empty and the demand exceeds the supply. This indicates the necessity for stores to meet the emergency demands. While providing these, it would be well if the labour in handling could be reduced by constructing these stores underneath sidings well above the roadway, so that on opening the sides of trucks the coal might fall down, slide into the stores below, whence it could be taken in a similar manner, when required, to the delivery lorry, before or after sacking, according to the facilities for delivery at the destination.

It might be argued that such methods would produce much coaldust, owing to the increased attrition involved by this process. Even if this could not be overcome by well-designed shoots, there is good use for the dust (by-products, fuel blocks, etc.), and the loss in value should be more than covered by the saving in labour.

London's coal (about 16,000,000 tons a year) comes in half by sea and half by rail. Stores have therefore been placed by the riverside at Beckton, Woolwich, Deptford, Wandsworth, Lots Road, and Brentford to receive the seaborne coal.

The others are placed near the present distributing centres on the main lines of railway.

Generally, on the question of heavy goods traffic we consider that the essentials to an efficient service are:

1. Adequate sorting sidings in the right places, with as many labour-saving devices as possible. This includes plenty of "humps" (for shunting by gravitation) and well planned lines.

In our opinion, all the main lines are well provided in this respect, except the L.S.W.R., the G.W.R., and the Cambridge line of G.E.R.

In the first instance, Nine Elms, which combines sidings and goods station, is too near the terminus and the wrong side of Clapham Junction, and is a dead-end and therefore involves more shunting. Our suggestion is for new main sidings at Raynes Park and also at Hounslow, leaving Nine Elms as a goods station only.

For Great Western use, Old Oak sidings are also a dead-end and awkwardly situated, and we suggest new sidings at Greenford, retaining Old Oak as goods station.

The great increase in Lea Valley goods traffic and the closeness of Temple Mills to the central area render a new siding on this line necessary, and we have indicated one at Brimsdown.

Another new siding proposed is at Harrow, on vacant land at the junction of L.N.W. and G.C.R., to relieve Camden Town (already overlarge for its present use and closely built up to), and also to relieve Neasden, which is too good a position residentially for a vast siding, such as it would become in due course if present arrangements continue.

2. Reduction of the number of goods termini. We have already referred to the proposal to close Bishop's Road goods and substitute Marylebone as the main western goods terminus.

   In the east we should suggest closing Broad Street goods, which is already too small and too valuable in position to be so retained. In its stead we suggest an enlarged Bishopsgate.

   In the north we have to-day St. Pancras, Somers Town,

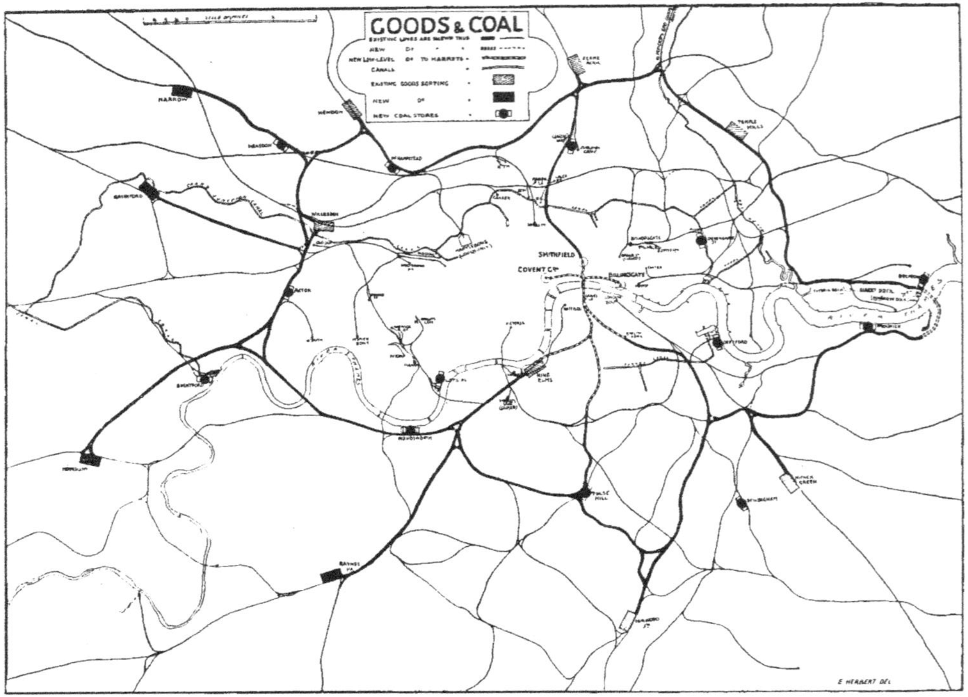

SUGGESTIONS FOR DEALING WITH GOODS AND COAL.

(Drawing prepared by H. J. Leaning, F.S.I., and Ernest Herbert.)

To face p. 86.

York Road, Chalk Farm, all of which deal with heavy volumes of traffic. It would be a very difficult and expensive work to merge all these into one, but we certainly think it the right thing to aim at. The removal of the gasometers behind King's Cross Station (now only used for storage purposes) would facilitate this, and if it could be ultimately contrived, as we believe, the fusion would certainly greatly decrease the cost of administration.

In the south-west we now have Lambeth (G.W.), Stewart's Lane (L.B.S.C.), and Nine Elms (L.S.W.) all close together. The amalgamation of these into one new station, either at Lambeth (where there is ample room for extension over the old reservoirs) or at Nine Elms, would, we consider, be ultimately justifiable. In the south-east, Willow Walk (L.B.S.C.) and Bricklayers' Arms (S.E.R.) might properly be amalgamated. The Dock stations would have to be retained and improved as the new circumstances require.

3. Easy intercommunication by rail between the various main sorting sidings. Under a unified ownership this should not prove a difficult matter. The plan shows that this can largely be done with existing lines, with the exception of a connection under the Thames east of Woolwich and flying connections at the crossings of various main lines.

4. An adequate and efficient through connection between north and south.

The present connections are:

via East London Railway at Shadwell.
via L.C. & D. at Blackfriars.
via West London Railway at Barnes.

The second, which has the best connections, is physically so inferior owing to the gradient at Snow Hill, which limits a train to twenty-three trucks against a normal sixty-three, that it hardly counts.

The first is of two tracks through the Thames Tunnel and largely occupied by passenger traffic.

The last is that most used, but to use it from the Docks a journey of $17\frac{1}{4}$ miles has to be made.

Now, the second of these routes has this feature about it,

that it runs very near to all our principal produce markets, and if carried under the river instead of above, it might be made to serve them all by means of branches to Covent Garden and Billingsgate: Smithfield already lies on the route.

This proposal raises the whole question of London's markets. Various unsuccessful attempts have been made to move them, particularly Billingsgate. The City Corporation actually erected a new fish market at Smithfield, but it was closed after a short time and converted into a poultry and game market.

The vested interests are still very powerful, and the Traffic Commission did not dare to make any proposals for change.

The only change that seems possible is that Covent Garden might cease to receive bulk vegetables, such as potatoes, cabbages, etc., which might be sold at the termini where received, only the vegetables and fruits *de luxe* going to Covent Garden. Notwithstanding any such change, it will always be a consummation devoutly to be wished that the streets approaching Covent Garden shall be as other streets, and not blocked with tons of produce, sometimes highly odoriferous.

As to fish, it was recently stated in evidence by the General Manager of G.C.R. that the quantity of fish carted daily from Marylebone to Billingsgate was 44 tons. Further quantities are similarly carted from other termini. The proposed line would obviate all this.

It would probably have to be a six-track line, as we have reason to believe it would be used very heavily by the Port of London Authority in disposing of the produce taken from ships in the river which is destined for the west or north-west.

Once constructed, it would of course be available for suburban connections and also for through Continental or other services. For these latter purposes alone it would not be justified, but for the combined purposes described would constitute a very substantial gain to the traffic facilities of London.

5. Greater use of the Thames and Regent's Canal.

The number of lighters annually licensed to ply on the Thames has been stationary for many years. These are mainly used for discharging ships which carry goods consigned to London wharves. By unloading in the river they avoid dock dues, which is a considerable saving. If there were suitable up-river railway wharves, many ships now going into dock would do this and send their goods direct. We are suggesting such a wharf at Brentford, where in 1914 the G.W.R. were intending great extensions, probably with that idea.

With regard to the Regent's Canal, although we do not agree with the Majority Report of the Canal Commission as to canals in England generally, we do feel that, having got a canal already made through 11 miles of closely built London premises, it would be folly not to make it serve as a proper distribution artery. It certainly is not that to-day. It only pays about 1½ per cent. on the capital, but if properly developed to take 100-ton barges, and with the banks covered with warehouses, as they probably then would be (a very small proportion of the frontages are now occupied), the canal should be a profitable and useful property. It should, if so treated, be *handed over to and operated by the Port Authority.*

IV. PARCELS TRAFFIC

The principal remaining classification of goods traffic is that known as miscellaneous goods—that is, small parcels.

As to these, the railways have now very little to do, as most of them are carted. Mr. Gooday (General Manager G.E.R. in London) gives the figures of Walthamstow (24 lb. per head per annum) and Edmonton (12 lb. per head per annum) to compare with those for Chelmsford (1,603 lb.).

These figures show either that the railway cannot take this traffic or that its cost is prohibitive.

In Central London we are now inaugurating a new method of transmission of mails by pneumatic tubes. The Post Office has commenced the experiment by lines connecting Mount Pleasant with the Eastern District and Western District offices.

No doubt this will be followed by lines connecting north and south, and finally the intermediate districts.

When this has been done and the system is fully organized, we suggest further connections between the main railway termini and the pneumatic system, and that the Post Office should accept parcels up to 1 cwt. and consign and deliver by this means.

Eleven pounds is a very low limit of weight for a parcel, and in adopting 112 lb. we should only be following Continental example.

If such a scheme were adopted, it might reasonably be extended to include the personal luggage of railway passengers arriving at the London termini, either for transit across London to another terminus or for delivery to hotel or residence from nearest district office. The inevitable result of such a system would be a great decrease in the number of taxicabs serving the London stations.

A great advance has been made during the war towards scientific collection and delivery of parcels delivered by road by the pooling of motor vehicles, whereby, instead of several deliveries to one district of small consignments, the whole of the daily delivery is assembled at one place and dispatched in one delivery.

CONCLUSION.

In presenting this outline of a scheme for the unification of London lines—the first complete scheme, we believe, that has been formulated—we venture to hope that some contribution has been made towards the solution of this complicated problem. It has been under the consideration of the Ministry of Transport for some time, and it is gratifying to find that, having anticipated the decision to group London railways together as one unit, the realization of many of these proposals is rendered more possible than before.

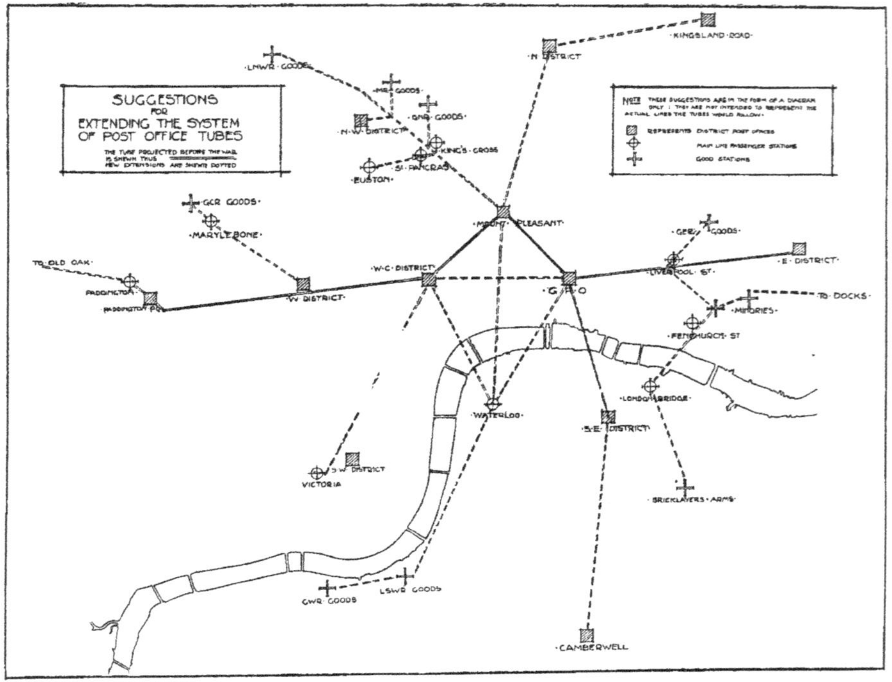

SUGGESTIONS FOR DEALING WITH THE PARCELS TRAFFIC.

(Drawing prepared by H. J. Leaning, F.S.I., and Percy W. Lovell.)

To face p. 90.

COMMERCIAL AVIATION AND LONDON

THE LORD MONTAGU OF BEAULIEU, C.S.I.

CHAPTER V

COMMERCIAL AVIATION AND LONDON

LONDON, the heart of the British Empire, will of necessity be one of the chief centres from which commercial flying will start and arrive in future. At the present moment the number of journeys per inhabitant per year in London is not so great as in the case of New York. But this difference is more due to local than national reasons. As commercial aviation becomes established as the most rapid means of communication between distant centres, such as Paris, Ostend, Brussels, other places more distant and London, so the traffic between these centres will increase and travelling by air will become common enough.

The comparative certainty and safety with which these journeys will be conducted will eventually be recognized, for already the Cross Channel services have surprised those who were not aware of the possibilities of regularity as well as of speed in the case of the aeroplane. In a few years the departures for Continental and oversea destinations every day, and perhaps two or three times a day, will become just as much a matter of course as the departure and arrival of trains at any of our great metropolitan stations.

London is, however, badly provided at present with aerodromes and landing places near its centre. The closest and most convenient regular station at present for departure and arrival is at the Hounslow aerodrome, about 11 miles west from Hyde Park Corner. It may be interesting to give here a list of the aircraft landing grounds near London on October 1, 1919.

AIRCRAFT LANDING GROUNDS NEAR LONDON.

PRINCIPAL AEROPLANE LANDING GROUNDS.

Hendon, Grahame White Company
Kenley, R.A.F. .. .. .. 15 miles from Charing Cross

Hounslow, Government	13 miles from Charing Cross
Northolt, R.A.F.	Near Hounslow
Cricklewood, Handley Page Company	
Whitehead Park, Feltham	

AIRSHIP STATIONS.

Wormwood Scrubs	For small airships
Pulham	For rigid airships; 80 miles from London
Bedford	For rigid airships; 50 miles from London
Kingsnorth	For large airships; 30 miles from London

It is clear that some day a big landing ground as near as possible to the centre of London will have to be established. I have already suggested that an elevated landing ground may have to be built, over a part of one of the parks, with, say, a winter garden underneath—the landing ground will be made of a platform of thick glass with open sides—or a similar structure over some area of London, say north of Oxford Street. The area will perhaps embrace 40 or 50 acres at a height of 150 feet, high enough to allow air to pass freely between the houses and the platform. The inhabitants living below would only feel the difference caused by slight diminution of heat from the sun's rays in the summer and some increase of temperature in the winter caused by the decrease of radiation which such a roof would prevent. On the other hand, the inhabitants of this area would never be snowbound or suffer from mud or rain-wetted pavements. The glass landing ground would rest on concrete or steel pillars. A solution of this kind, though it may seem strange to-day, is in my opinion the only way of securing an adequate landing stage for aircraft near the heart of London. The destruction of house property which would be needed for a landing place on the ground itself makes such a solution obviously impossible, on account of its cost and the disturbance and rehousing of the population. Also, any serious interference with the open spaces of the parks is highly undesirable, in view of the necessity of maintaining them as the lungs of the community and the playground for London's children.

But, whatever may be the development of such an idea in the future, it is clear that for the time being there is urgent necessity, from the point of view of aircraft leaving and arriving near London, of better communication by road or rail with the landing grounds which already exist. To get to Hounslow or Croydon by road is at all times a work of weariness, on account of the multiplicity of slow traffic on the road and the obstructive character of the tramway traffic through narrow streets. Hendon is situated more favourably in this respect, for the Edgware Road is nothing like so crowded and is of a fairly good width throughout. Northolt, between Harrow and Southall, is not of much importance and the road thither is twisty and bad. Whitehead Park, Feltham, is forty-five minutes by road from London on an average day, or, to put it in another way, it takes one-third as long as the whole average journey from London to Paris, namely 2 hours 15 minutes. Cricklewood is nearer the north and north-west of London than almost any other aerodrome, but here again the Edgware Road with its traffic has to be encountered.

But we must not forget also the possibility of using the Thames as an alighting place with "amphibians," which are certain to become more and more used as years go on. Already these aircraft have been successful in using the Thames, and on any reasonable distance between bridges can use this great London waterway.

When we come to consider the airship stations, the larger ones are far too far off from London to be of any practical use, Kingsnorth, the nearest, on the north coast of Kent, being no less than 30 miles away. It is essential that one big airship station should be established in or near London. Wormwood Scrubs is the obvious place for this, being in a favourable position for identification from the air, close to the Great Western Railway, which forms an excellent guiding mark, and containing room enough for the biggest airship if sheds were provided. But sheds for the future airship traffic of London will have to be many in number and occupy a great deal of ground. But these sheds should be looked upon rather as docks for aircraft than as places of arrival and departure, for the mooring mast system has come to stay and vast sheds are no longer needed for ordinary arrivals and departures.

In regard to the general use of aviation by Londoners, I am not one of those who believe that journeys of under 100 miles will be usually or usefully performed in the near future, except for special purposes. Journeys like London to Brighton, now performed from terminus to terminus by rail in an hour and by motorcar in less than two hours, would not be a long enough distance to make the superior speed of aircraft a real factor. London to Liverpool, Manchester and Yorkshire manufacturing centres, Scotland, Ireland and places west of Salisbury, Southampton and Oxford would, however, gain greatly by the use of aircraft transport. But, on the other hand, one must admit that foggy days, exceptionally stormy weather, and other climatic conditions will render the use of the air occasionally unsatisfactory and often impossible, so, in the matter of these places, transport on the ground, whether by road or rail, will still obtain for the majority of ordinary traffic.

But there is one kind of traffic to which aircraft is specially suited, namely the transport of mails, or, as I should prefer to call them, "airgrams," to really distant places. The airgram will be a combination of a letter and a telegram. That is to say, within the compass of an ounce of weight at least four thousand words can be sent at a price of 2s. an ounce. Such a letter will in many cases surpass the present speed of the telegraph service, and can only be equalled by telephonic communications, for which the charges would be very high and the service at present unsatisfactory. Most great London firms will probably send airgrams in the coming years to their branches abroad. And for this purpose a solution must be found, so far as London is concerned, of the difficulty of getting the airgram to the point from which the aircraft takes its departure. Either a pneumatic tube conveying mails from a certain number of conveniently situated post offices must be provided, or by means of the telephone the airgram must be repeated to a person at the point of departure, where the message would be taken in shorthand, transcribed and typewritten, and dispatched by the first aircraft leaving for a particular centre. For long messages, where the cost would be high, photography will no doubt be used, and the original manuscript or typescript will be photographed in a much reduced size, so as to occupy an exceedingly small compass, and enlarged again by the recipient at the other end.

The day also may come when aeroplanes will be able to alight in a much smaller space than we realize to-day, say an area represented by 200 square yards. If this comes about, then certain areas may combine together to roof over their houses and provide an area of their own of adequate size, which will form a landing and departure ground for their own planes, which will be kept at some place outside London and be flown in to pick up their owners, in a way similar to that in which motor-cars are kept in garages at some distance from the owner's residence to-day.

Whatever the future of commercial aviation may be, and I for one believe it to be almost limitless, London will always remain one of the chief brain centres in the world, and London, by virtue of its political, social and commercial importance, deserves, and should eventually get, the best aircraft service in the world.

THE BRIDGES OF LONDON

1815–1920

SIR REGINALD BLOMFIELD, R.A., Litt.D.

CHAPTER VI

THE BRIDGES OF LONDON

1815–1920

Bridges over running water seem to possess a certain vitality peculiar to themselves. Whether this impression is due to the springing arch, or to the suggestion of being above the earth and to that extent aloof from it, or to the movement of the water, they affect one differently from other buildings, and from time immemorial seem to have had an irresistible attraction for mankind which it is not easy to explain. Why, for example, in mediæval times, should people have insisted on building their houses on bridges, in spite of the extreme inconvenience to themselves and others, the risk of fire from their ramshackle houses, such as the disastrous fire on old London Bridge, when three thousand people were said to have perished, the dangers to the fabric of the bridge and other common-sense reasons, all of which were impartially ignored, in some vague anxiety to put as great a distance as possible between one's habitation and the noisome things of earth? Why, again, was the head of the Roman College of Priests called the "Pontifex Maximus"? Was he a bridge-builder to heaven, like the Pontifex Maximus of later date, or was he in the first instance a builder of actual bridges, the man of skill and genius who met and conquered the forces of nature for his fellows? We must leave these questions to the student of primitive religion and content ourselves with the fact of the indefinable fascination of bridges over running water, and one other fact, that in the twelfth and thirteenth centuries the "Frères Pontifes," the brethren of the order of S. Bénézet, were actually the men who built and maintained the few bridges that existed. The great bridge at Avignon, 900 metres long, now in ruins, the Pont Saint-Esprit across the Rhône, 919 metres long,[1]

[1] The length of Waterloo Bridge between the abutments is 1,240 feet; Westminster

still in use, though much altered, were carried out by these indomitable brethren. Probably old London Bridge, built in the last quarter of the twelfth century and attributed to Peter the priest of Colechurch, was the work of the Brotherhood. From the clergy, bridge-building passed into the hands of the military engineers, but its design was recaptured by architects at the Renaissance, and remained with them till the middle of the eighteenth century, when it passed into the hands of the specialized engineer. All the finest stone bridges of the seventeenth and first half of the eighteenth century seem to have been designed by architects, and it is a matter for regret that the designing of bridges should ever have passed out of their hands, but architects were themselves partly to blame. That arch-impostor, J. H. Mansart, undertook bridges, as he was ready to undertake anything else, but the total collapse of one of his bridges within a very few years of its being built was one of the reasons that led to the establishment of the "Ponts et Chaussées" in France and its complete reorganization by Perronet in the middle of the eighteenth century. To Perronet and his school were due some of the finest bridges in France, but the specialization of construction, the severance of engineering from architecture, had already begun, with disastrous results to both, and the process was completed by the introduction and development of iron, and later of steel, construction in the last century. One could wish for a class of Frères Pontifes amongst us now, men equally conversant with construction and design, men capable of getting the utmost possible out of material, both for scientific and æsthetic purposes, who out of their construction would evolve forms that are beautiful to look upon, instead of plastering on to their construction ridiculous attempts at ornament. For a bridge-builder it is not enough to be a master of construction and building processes. These ought ye to have done and not to leave the other undone, and that "other" is of the very essence of the work—the grasp of the imaginative problem as a whole, the realization of what the bridge means, not merely as a means of transit but as a symbol of the life and civilization of the people who use that bridge; and it is here that our modern bridge-builders so lamentably fail. Some years ago it was necessary to construct a bridge above the Pool of

Bridge is 810 feet long between the abutments, little more than one-fourth of the length of the *Pont* Saint-Esprit. The *Pont* Saint-Esprit is about 40 kilometres above Avignon.

London, the very centre of business of the waterway of the greatest city of the world, and all we could produce was that monument of artistic ineptitude, Tower Bridge, with its towers like a confectioner's cake and the clumsy curves of its suspension bars. I make no criticism on the engineering solution of the problem. It answers its purpose efficiently, and is no doubt very well done, but the æsthetic result is patent to anyone who looks eastward from London Bridge. What is forgotten nowadays in dealing with monumental problems of design, such as bridges and the like, is that, after all, technical knowledge of construction, though indispensable, is not the whole of the equipment necessary. Imagination, passion, fine ideals and a range of thought that lives among the higher spaces of life are equally vital, are in fact the essential basis of great design. Our bridges, serviceable enough as a means of transit, have a distressing habit of lapsing into bathos. The artist is wanted here not less than the scientific constructor. Where the latter sees only his calculations and formulæ, the artist will see possibilities of emotional expression. He is trained in the appreciation of form, line and mass, in selection, in sacrifice, and it is his business to interpret the æsthetic qualities that lie latent everywhere, not by superadding things that have no relation to the essential purpose of his subject, but by searching out the beauty that is inherent in it. The best solution, no doubt, would be to combine the two faculties in one man; but if that is not possible in view of the intricate complexities of modern construction, the engineer and the artist might at least co-operate. After all, a bridge is about the most prominent object it is possible to construct anywhere, and as it is impossible to escape it, the æsthetic effect of the bridge must be a vital part of the problems of its design. There ought to be no difficulty in the co-operation of engineers and architects if both of them know their business and if only they are ready to pull together.

It is not very easy to say where the London bridges begin. They end with Tower Bridge, but up the river the interminable houses extend on both sides of the river up to Putney, with the welcome break of Hurlingham. Strictly speaking, the London bridges extend from Tower Bridge up to Hammersmith, and of these Tower Bridge, London Bridge, Southwark and Blackfriars are under the control of the Corporation of the City of

London, and Waterloo Bridge and the bridges westward, up to, and including, Hammersmith Bridge, are under that of the London County Council. With the exception of Westminster and Chelsea Bridges, which were built for the Government, all the L.C.C. bridges were in the first instance built and maintained by private companies under powers conferred by Acts of Parliament, and the cost was to be recovered from the tolls. In 1877 an Act was passed empowering the Metropolitan Board of Works to buy out these interests and free the bridges to the public. This was done at a cost of £1,376,825, the control passing finally to the L.C.C. in 1895.[1] It must be admitted that with all its faults of omission and commission the old Board of Works rendered two admirable services to the public—the freeing of the bridges and the construction of the Victoria Embankment. Unfortunately, the bridges so acquired displayed a want of taste and knowledge inconceivable in any period but that of the second half of the nineteenth century. To Peter Bell,

> A primrose by a river's brim
> A yellow primrose was to him,
> And it was nothing more.

So to these engineers a bridge seems to have had no symbolism, it was just a means of getting from one side of the river to the other; but had they been content to leave it at that, one would have gladly acquiesced in their bare construction. The municipal authorities of the time seem to have thought it necessary to make some concession to æsthetic demands, and instead of consulting some competent artist, the engineer, with sublime self-confidence, launched out into uncharted seas, and produced the abominations of the Hammersmith Suspension Bridge and Chelsea Bridge. The L.C.C. *Report on Bridges* says that Hammersmith Bridge was the first suspension bridge over the Thames. It was designed by Mr. William Tierney Clarke, and was opened on October 7, 1827. When the Metropolitan Board of Works acquired it in 1880, the bridge was found to be unsafe and too narrow. A new bridge, opened in 1887, was designed by Bazalgette, and the *Report* continues: "The only portions of the original structure which were allowed to remain were parts of the towers below the road and the abutments." The

[1] See the *Report on Bridges*, printed for the L.C.C., 1914, P. S. King & Son, 2 and 4 Great Smith Street, S.W., to which very useful pamphlet I am greatly indebted.

old masonry towers were replaced by "lighter ones of wrought iron." I do not know what the old "towers" were like; they are described as having had openings for traffic only 14 feet wide, and were no doubt extremely inconvenient, but anything more mean and commonplace than Bazalgette's "lighter ones of wrought iron" it would be difficult to conceive. They are as bad as the deplorable towers of Chelsea Bridge, two of the worst eyesores in the whole length of the river. If only the engineers had learnt to leave well alone!

Battersea Bridge seems to be a reasonable limit for the London bridges. To the west of it the river sweeps round Chelsea Bay and then turns southward in a long reach to Wandsworth Bridge. Moreover, older London stops at Chelsea and Battersea, with their memories of the eighteenth century, and the old bridge of Battersea will always live in the work of a great modern painter. The old bridge was constructed for Lord Spencer in 1771–2. It was formed entirely of wood in nineteen spans, and after having valiantly done its work for a hundred years, it was purchased by the Metropolitan Board of Works, who found its condition so unsafe that they had to set about rebuilding it at once. Bazalgette designed the new bridge, which was opened in 1890. It is a singularly ugly structure. Five segmental arches of cast-iron ribs on stone piers span the river, and above the arches is a large cove which the engineers believed would give "lightness to the design of the bridge." Its result is to make it look weak, and the L.C.C. *Report* says that on foggy nights it has led to accidents, because bargemen mistake it for the outline of the arch. Above this cove there is a preposterous little balustrade of a Moorish design, reminiscent of the Alhambra—the Alhambra, that is, of Leicester Square, not of Granada. Altogether it is a poor design. The work of the engineer of the Metropolitan Board of Works was, to say the least of it, puzzling. Some of it was very good, as, for example, the Victoria Embankment,[1] and some of it very bad, as, for example, the Battersea Bridge and the Chelsea Embankment.[2] The difference is so great that it seems inconceivable that they were all designed by the same hand, and that the man who could design the splendid detail of the Victoria Embankment could also have been responsible for the coarse and

[1] Opened in 1870; J. W. Bazalgette engineer.
[2] Opened in 1874; J. W. Bazalgette engineer.

ignorant detail of Battersea Bridge, or, for the matter of that, of the Chelsea Embankment. The details of the latter are very inferior. The mouldings are ignorant and have no meaning, and the engineer perversely rusticated the retaining walls of the embankment on the side of the river, thus affording a convenient resting place for all the garbage of the river. Battersea Bridge has, however, one merit. It is approached by long straight roads, which, though not quite axial on the north side, are nearly so, and as the gradient of the bridge is low, a fine long vista is obtained across it southwards.

There is little to detain us in the Albert Suspension Bridge, hung like a great spider's web spun across the river. It was designed by Mr. R. W. Ordish, C.E., in 1873, and the only remarkable thing about it is the width of the centre spans of 383 feet and the height of the towers, 101 feet above high water. The *Report* says, "The whole structure is from an engineering point of view very unsatisfactory," and from an artistic point of view it is worse than that. It looks like a temporary gangway flung across the river, and in fact is not very much more. Both on this and the Chelsea Bridge, troops have to break step in crossing, and no load above five tons is allowed.

The Chelsea Suspension Bridge is even worse, because it is more ambitious. This bridge was built in 1851–7 from the designs of Mr. T. Page, C.E. Its kiosques and gilt finials, its travesty of Gothic architecture in cast iron, its bad construction and its text of "Gloria in excelsis" above the arch between the piers are redolent of 1851, the year of the Great Exhibition, the *locus classicus* of bad art, false enthusiasm and shams. In spite of its pious aspirations, the bridge had to be strengthened six years after its completion and again in 1880, and even so will not carry more than a load of five tons. The worst of it is that this bridge blocks the view of Chelsea Hospital as one enters London by trains crossing Grosvenor Bridge. Instead of wasting money on paint and patching, it is to be hoped that this bridge will some day be replaced by a permanent structure. The approach on the south side next Battersea Park is a fine one, and that on the north side could be improved without much difficulty. This matter of the approaches to our bridges has been far too much ignored from the very first. It is a point that was never overlooked by the best French bridge-builders.

The next traffic bridge down the river is the important bridge of Vauxhall. This is so far the last completed of the London bridges, and though it is open to criticism, it is notable as being the first serious attempt in recent times to regard a great bridge as something more than a mere engineering problem. There was an earlier bridge at Vauxhall, built in 1811–16, at a cost of £296,998. This bridge, designed by John Rennie, consisted of nine iron arches of a span of 78 feet, and was the first iron bridge across the Thames. It was taken over by the Metropolitan Board of Works at a cost of £255,000, but a few years later was found to be unsafe, and in 1895 the L.C.C. obtained powers to rebuild the bridge, and the work was completed in 1906 from the designs of Sir Maurice Fitzmaurice and Mr. W. E. Riley, superintending architect to the L.C.C. The bridge is in five spans, with steel arches on granite piers and abutments. A bold ovolo moulding projects above the crown of the arches, carrying a light iron balustrade. On the piers above the cutwaters are steel recessed panels, four on each side, filled with bronze figures of heroic size by Mr. Alfred Drury, R.A., and Mr. F. W. Pomeroy, R.A., representing Local Government, Education, Science, Fine Arts, Pottery, Engineering, Agriculture and Architecture. The bridge is of fine width—80 feet—and of a good outline, and has the merit of showing its steel construction without any attempt to make it look like masonry. In order to get headway without too steep a gradient, the arches had to be kept very shallow, and it was to correct this thinness that Mr. Riley designed the unusual balustrade of iron bars with a secondary rail, carrying through the top of the piers. Though perhaps the treatment is rather light and hardly in scale, it is a metal treatment, and a break away from the habit of trying to get the effect of stone ornament in cast iron. The figures themselves are dignified and impressive, but their position on the piers is open to question. It is doubtful whether in any case it is right to put figures below the bridge level and on the face of the piers instead of on the top of them. In this position it is difficult to get them into scale with the bridge itself, as can be seen from the failure of the figures on the Pont de l'Alma at Paris, where the effect is almost grotesque. In the Vauxhall Bridge the setting is hardly adequate for the figures, and the only people who can see these figures are the crews of the tugs and barges that go up and down the river, as the Embankment stops short on either side and the nearest point from which the bridge can be seen is the Embankment in front of the Tate Gallery. Moreover, the figures, being of bronze against a dingy green paint, are lost against the background. When the sun is west of the bridge, these figures are hardly visible at a distance, and it ought to be almost a rule in our climate that when bronze is used in the open it should be set against a light background, such as Portland stone. Here, however, at any rate, a serious effort has been made to treat the bridge as a great public monument.

There is nothing to detain us on our way down stream till we come to Westminster, for the Lambeth Suspension Bridge is an insignificant affair; its end bays are sagging seriously, and for over twenty-five years it has been practically condemned. In an important part of the river, such as this, a suspension bridge should never have been allowed. Looking down the river from Vauxhall Bridge, the outline of the Lambeth Bridge cuts the lines of Lambeth, St. Thomas's Hospital, the Houses of Parliament and Somerset House beyond in the most disagreeable manner; but the bridge-designers of the last century seem to have thought it unnecessary to consider the bearing of their design on its setting and surroundings.

With Westminster Bridge begins that splendid series of bridges, embankments and buildings which makes the view from Westminster Bridge the finest thing in London, perhaps in the world. The old Westminster Bridge was begun in 1739 and completed in 1750, from the designs of Labelye, a Swiss engineer, at a cost of £389,500. Labelye seems to have been careless or over-confident about his foundations, for he omitted any piling under the piers and built them in caissons, directly in the soil, at a depth of from 5 feet to 14 feet below the bed of the river. The piers were constructed of huge blocks of Portland stone, weighing from one to three tons and fastened with iron cramps. There were thirteen large arches, the largest 76 feet in span, and two small ones at the ends, the total length of the bridge being 1,223 feet and the width 44 feet. It must have been a fine-looking bridge. I saw recently in a print-shop a beautiful aquatint in blue and silver of old Westminster Bridge. The view was taken from the site of the new L.C.C. buildings before the Houses of Parliament were burnt and rebuilt, and shows Westminster Hall rising above the arches of the bridge, and beyond it the towers and roofs of the Abbey. Fine as Barry and

Pugin's design is in some ways, it blocks the Hall and the Abbey, and it seems to have lost us one of the most beautiful architectural compositions that ever existed in London. But Labelye's construction was faulty, and in 1831, after the removal of old London Bridge, the increased scour gradually washed away the foundations of Westminster Bridge, until its rebuilding became inevitable. The work was entrusted to Mr. Page, the engineer of the Chelsea Suspension Bridge, and was completed in 1862. It is a great improvement on the Chelsea Bridge, and though at a far lower artistic level, is, next to Waterloo Bridge, the most satisfactory of the later London bridges. The bridge is in seven spans, formed with iron arches varying from 94 feet 9 inches at the sides to 120 feet wide in the centre arch. The piers and abutments are of granite, and though the details are rather absurd, it is a solid and by no means undignified structure, being of ample width (84 feet 2 inches between the parapets) and having the great advantage of important buildings on either side of the approaches at each end. It is true there is no sort of balance in these buildings; at the south end, St. Thomas's Hospital and the new L.C.C. buildings are too close in to the bridge, and at the north end the business premises are unequal to the task of standing up to the Parliament buildings across the road; but seen from Charing Cross Bridge, with Shaw's splendid Scotland Yard in the foreground, the bridge and the Westminster buildings make a noble group. The lattice girders of the South Eastern Railway bridge block the view, and till this is removed, Londoners will not realize what they possess.

Waterloo Bridge is the last of the L.C.C. bridges eastward, and by universal consent is architecturally the finest bridge in England, if not in the world. Its history is curious and characteristic of our English methods. In France a bridge of this importance would, as a matter of course, have been undertaken by the State. In England it was the work throughout of a private company. In 1809 an Act of Parliament authorized the formation of the "Strand Bridge Company," with a capital of £500,000, increased in 1813 to £700,000, and again increased in 1816. The bridge was designed by John Rennie; the first stone was laid on October 11, 1811, and the bridge was opened by the Prince Regent on June 18, 1817, the second anniversary of the Battle of Waterloo. The name had already (1816) been changed from Strand to Waterloo Bridge, and the words of the Act of 1816 are memorable: "The said bridge when completed will be a work of great stability and magnificence; and such works are adapted to transmit to posterity the remembrance of great and glorious achievements." It was therefore decided that "a name should be given to the said bridge which shall be a lasting record of the brilliant and decisive victory achieved by His Majesty's Forces," and no monument could more fully express the grim and enduring courage of the British soldier of 1815. The total cost of the bridge and approaches was £937,392. In 1877 it was acquired by the Metropolitan Board of Works for £474,200, when the toll-gates were removed. With the exception of certain works necessitated by the scour of the river in 1882, the removal and subsequent return of the original iron lamp-standards, and the skilfully executed alterations for the tramway on the west side, this great bridge has stood its hundred years without any alteration or failure, and, unlike the new bridges across the Thames, there is no limit to the weight of vehicles using the bridge.[1]

The bridge is so familiar that no description is necessary. It is a standing example of what may be done by a good man with the simplest possible means. There is no ornament, except the modillion cornice and the coupled columns above the cutwaters, but the whole design is so admirably balanced, the proportions are so perfect, the details, simple as they are, so exactly right and so instinct with knowledge in reserve, that criticism is ungrateful to one who day after day has passed under its arches and watched it, immutable, yet never the same under the changes of our restless skies, gathering up into itself all the elements of romance—the storm, the sunshine, the power and the tragedy of London's glorious river. Yet I confess to an incessant curiosity as to who really designed the form and fashion of this bridge. That Rennie was the engineer, and an extremely able one, we all know; but Rennie also designed London Bridge a few years later, and this is so

[1] L.C.C. *Bridges, Historical and Descriptive Notes*, p. 56. The bridge is constructed of granite in nine elliptical spans, each of 120 feet with a rise of 35 feet; the total length is 1,240 feet, and the width between parapets 42 feet 6 inches. The bridge of Neuilly, constructed from the designs of Perronet in 1772, though in five arches only, has very similar proportions. The arches are 120 feet wide with a rise of 30 feet. The piers are 13 feet thick as against the 20 feet of Waterloo, and the width is 45 feet out to out, almost identical. It is a testimony to the soundness of the work of the English engineer that, whereas the arches of Perronet's bridge settled some 8 inches after the centres were struck, the arches of Waterloo Bridge only settled 1½ inches.

inferior and his treatment of his iron bridges was so unattractive, that, as in the case of the Victoria Embankment, one cannot help asking who helped the engineer. There is a legend in the Temple that Rennie got the designs from some broken-down architect in prison, and the hand of an architect, and of a very good one, is written all over it. When Waterloo Bridge was built architects were still enthusiastic for the severest forms of Greek architecture. Were any of the leading architects of the time consulted? Did Soane or either of the Inwoods or Decimus Burton lend a hand; or do we owe the Sicilian Doric of the columns, the fine and even learned profiling of the cornice, the admirable spacing of the rustications, to some unknown draughtsman, some forgotten and unrecognized genius in Rennie's office? The motives of these columns in this position and the modillion cornice were undoubtedly due to an architect, for in the old Blackfriars Bridge, begun in 1760, Robert Mylne, the architect, had also placed pairs of columns above the cutwaters and a modillion cornice with the architrave omitted above the arch, exactly as in Waterloo Bridge. Mylne had used rather attenuated Ionic columns, and the general scale of the Blackfriars Bridge was inferior to that of Waterloo; but whoever it was, whether Rennie or his draughtsman or another, the designer took this motive and handled it with the audacity of a master. In one point only the design seems to me open to criticism: the voussoirs in the crown of the arch are not quite deep enough. With one more effort of audacity the designer might have broken through his frieze and carried these voussoirs through to the soffit of the cornice. The central voussoirs appear to be about 4 feet to 5 feet deep. According to Belidor's rules for the depths of voussoirs in an arch of 120 feet span they ought to be 8 feet deep. In the crown of the arches of Waterloo Bridge they are too shallow for effect.

With Blackfriars begins the series of City bridges. The existing bridge is a standing example of foolish ornament. About forty years ago these stumpy little columns, about two to three diameters in height, with their enormous capitals doing nothing, were rather the fashion, apparently an attempt to catch the Romanesque manner of Burgess. Here they carry nothing, nor have they any relation as a motive of design to the iron arches. If one is going to use steel or iron in bridges, the least one can do is to attempt to make the most out of its essential qualities, its capacity to do a great amount of work with a relatively small amount of material; and if stone or granite or softer material is used in connection with steel or iron, the design should subordinate itself to the character of the harsher material—it should eschew all florid detail and make up in mass what it lacks in concentrated strength. In the old Southwark Bridge, now destroyed, with its three great iron arches and massive stone piers, Rennie managed the combination perfectly well, but modern engineers will never learn to let well alone. Tower Bridge is an even worse example than Blackfriars of the same failure in ideas, though candour compels me to admit that the Gothic towers and gateways were designed by an architect. Since the building of St. Paul's no finer chance has offered itself in London for a great monumental design. With the Tower of London to set the scale, with the splendid waterway it was to span, with all the past and present of the City of London to symbolize, this bridge might have been a monument of the greatness of the British Empire; and it is—what it is. Let us hope that the new Southwark Bridge will redeem the reputation of the City Fathers.

London Bridge completes this short survey.[1] Till nearly the middle of the eighteenth century the old bridge was the only bridge possessed by London, and it is amazing that, constructed as it was, it should have lasted for over six hundred years. It was begun in 1176, and appears to have been finished early in the thirteenth century. It was 926 feet by 20 feet wide, and formed with twenty arches, with a drawbridge in the centre. The citizens of London at once proceeded to load it up with houses, and the multiplication of piers so blocked the waterway that the bridge was in constant danger of being washed away by floods. Five arches went in 1282, destroyed by drifting ice. The houses caught fire from time to time, and the passage under the bridge became more and more dangerous. In the aquatint view of London Bridge by Milton, the water is shown rushing through like a millrace. In the middle of the eighteenth century an Act of Parliament was obtained for the removal of all buildings on the bridge, and in 1759 Dance, the City architect, and Taylor converted two of the old arches into a large central arch. Finally, some six hundred years after its building, it was decided to remove old London Bridge and build a new one close by. This

[1] See Britton and Pugin, *Edifices of London*, ii. 303–13.

was before 1801, but it was not till 1824 that the new bridge was actually begun from the designs made by John Rennie and under the superintendence of his son. The *Sunday Times* for November 23, 1828, records that on November 23, 1828, the keystone of the last arch " was slowly lowered amidst discharge of cannon to its place. The Lord Mayor took a mallet in his hand and struck the stone three times. On the third stroke the whole assembly gave three cheers." In the Guildhall there is a collection of admirable pencil drawings by E. Cooke, R.A., showing the old bridge in various stages of demolition and the construction of the new.

The bridge is on five arches of unequal spans, instead of the nine of Waterloo Bridge. Rennie increased his span from 120 feet to 150 feet in the central span, a daring piece of construction which J. H. Mansart had foolishly attempted in a bridge over the Allier at Moulins, which totally collapsed within ten years of its being built. Yet London Bridge is disappointing. Instead of keeping his courses the same depth, Rennie, following Mylne, reduced them as they ascended. He omitted any solid walling above the piers, carrying his balustrade through without a break ; in both cases with most unfortunate effect. It is probable that these alterations were forced upon Rennie, or introduced by his son as the work proceeded, as they do not show in the contemporary illustration in Britton and Pugin ;[1] but the design throughout is dull. If one stands on the Old Swan Pier and looks up the river, there is the South-Eastern Railway bridge to Cannon Street. It is not lovely, nor does it affect to be anything but what it is, a solid, ugly railway bridge; yet when the tide is running out and the wind is in the sky and the grey water comes swirling under these piers, this bridge, too, has its quality—it sends the imagination roving to other lands and far-distant ages.

The bridge problem is a serious one. So far, with one or two not entirely successful exceptions, it has been considered mainly from the engineering point of view, or rather as an affair of construction plus ill-chosen and ill-adjusted ornament, instead of being thought out as a problem of practical conditions translated into beautiful forms by the ability of the designer. A great bridge should be something more than a mere means of transit. It is not

[1] See Britton and Pugin, *Public Edifices* (1828). A parapet wall is shown with breaks over the piers, greatly to the improvement of the design.

enough to throw a girder across a river or suspend a roadway with steel cables. A bridge should have an imaginative significance, not lost sight of by the great bridge-builders of the past and still waiting to be recovered. Where the bridge over is impossible, there is still the tunnel under, and this too requires thought and imagination in its approach and frontispiece. Both bridge and tunnel will be wanted. During the war a temporary bridge was thrown across the Thames at Gravesend, and at this vital point it is essential that some means should be provided for getting from one side of the river to the other. The ferry service at Woolwich is another case in point. This too should be replaced by a road tunnel, designed as part of the general plan of development suggested by The London Society in connection with the East London Dock systems. There is no reason why the entrance to a tunnel should be ugly; on the contrary, it is a fine opportunity for design, e.g. the tunnel under the Quirinal at Rome or the entrance to the tramway tunnel at Waterloo Bridge.

New bridges, too, will be wanted, small and great. The River Lea still forms a barrier, so does the Wandle, and lastly there is the crying need of the great roadway bridge across the river from Charing Cross, with the unequalled opportunity it may provide for a fitting Memorial *urbi et orbi* of the Great War. Five years ago, with Sir Aston Webb and Mr. John Burns, I put forward a tentative suggestion for the line this bridge might follow, having the spire of St. Martin's in the Fields at the end of the vista looking north. On some such lines as that a great scheme might be worked out, with noble approaches and vistas, "Places" and triumphal arches at either end, the best of our sculpture, the finest of our architecture, to speak to future ages of the heroism and sacrifice of the unnumbered dead and of the patient devotion of those men and women who worked at home, without reward, from simple faith and patriotism. Waterloo Bridge, though not built for that purpose, is still the noblest monument of the men of 1815, and in its perfect scale and admirable restraint shows us the way. We have passed through the fiery furnace, and the record of this war shows that the spirit of 1815 lives stronger than ever throughout the Empire. What finer symbol of that spirit could there be than some great bridge such as Waterloo, if only we can rise again to the level of our opportunity.

LONDON AND THE CHANNEL TUNNEL

SIR ARTHUR FELL, M.P.

CHAPTER VII

LONDON AND THE CHANNEL TUNNEL

CHARING CROSS is distant more than 70 miles from the entrance to the Channel Tunnel, which will be situate on the chalk downs behind Dover, but the construction of this tunnel will have an immense influence on the future of London, an influence which it is hard to realize at its true value.

London is at present crammed to overflowing, and with all the shops and theatres doing a record trade and with every means of locomotion overcrowded. People may well wonder, under these conditions, if anything could render London more popular and more prosperous than it is, and if any change can be needed to draw more people and more money to it as the centre of our Empire.

The answer to this is, the present boom, which is world-wide, will pass away, and competition will arise again, and the country or city which stands still and which merely beats time will assuredly be passed in the struggle and lose its pre-eminence in the world.

London has perforce stood still for the five years of the war, as have the other capitals of Europe, but the question now arises, Is London to continue to stand still, or what does it propose to do now that the war is over? What great plans and improvements are contemplated and what great works are to be undertaken?

The great drapers, in numbers, intend, it is reported, to rebuild their premises and increase their stores; new theatres and music-halls and cinemas and new hotels will be erected, Devonshire House, in Piccadilly, may be pulled down and a great caravanserai built in its place; but all these improvements simply mean that London will be a little larger. A little more of everything will be provided for the people, but nothing more.

Paris, on the other hand, has decided to undertake a memorable work. It will remove the walls and fortifications which encircle Paris. The visitor hardly notices these fortifications as the trains cut their way through them. When he drives out of Paris to the Bois de Boulogne, he may perhaps notice the grassy slopes of the Enceinte, the walls and dry moat and the glacis on the other side, as he passes through the Porte Maillot, but he takes little heed of them. These fortifications are some 30 miles in circumference, and although but a hundred yards or so in breadth they cover in the whole an immense acreage of most valuable ground. This regained land is partly to be laid out in gardens and partly to be built on, and new great streets and boulevards will be made; and when we think of the magnificence of French buildings and the grandeur of the broad streets the French lay out, we may realize that a new Paris will be created and that the victorious war will be thus fittingly commemorated. The grand boulevards of Paris, stretching from the Place de la Concorde to the Bastille, are on the site of the old walls and fortifications of Paris, and we appreciate what their removal has meant to modern Paris.

We have in London made no great improvement since the construction of the Thames Embankment. Some new streets have been driven through the poor and crowded district between Oxford Street and Piccadilly and the Strand, but they are nothing noteworthy. We may build half a dozen Shaftesbury Avenues and Kingsways, which will to some extent relieve the traffic and provide sites for new hotels and theatres, but that is all. They will make London bigger, but they will not make it greater or more worthy of its position and pre-eminence as the biggest city of the world and the capital of the greatest Empire.

The prospect of the early construction of the Channel Tunnel, which now seems nearer of accomplishment than at any previous time, holds out possibilities of a new and great future for London—a future which will leave its mark upon it, and, if taken advantage of wisely, will create a new London for our children, which will assure its position in the Empire for all time.

The Channel Tunnel means two tubes under the Straits of Dover, about 30 miles long and 20 feet in diameter, connecting the Chemin de Fer du Nord of France and the South-Eastern and Chatham Railway of England. These tubes seem but a small thing to effect all that is expected of them.

To many this tunnel means but an easier and quicker means

of getting to Paris. The journey will be made without sea-sickness, the trouble with hand luggage at Dover and Calais, and the exasperating struggles that take place in the Custom House and in getting seats in the trains at Calais and Boulogne. The tunnel means, however, very much more than this. It will affect the position of London as the great railway centre of Great Britain and make it the great world terminus of Europe, Asia and Africa, the gateway of the East, the starting point of the great express trains for India, for Palestine and Africa, which will surely follow on the opening of the tunnel. Upon it will depend the direction of the flow of the great Transatlantic travel. Will this travel pass through London, or will it give it the go-by and pass direct to the Continent through the great seaports in France, Belgium, Holland and Germany, which will all be competing for it? Will London, in fact, be *side-tracked*, as the Americans call it, or will it secure the full benefit of the prize which will be at its feet?

There will be for a very long time—possibly for fifty or a hundred years—a steady, continuous stream of travellers who will visit the scenes of the Great War. It was the World's War, and they will come from every quarter of the world to see the battlefields, which will be described in countless books to be written in increasing numbers every year. There was a never-failing stream of English visitors to the Field of Waterloo right up to the very time of the Great War—and on the field of Waterloo only fifty thousand British were engaged, whilst on the battlefields of France ten million French, British and Americans were engaged against the eight million soldiers of Germany and Austria. There is no one who has not had relatives fighting, and few who have not relatives who have found their graves in France. The widespread interest will create the greatest travel, the greatest movement of passengers and travellers the world has ever witnessed.

So far as England is concerned, this movement will flow from England to the Continent and back to England without any change being made in our means of communication, but what route will the passenger traffic from other lands take? Will the travellers from the Western World pass through England and via London, or will they go direct to the Continental ports instead? If the Channel Tunnel is not built and every facility offered to travellers from the United States and South America, they will not come to England.

They will not land at Liverpool or Southampton, travel up to London and then cross over by steamer to France, and then travel by train to Paris or the battlefields, but will rather go direct to Havre or Cherbourg or St. Nazaire, and so avoid the Channel crossing. This crossing is, to many, a bugbear worse than an Atlantic voyage. An English Admiral said the other day that he was never seasick on a man-of-war, but that he never could cross the Channel without suffering agonies; and many Americans cross the Atlantic in the liners without a qualm, but succumb to the Channel crossing. This Channel crossing must always remain about the worst sea passage in the world. The gales and fogs and small harbours in France make it exceptionally difficult to maintain the service. In September 1917 it was interrupted by storms for four consecutive days. One of the small paddleboats which are always used in rough weather started on the second day of the gales from Folkestone, full of troops, but could not enter the French harbour and had to return, and a similar experience happens every year.

The Channel Tunnel will, however, do away with all these difficulties and make the Continental system of railways a part of our own. The two tubes, with the up and down lines, will be able to carry an enormous traffic. Thirty thousand passengers and thirty thousand tons of goods can be conveyed through them in twenty hours, leaving an interval or margin of four hours each night for repairs and renewals and change of staff. This would mean they could convey to France nearly eleven million passengers in a year, whilst the passenger traffic, judging from the pre-war figures, would amount to about two million only in the year.

The traffic to the Continent will certainly double on the opening of the Tunnel, but it will be many years before it can have outgrown its carrying capacity.

The tunnel will assuredly be built, and the passenger traffic will multiply probably beyond all expectations, but the question remains, How will London deal with it ? Can London cope with it, and conduct it with comfort and give the facilities demanded by modern civilization ?

The answer must be that with the existing stations and railways this will be impossible. The stations available are Charing Cross, Cannon Street, Victoria and the Holborn Viaduct. They are all now working to almost their full capacity, and they could not possibly, in addition to their present traffic, accommodate an addition of even hourly great Continental trains with their sleeping-cars, their dining-cars and huge baggage-cars.

The platform accommodation is quite inadequate, and the access to the stations by the existing roads would prove a problem which no police could solve. The stations can just about manage the English traffic to the South Coast towns and the growing suburban traffic, but the addition of, say, from twenty to fifty great European expresses to their daily service of trains would be an impossibility, and the block in the streets in the neighbourhood of the stations would create a position which would be intolerable.

What can London do to meet the situation which will arise, and accommodate the great world traffic and meet the requirements of shoals of Americans and Colonials, who will certainly come to London if they can proceed to the Continent, and to Palestine, Egypt and the East, with proper comfort and facilities ? If they do not get these facilities, they will most certainly avoid England and London and go direct to some Continental port.

There are, however, some shrewd and far-seeing Londoners who say that London can rise to the occasion and do all that is necessary to make it the railroad centre of the Old World and the starting point for all the trains that will run, not only to Paris, Switzerland and the Riviera, but to Constantinople and the East, to Moscow and Siberia, to Italy, to Spain and Morocco, and even to Berlin and Vienna.

They propose to build a great Empire Station over the water in Surrey, somewhere in Southwark or Blackfriars, more than double the size of any of our present stations, with a magnificent high-level bridge across the River Thames on the site of the present Charing Cross railway bridge, opening out on the Strand and Trafalgar Square at one end and with the Empire Station at the other end—a roadway and bridge like the Pont Alexandre at Paris, about half as wide again as Westminster Bridge. Along this bridge would roll the motor-cars and taxi-cabs carrying the passengers and their luggage to the station, whence the trains would run to all parts of the world, whilst beneath the Thames would be tubes to connect up all parts of London with this Empire Station.

This scheme, if carried out, would not only provide London with the finest bridge and road in the world, starting from the very heart of London, but it would open up to Londoners the unknown regions of Southwark and Blackfriars and the populous and neglected districts of the south, and make them really a part of London, and incidentally, as a result, would probably double the value of all the houses and property there.

The River Thames makes a great bend between the City and Westminster, and the Embankment and Fleet Street, the Strand and Whitehall are all on the outer circle of the great bend of the river. The usual routes from east to west are thus all greatly lengthened by their position on the outside of this bend. If you take the map of London and a pair of compasses, and start from a point at the middle of Roupell Street, between Waterloo Bridge Road and Blackfriars Road, you will find how central that spot is, and how short is the distance from that centre to St. Paul's on the east and Westminster on the west—the streets over the bridges radiate from it almost like a fan—and that, as a matter of fact, with the new bridge and road over the Thames to Charing Cross, it will be the most central spot for the new great terminus that could be found in London. From it a taxi-cab would take you in ten minutes to any part of Inner London, which could not be said of the positions of any of the great stations on the northern side of the river.

To clear this site no buildings of any importance would have to be sacrificed. It is a neighbourhood which the majority of the inhabitants of London have never seen. Some pass over it on the South Eastern Railway, and some pass under it in the tube from Waterloo to the Bank, but few Londoners have ever walked through it or know anything of it. How many know the wooden houses which are certainly two hundred years old and which may be found at the end of Roupell Street where it joins Blackfriars Road? They are a monument of good timber and building, and in one of them resided recently a man whose trade was that of a professional "knocker-up"—a man who for a small weekly fee called persons in the neighbourhood at any hour of the day or night! His business card hung in his window. The neighbourhood is dull and monotonous, and has been growing steadily worse and more dull and hopeless every year.

When Londoners think of London south of the Thames and compare it with other cities—with Paris south of the Seine—they may well feel ashamed at the way that great part of London has been neglected in the past.

Paris has its finest monuments across the river. They are too numerous to mention, but the Panthéon, the Invalides, the Luxembourg, the University, the Eiffel Tower, the Chamber of Deputies, are a few that every travelled Englishman knows. Is there any ordinary Londoner who could name any buildings or monuments south of the Thames beyond St. Thomas's Hospital and Waterloo Station? Some may know of the Oval, the Elephant and Castle, Bethlehem Hospital and Spurgeon's Tabernacle. The London County Council Town Hall, when finished, will be a beginning, and when the new bridge and great station are added, the very heart of this neglected London will be opened up and other improvements will follow, and the south of the river will be raised from the deadly torpor which has overshadowed it for the past forty years.

It was quite different fifty years ago. At that time Astley's Theatre was fashionable and all London flocked to see Miss Ada Menken as "Mazeppa" on her barebacked steed. The "Old Vic," as it was called, drew all London for its pantomimes and its transpontine blood-curdling dramas—farther back, Vauxhall Gardens was the centre of fashionable London.

From an artistic point of view, the present Charing Cross railway and foot bridge has always been criticized. Mr. John Burns expressed a particular antipathy to it and described it in the House of Commons as a Behemoth or monstrous erection which ruined the view from Westminster Bridge and from the Embankment.

The proposed new bridge and approach will do away with this railway bridge and Charing Cross Station.

A picture recently published represents a proposed low-level bridge at this spot, crossing the Thames from the back of the Embankment at the end of Northumberland Avenue.

A high-level bridge is, however, more favoured now—a bridge on the site of the Charing Cross bridge, carried on the level of Trafalgar Square and the Strand, and passing over the Embankment as Waterloo Bridge crosses it on the high level a quarter of a mile lower down the river.

Whatever plan is adopted, it will do away with the present railway bridge and the station and the railway carried on arches on the other side of the river, and replace it with a magnificent bridge and road which will have no equal in England or in the world.

This is the great proposal put forward for London as a fitting work to be undertaken to commemorate the peace and the commencement of the Channel Tunnel which will unite us to our Ally, France. Friendship and commerce will go hand in hand, and will both be assisted by this great work, which will assist the two countries to recover from the effects of the war and give Englishmen and Londoners something great to look forward to.

THE SURREY SIDE

PAUL WATERHOUSE, F.S.A., P.R.I.B.A.

CHAPTER VIII

THE SURREY SIDE[1]

To many born Londoners the south side of the river exists merely because any river must have two sides to it. But it is as remote from them and their lives as though it were in the Antipodes—more so indeed.—ELINOR MORDAUNT: *The Park Wall.*

THE future of the Surrey side of the Thames offers a problem which demands very serious attention. The present utilization—one might say the present misuse—of the land which borders the right bank of the Thames from Lambeth to Southwark is the result of a strange combination of historic facts and of—sentiment.

Probably sentiment, or the survival of certain illogical ideas, has more to do with the existing condition of affairs than have any real facts or any reasons based upon necessity and convenience. The Thames was, in primitive London, a definite barrier between shore and shore. To-day it is spanned by many bridges; these bridges are crossed daily and hourly by swarms of traffic; moreover, the bed of the river is burrowed under by three lines of railway; and yet the barrier remains a barrier. This is the more remarkable when we realize that throughout a great part of the Middle Ages and up to a late date in the eighteenth century the waterway was actually a highway of traffic.

The river was not merely a channel for goods traffic, but was the gentlemanly route from east to west. The private carriage of a nobleman was in former days a sumptuous barge; the cab of the middle classes was a waterman's boat; so that there was

[1] It will be observed that the projects set forth in the following article are not in close accord with certain other intentions of the Society as set forth here and elsewhere. In fact, the proposals of the writer are rather parallel to than allied with those of his colleagues, and the article is published as exhibiting a line of thought which is in some respects independent.—ED.

no visible reason why Surrey land should have been more meanly occupied than the land of Middlesex. One might as well expect to find in modern London clubs on one side of Pall Mall and fried-fish shops on the other.

It was as easy for these old-time wayfarers to land on one side as on the other; and the only explanation one can offer is that, as the necessity for town expansion in the past was not what it is to-day, the pre-existence of the City and of Westminster on the left bank perpetuated the neglect of the semi-rural right-hand shore.

The prevalence of the Thames as a waterway gradually lapsed after the Great Fire. This change of habit on the part of London travellers was largely due to the improvement of the City's streets when rebuilt; for at least one of the reasons for the frequent use of the river was the squalor of the byways and narrow streets of the town.

But it still remains a subject for amazement that, after London Bridge was supplemented by the bridges of Waterloo, Westminster, Southwark and Blackfriars, the avoidance of the Surrey shore as an integral part of the building land of Central London still continued and continues still. I expect that the tidying-up of the Middlesex side by the formation of the Embankment, contrasting as it did with the primitive wharfage still occupying the Surrey frontage, had something to do with emphasizing the prejudice against Surrey as building land. Surrey seen side by side with the smartness of Middlesex sank in its shabbiness into the rôle of the poor relation. Certain it is that when modern building did begin to flourish in the Borough regions it took the form, as in Southwark, of warehouses and gloomy business establishments to which the name of architecture may enthusiastically be denied.

It will be noticed that this article is headed the "Surrey Side," not the "South Side," and I have so named it with a purpose. I want to emphasize the fact that this Surrey territory is very intimately and integrally connected with the heart of London, and I also want to point out what is so often forgotten, that Westminster Bridge, in crossing from Westminster to the opposite bank, does not proceed southward, but absolutely due east. It would astonish many Londoners to be told that the square mile of which the western side runs from Drury Lane to the House of Lords and which has its north-east angle in St. Paul's Churchyard contains more of Surrey than of Middlesex.

The importance of this (neglected) proximity of Southwark to London and of the fact that it is so encircled by the bend of the river between London Bridge and Lambeth is very great. It has a forcible bearing upon the solution of various London problems, and it is necessary that it should be taken very seriously into account. In this connection it is well to give emphasis to certain considerations which can easily be overlooked but cannot possibly be denied.

1. The shortest way from Westminster to London Bridge lies through the Surrey district.

2. The long neglect of Surrey as desirable building land for other than comparatively mean commercial buildings has resulted in the fact that we have within a mile or so of the Bank of England on the south side land much cheaper than that which can be found within three or four miles of the same spot on the Middlesex shore.

3. Whether we pay any attention to the development of the Surrey side or not, the Surrey side will be developed. The arrival in Lambeth of the new buildings of the London County Council alone assures the improvement of the meanly occupied sites in its immediate neighbourhood; and it seems essential to those who love London that such development should be watched and guided. Some people say, " Why envisage large schemes which will involve large expenditure ? " The answer is that the large expenditure will inevitably come, and the important point which we have at heart is to see that that large expenditure is made subservient to some well-ordered plan.

4. The shore of the Thames is occupied almost throughout the region here discovered by small or comparatively small wharves. Their appearance is undoubtedly picturesque. In some cases their picturesqueness is rather squalid. In other cases it is obvious that the beauty is due to a mixture of neglect and decay, which, however greatly one may admire it, cannot possibly be made permanent. It may, in fact, if not guarded, guided and protected, give place to the shameless inelegance which casts a gloom over Thames Street. It is understood that these properties are less moribund than they appear.

5. Apart from building problems, London is afflicted with traffic problems. The improvement of free locomotion in east and

west direction has for scores of years been one of the most urgent and difficult of public duties. It has been constantly hampered and thwarted by the great cost of interfering with the buildings or purchasing the land on the north side of the Thames. The Surrey side offers splendid opportunities for effecting at less cost, and sometimes with greater directness, those improvements which on the City and Westminster side seem almost unattainable.

If I venture here to offer some suggestions of a practical and constructive nature for the carrying out of definite schemes, I do not do so altogether with the presumption of an individual agitator. It was my privilege to act for many months before the war as chairman of a committee of The London Society which not only had these problems very much at heart, but gave to them a concentrated attention which was all the more acute because almost every member of that committee contributed his own views and his own personal investigations of the facts and probabilities. The suggestions, therefore, which I shall offer are largely based upon the conclusions of that committee, though I do not claim that they would father all I may have to say.

The problem can be divided into the foreshore question, the question of bridges, the question of traffic generally on the Surrey side, and the larger question of the development of the Surrey land as sites for important buildings. All these aspects of the case interlock with one another; and, though I shall endeavour to make use of this division of the subject as a convenient method of handling, it will be found impossible to deal exclusively with any one heading without constant reference to and introduction of the others.

To start, then, with the shore problem. It was surmised by some of my colleagues that no great harm would be done to the River Thames or to its business as a waterway if the stream were narrowed along the Surrey bend by throwing the shore forward. In other words, the advocates of a roadway embankment along that shore suggested with some confidence that for a considerable portion of its length the intended embankment might be constructed not *within* the lines of the present shore but right out upon the mud-bank. Inquiries were made in an authoritative quarter on the question whether such an encroachment would be likely to result in the formation of a new mud-bank outside this new embankment. A most reassuring answer was received, and it therefore became

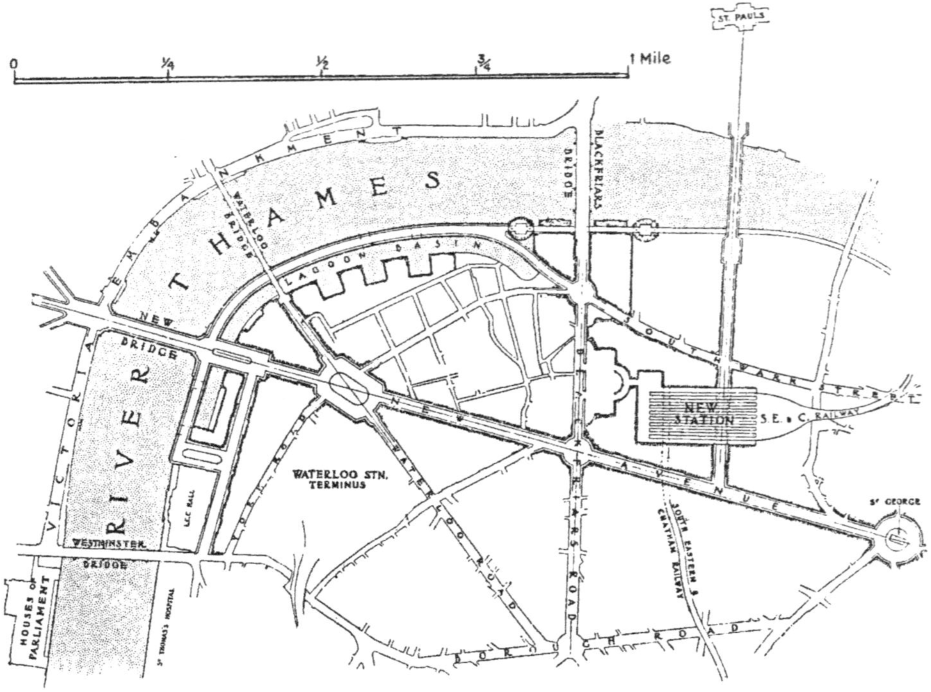

PLAN EXPLANATORY OF CHAPTER VIII, SHOWING SUGGESTED NEW AVENUE, NEW EMBANKMENT, LAGOON BASIN AND POSITION FOR S.E. AND C. RAILWAY STATION.

To face p. 130.

possible to make schemes for planning an embankment roadway actually clear of the existing wharf frontage. This opened up a new idea. If it is uncertain whether these wharves can be given up, why not retain their waterside privileges by the expedient of letting the water remain in spite of the embankment roadway? This gave rise to the idea of the so-called lagoon-dock—an enclosed stretch of water bounded on the Thames side by the embankment roadway and on the shore side by warehouses. We contemplate naturally a rebuilding of the places of business, whose frontages, running down sheer into the water, might become a feature as beautiful in their modern bravery as their predecessors are in the garment of decay. It was realized, of course, that the gradients of the embankment would have to be so contrived that at one or more points barges and boats could pass under the roadway into the lagoon, and also that there would have to be free inlet and outlet for the tidal waters to pass through and scour the channel. It is conceivable that if these new warehouses were adroitly disposed, with their frontages recessed at intervals to allow space for large basins or inlets, there would result not merely a great increase of wharfage space but also a great scope for attractive design in the façades. London has always hitherto been ashamed of its wharves. Let us have here some wharves that know no shame.

Of course, a question at once arises as to the extent of the embankment and its level. It may be taken for granted that it will have to pass under Waterloo Bridge, using as a land arch what is at present the first water arch on the Surrey side.

This settles one point in connection with the levels, and it accords well with the views of a good many people on the subject of the new Charing Cross Bridge. (At this date there is, I hope, no harm in speaking of the abolition of the railway bridge and the establishment of a road bridge as blessings which the future is sure to bring.) The advocates of this new bridge and the various designers of its approaches have divided themselves into two schools—the high-level school and the low-level school. I am assuming in this article that the low-level enthusiasts have their way and that the new bridge will start from the Middlesex shore at the level (slightly modified) of the junction between Northumberland Avenue and the Victoria Embankment, and that it will expect a welcome from an embankment of similar level on the Surrey side. So far so good.

Up-stream the new embankment cannot proceed farther than the new County Hall, because the London County Council has appropriated the shore opposite its new home. So the embankment must terminate there. I suggest it should end in a fair-sized square or "Place," flanked by the (almost) north elevation of the County Hall. Its termination at the eastern end is open to greater doubt. We have to face the question whether the embankment road should pass under an arch of Blackfriars (road) bridge, just as it would pass under Waterloo Bridge. Blackfriars Bridge, it is true, is nominally a low-level bridge, insomuch as it starts from roadway level at the end of the Victoria Embankment. But it stands high in relation to the land at the Surrey end, and the way through could probably be managed if the roadway be at this point reduced in width. So I have contented myself by forming a comparatively narrow commercial quay or wharf road from Blackfriars eastward, and have allowed the main road to curve itself southward so as to become a continuation of Southwark Street. Southwark Street is unredeemably hideous; but a life of new traffic might put new heart into it. Some day, who knows, some of its buildings may become obsolete, and at least they can never be rebuilt in the horrible period that gave them shameful birth.

The bridges question is mainly the question of the new Charing Cross Bridge. But there are two other points to consider. If any new road bridges are ever brought into being, they will probably be the Temple Bridge and the St. Paul's Bridge. The other, a more important point, relates to railway bridges. Charing Cross railway bridge will, as we all hope and believe, disappear. Some of us go the length of depending on the removal not only of Blackfriars railway bridge, but also of that horrible iron approach to Cannon Street Station. For Cannon Street Station must also in the long run go. Of this more hereafter.

And now we come to the problem of traffic on the Surrey side. In this division of the subject I am bold enough to deal with railways as well as roads, and what I am about to say will be at variance with the views of many of my friends in The London Society; at variance also with opinions suggested in this book. I expect that there will be no harm in this divergence of outlook. It may be said in general criticism of the Lambeth-Southwark-Borough region that what it needs in the way of traffic facilities is more convenient through-routes. The curve of the river naturally makes the lines of the bridges converge like the radii of a circle. The main roads coming in from the south similarly converge, and convergence of this kind, which gives no great trouble in a small town with a moderate business, becomes intolerable in a large town of supreme industry. The planning of the Surrey region having been left largely to chance, no effort has in the past been made to counteract this nuisance. In fact, it has been accentuated and concentrated rather than combated. The roads are drawn together at two foci, the Elephant and St. George's Circus. Thus the main traffic from the south to London is quite unnecessarily brought into a double congestion before it is permitted to select the bridge which will best serve on its way into London. And there is a worse trouble still. The Surrey territory should from its position and shape form a convenient link between Westminster and the City, but the provision of any good east to west road across this tract of land has always been postponed or ignored. The present is the time at which we ought to consider how these inconveniences and anomalies can be remedied.

Let us go back for a moment to the Charing Cross Bridge scheme. What is the great road across that bridge to lead triumphantly up to? A chorus of voices cries: "Why, straight to the new Charing Cross Station, of course." I think we have been a little too ready to assume the indisputable desirability of this arrangement and of the kindred assumption that the new station must be as close as possible to Waterloo.

A moment's thought will show that if a single central station in the centre of London is an impossibility—and I for one am entirely satisfied that it is—there is everything to be said for the plea that all the great termini should be kept at a convenient and fairly uniform distance from the centre. Also, it is obvious that there are advantages in keeping these termini reasonably distant from one another. A traveller passing through London may regret that King's Cross is not close to Waterloo, but much less regret is felt at the present separation of Waterloo from Charing Cross. Two big termini near together hamper one another, because the streams of road traffic necessary to each station converge upon and mingle with one another. I suggest, therefore, that there is more to be lost than gained by making the new Charing Cross terminus sit in the lap of Waterloo. Why should it not occupy that triangle of ground (with additions) which is already rendered desolate by railway arches? I refer to the spot just east of the Blackfriars Road through which runs Gravel Lane. Once grant the practicability of this and there becomes possible a new prospect and a new career of usefulness for the great new street which is to cross our river by the great new bridge. A "straight-edge" and a map will show that the line of axis already assumed, viz. the centre line of Northumberland Avenue, is heading for the Church of St. George, which stands with a good deal of quiet majesty at the end of Borough High Street, just at the point where that thoroughfare is joined by Great Dover Street and Long Lane. Let us boldly take our great street to that point and see what we gain.

In the first place, we have secured an easy connection for the new great station with both the City and the West End.[1] It will by means of this street get a straight run to Westminster and the West End, and will also have an easy approach to London Bridge (as well as a ready use of Blackfriars Bridge, Southwark Bridge, and, if it ever comes, St. Paul's Bridge). Secondly, we shall be planting hope and the chance of prosperity in the very heart of a derelict region which has never yet enjoyed the opportunities which its close proximity to London proper deserves. This great avenue would have a straight course of exactly a mile and a half between Trafalgar Square and the Borough. It would be more or less parallel to the course of the street variously known as Holborn, Holborn Viaduct, Newgate Street and Cheapside, and would be at the same average distance from the river, viz. between a quarter and a third of a mile. The new Charing Cross Station would stand on its north side roughly half-way between London Bridge Station and Waterloo. London Bridge Station would probably, on the completion of the new station, die of jealousy and chagrin. If it did not, it would sooner or later succumb to the forces of its own manifest inconvenience and of natural decay.

That it should either be abolished or rebuilt is an essential of decency. Its squalor is quite intolerable.

[1] Earlier writings of mine have advocated a great eastward road from Westminster Bridge. Such a road is shown on the Development Plan of The London Society. The road I now propose is perhaps nobler and more direct.

Of course, it will be understood that I am contemplating the entire removal of Blackfriars Railway Bridge. I urge this chiefly because of its supreme ugliness. I urge it also because I believe that the space occupied by Holborn Viaduct Station and the stations of St. Paul's and Ludgate Hill could be far more profitably occupied. The misuse of the land along the east side of New Bridge Street is evident to all.

Against the removal of this cross-river railway connection will be urged the value of the through goods traffic carried by this bridge and the usefulness of the three above-mentioned stations to passengers. The answer is that the through goods traffic can be much better arranged by an underwater connection in the future, and that the kind of passenger traffic catered for by these three stations had much better be conveyed by the underground electric system, which will no doubt in the near future be vastly extended.

Does it occur to anyone that the hideous overcrowding of the tube railways now prevailing is not an argument against these means of transit but an overwhelming proof of the success of the tube system and of the urgent necessity for its development?

And what about Cannon Street Station with its bridge? I have been told that the continued existence of these two appliances is essential, that the healthy life and activity of London depends upon them. Do they? One thing is certain, that they will some day need reconstruction. Will anybody, when that day comes, think the reconstruction worth the expense? I doubt it. Yet another thing is certain. The centre of gravity of London is going to shift southward. I do not suggest that the heart of London will cross the water, but I do suggest and prophesy that the occupation of Surrey land by official, Imperial, national and influential tenants is sure to come and to come quickly. That is one of the reasons for which I urge that the great new road should carve its way right through the very heart of this promised land. It is new to us, but it is ancient. The road will be for a time a *vox clamantis in deserto*. But the voice will not cry for long. The desert will soon blossom.

To go back from these aspirations to a little bit of detail. It is of course a fact that one of the lines of rail that join up in the triangle by Blackfriars Road (which I am dedicating to the new station) is the London, Chatham and Dover line coming northward through Camberwell and Walworth. It crosses over the South-Eastern main line within the triangle. I see no reason why it should not be provided for within the buildings of the new station by a small terminus about the size of Holborn Viaduct Station, built transversely at a higher level than the main terminus and with its rails and platforms at right angles to the main platforms of the station. In any case, the main platforms of this station will be at a higher level than the road entrance to the station, and there will essentially and necessarily be lifts for passengers and luggage. Our new station will in fact be like the station on the Quai d'Orsay in Paris, but reversed, i.e. the trains will be upstairs instead of downstairs.

It will, I hope, be understood that I involve none of my colleagues in The London Society in the suggestion that the great new road should travel on to the Borough. The embankment road and the enclosed dock and basin between Waterloo Bridge and Blackfriars Bridge are, however, distinctly schemes backed by the members of The London Society. So also is the suggestion that the new bridge should have its axis on the line of Northumberland Avenue and that it should be a low-level bridge. But this last statement must be made with the utmost reservation, for the division of healthy opinion within the Society (and, indeed, within the South Side Committee) on this subject has been very equally balanced. Excellent schemes and excellent arguments have been put forward to favour the idea that the approaches to the new bridge should start on the Middlesex side from the level of the Strand, and that the bridge itself, maintained at a high level, should pass over the embankment roads on both sides of the river, and thus be better fitted to join the new railway station at the level of its present permanent way.

I have just touched upon the subjects of the suggested Temple and St. Paul's Bridges. Against the latter the criticism has been uttered that its Surrey-side approaches were not so arranged as to make it useful to the full. There are two essential points about this bridge. It must align directly on the Dome of St. Paul's and it must cross the Thames (any bridge must) at something reasonably like right angles. If these points are kept in mind it will be found that the main road to the bridge could join Southwark Street at a point close to my site for the new Charing Cross Station. But there are some level difficulties, and I am not sure that the bridge is really wanted.

The Temple Bridge would be necessarily a communication from one embankment level to the other. At the time (1905) when the irresponsible dreamers of the Traffic Commission contemplated a continuation southward of Gray's Inn Road (which would have crashed through Staple Inn, the Patent Office, the Record Office and the Temple) there would have been something to say for a Temple Bridge as a means of through communication north and south. As matters now stand, the most likely use for a bridge in that position would be to provide cross-river communication for passengers already on the Victoria Embankment, who cannot cross Waterloo Bridge without working back to the higher ground of the Strand. For such purposes a bridge there would be of value, specially since the new south embankment by its connection with Southwark Street and with the great new road is in easy access to various Surrey-side outlets.

One might suggest in this connection the return of Temple Bar from its seclusion in Theobald's Park to the place assigned for it in my late father's perspective drawing for the Law Courts. It would stand well in the Temple Gardens facing down the new bridge.[1]

I have left to the last the subject of the development of the Surrey land as sites for important public and business buildings, only to find that I have already dealt with it by inference. Of the demand for such land, the bold step of the London County Council in choosing their new site is a proof already in the past. As to the future, one can only say that the indications derived from common sense have already been fortified by more than one semi-authentic hint from responsible quarters that even the Government will not shrink from placing on that shore buildings of greater importance and value than the Stationery Office (off which I sadly fear my road scheme has chipped a corner).

The great new road—by far the finest thoroughfare in London—would be a worthy site for buildings of the noblest architecture and the most important type. Our new phase of Government, which tends to a multiplication of Departments, might open the

[1] Since this was written the prospect of such a removal of Temple Bar has come almost into visibility.

proceedings by the establishment there of a second Whitehall, and the prestige thus given to a quarter of a mile of the new thoroughfare would ensure its value as frontage for the remainder of its course. Little by little the adjoining streets would share in the prestige, and the course of fifty years would find London the happier, the busier, the richer and the more beautiful by the simple discovery and development of property which she has long owned but never yet enjoyed.

CENTRAL LONDON

PROFESSOR ADSHEAD, F.R.I.B.A.

CHAPTER IX

CENTRAL LONDON

CENTRAL LONDON is an area rich in history and tradition. It is an area where innovation and preservation must clash. Less magnificent than Paris and less ambitious than Vienna, it nevertheless possesses irresistible attractions which are entirely its own. It is unapproachable in the picturesque assembling of its independent groupings, it is great in the scale of its river, and it is unique in the colour of its Portland stone.

To say that London as we see it to-day is an expression of our times is but partially true, for whilst amongst the conflicting interests of this great congeries of things new and old there are innovations of which we are a little suspicious, and which with our inherited conservatism we accept only with reserve, at the same time London for the most part is an old city, out at elbows, worn threadbare and sadly behind the time.

Science and invention always play havoc with old towns; they are very cruel in their treatment of old walls. New forms of construction, street widenings to receive increased traffic and new buildings erected for altogether new purposes are continually disturbing the repose and sedateness of old streets and squares. So that whilst improvement in London must mean innovation, it should be an innovation that is tempered with a respect for what is there.

Perhaps it is as well that there exists a reverence amounting almost to a religious fanaticism for the preservation of open spaces and parks. Perhaps it is well that churches, unable to justify their continued existence as such, should be retained and preserved. Perhaps it is well that the Temple and Gray's Inn should zealously perpetuate their old traditions. These are some of the aspects of London to be reckoned with in adapting it to the requirements of modern conditions.

LONDON OF THE FUTURE

No factor exercises so important an influence in bringing about change as transport, and whilst the suburbs and the surrounding areas of towns are more directly affected than the centre, as the pivot of the movement the centre is also affected, though in a different way. The central area of London is at the present moment passing through a process of scarcely noticeable but at the same time stupendous change. Changes in cities are scarcely perceptible within the narrow limits of a day-to-day experience; they are only noticeable in a comparison extending over decades, or in generations in the lives of citizens who have brought them about. The last quarter of a century has seen in Central London the erection of popular restaurants, palatial hotels, boarding establishments, municipal housing schemes, Imperial offices and tubes. Half a century has seen London torn to shreds by a railway system that has annihilated a cultured prosperity, and which has bred miles and miles of forlorn streets and embanked segments of confused happenings. A whole century has seen London converted from the polite Georgian town of Thackeray into a monstrous unmanageable machine.

But our march must be forward and not backward, and it is with adaptation, assimilation and conversion that we are to-day concerned.

When Sir Christopher Wren made his plan for the rebuilding of London, the centre was the Royal Exchange, and whilst the Royal Exchange must still be regarded as the historic centre of London, another centre of increasing importance has developed in Trafalgar Square.

Up to the end of last century London grew solidly, it pressed outwards as a solid body, and it was not until a suburban system of railways had become established, later to be supplemented by the tubes, that centralization became overtaken by decentralization. It overflowed more quickly than it filled.

The founding of new suburbs, the conversion of these into satellite towns, and adaptation of old towns within a radius of 60 miles from London into dormitories for the more restless of the middle class are aspects of London's development that confront us most prominently.

But this tendency towards decentralization, so conspicuously in operation in connection with the building of houses, is also to be noted in connection with the building of factories and business premises, though to a less noticeable degree. The need for more ample space about factories, the saving that can be effected in rates, always provided that the sacrifice of convenience is not too great, has meant that this class of property is strongly attracted to outlying areas around.

Central London is to-day no place of residence for the masses, nor is it a place for independent businesses and factories, but the kind of buildings that still flourish in Central London, and which will in the future monopolize or at any rate preponderate here, are hotels of all kinds, residential flats, big stores, head offices of important trading companies, public buildings of Imperial and national importance, restaurants, and shops for specialized wares. The demand for such buildings is ahead of the supply, and though rebuilding is continuous, nevertheless the change is not as rapid as it might be.

London is the centre of Imperial commerce and finance, and their transactions have developed enormously during the last century. Every insurance company, every banking concern, every shipping combine and every important business must have a head office in Central London, and attendant upon these Imperial houses there is needed a host of service buildings and Imperial hotels.

SUBURBAN TRANSPORT.

Of the many works to be undertaken in improving London, none are more important than those relating to the consolidation and completion of the suburban railway system. It is not our concern to review the system as it penetrates the outer area: our interest is confined to its terminals, and to the way in which they set down their passengers here. The test of a perfect system should be that passengers travelling on a trunk line should, either before entering the terminal or at the terminal, be enabled to change into a tube system that will deposit them, say, within a couple of hundred yards of any position in the central area, and passengers travelling on a suburban system should enter the central tube system without the necessity of a change. Generally this very desirable combination of systems exists at present; but there are gaps and important connections to be made. Perhaps one of the most obvious may be seen in the way in which the Victoria and London Bridge electrified system sets down its passengers at Victoria and London Bridge, leaving a most disconcerting connection to be made with the central tube system. Why could not this important line dive underground behind its present terminals and complete a circle via Victoria Street, Whitehall and the Strand? There exists a similar defect in regard to the termination of the electrified South-Western system. It should descend behind Waterloo and, crossing the central area, should emerge beyond the City to complete another loop in the north-east. Similar improvements might be made in regard to the terminals of the suburban systems in the north. The diurnal journeyings of the suburban passenger should be as easy and comfortable as possible. Nothing retards suburban development so much as difficulties to be overcome in getting from office to house. Passengers resident in the gathering grounds of an electrified railway are of the class who work long hours and can ill afford the time and energy necessitated by having to make changes, and who find it very distracting on arriving at a trunk terminus to have to push their way down long and crowded platforms, risk their lives in crossing station yards amidst a scrimmage of cabs, and ultimately have to enter a tube system through a maze of halls and passages; or, depending upon the means of transport with which nature has provided them, have to walk long distances along crowded pavements or have to force their way on to a crowded bus.

As mentioned, it is not within the scope of this article to do more than refer to suburban transit in so far as it is connected with what are distinctly central area transit systems. Let us therefore turn our attention to the central tube system, and consider in what way this could be improved. It needs improving both in regard to the design of its stations, the duplication of its lines, the construction of entirely new ones, and also in respect of its ventilation.

Ventilation is mentioned because the ultimate success of all underground workings must, when the competitive systems of overhead and underground travel are fully developed, be seriously handicapped unless greater attention is paid to it. But perhaps the greatest defect in the present tube system is to be seen in the confused planning of the stations. Notwithstanding the excellence and smooth working of the lifts, there are labyrinths of passages to be traversed, staircases to be ascended, and twistings and wanderings to be negotiated that are altogether so irksome and confusing as in many cases to completely discount the advantages otherwise obtained. It is obvious that in many cases the confusion referred to has been the result of adding new systems to old, rendering complicated junctions almost unavoidable. But much of the trouble exists, not at junctions, but at ordinary roadside stations. It could probably have been avoided had the lines been laid deep enough to take them under the buildings, and had it not been a condition that they be laid under the roads. Had they been laid directly under the stations, passengers might have entered the platforms direct from the lifts, an arrangement which so far as we are aware exists only at the Bank.

The separation of suburban trains from trunk trains would help enormously to ease the confusion that is at present seen at almost all our great terminals. We have only quite recently seen the reconstruction of Victoria and Waterloo, and it is a thousand pities that drastic alterations to these two stations were not carried out simultaneously with a sinking underground of the suburban system. But apart from this, and excellent as these two stations in many respects now are, each suffers from the lack of an ample, dignified, and direct approach. The construction of a new bridge for vehicular traffic at Charing Cross will assist in meeting the difficulty at Waterloo, but Victoria Station will never have a satisfactory approach until all the buildings standing aboveground on that obstructive island site which faces it are removed.

It should be obvious to everyone that, with the electrification of all railways, with the increased spending power of the lower classes, with the demand for hotels and the general recuperation of the nation, we are about to see an enormous increase in travelling, a condition of things that urgently calls for the modernizing of all our stations. We are slow to perceive that the old train sheds that did service for our grandfathers on their annual visit into the country are as out of date to-day as are the horse-buses and growlers that conveyed them and their carpet-bags from the stations to their homes.

Beneath every great terminal should be an underground non-terminal station through which the suburban passenger train should pass as it approaches and enters the central system of tubes. From immense waiting halls outside the trunk terminals giant staircases or sloping ways should provide a direct connection with the platforms of the suburban trains.

New York has in quite recent years constructed stations on these lines.

But better approaches and connections are not the only requirement. The ill-ventilated and crowded bars described as first-class refreshment-rooms need converting into tea-rooms, dining-rooms and waiting-saloons, and there should be writing-rooms, bath-rooms and, of course, hotels. All these things are gradually coming, and in a modest way are to be seen at Victoria and Waterloo.

With the nationalization of the railways and a bold programme of reconstruction, Euston, St. Pancras and King's Cross might with immense advantage be reconstructed and combined to make a terminus worthy to be described as the entrance to London from the North. Failing a scheme so drastic, King's Cross should be swept away, and we should have a reconstructed St. Pancras, consisting of a duplication of the present station on its eastern side, a scheme that amongst other things would involve a deviation in the St. Pancras Road.

The new Euston Station, as the main entrance to London from the North, would need an adequate approach, a processional way. Gower Street and Southampton Row are very well as bus routes and as short-cuts for tradesmen's vans, but their scale is entirely inadequate as main approaches into London. Our northern democracy must be inspired as it descends upon its capital, the largest city in the world and the capital of the Empire.

Such a reconstruction of Euston and of lands abutting upon its avenue of approach should be planned forthwith, involving, as it certainly should, most of the property situate between Gower Street and Woburn Place. The British Museum would stand on an island site, and would, on entering London, be the first great building towards which the visitor would direct his way. Incidentally it typifies the Empire, and thence the line of route would fork in a south-easterly direction towards Kingsway, and in a south-westerly direction towards Charing Cross and Whitehall.

Flanking this station approach would be the new University buildings and hotels of all kinds for democracy's vast crowds, who in the near future will descend upon London in increasing frequency from the North.

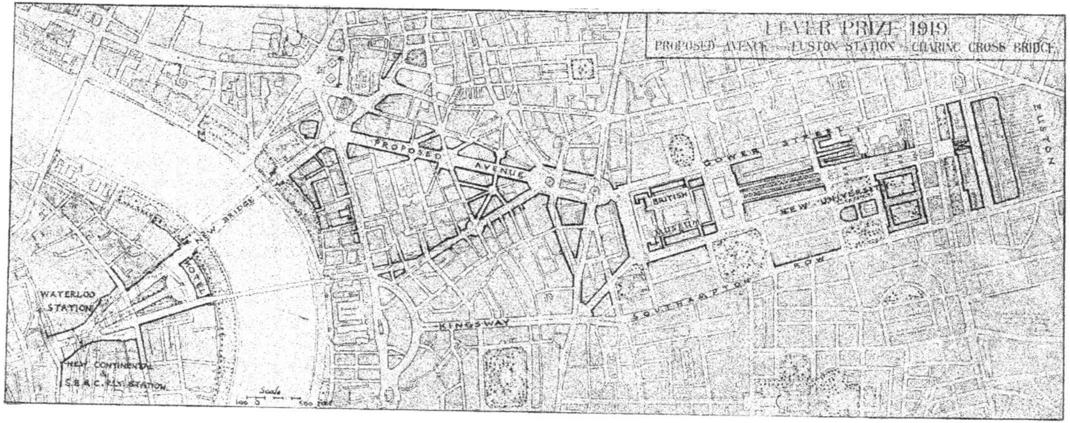

THE STUDENTS OF LONDON UNIVERSITY ARCHITECTURAL SCHOOLS STUDY THE PROBLEMS OF TOWN PLANNING. THIS WAS THE WINNING SCHEME SUBMITTED FOR THE LEVER PRIZE IN 1919.

(It is interesting to note that practically the same suggestion appeared in the Fifth Report of the Commissioners of Woods and Forests, 1826, under the heading, "Proposed New Street to the British Museum." The outcome, presumably, was Charing Cross Road.)

(Drawing by R. W. Lahey.)

To face p. 146.

CENTRAL LONDON

And now let us turn from the passenger train entrance into London to its goods entrance, and let us consider in what way improvements could be effected in regard to the conveyance of goods from the docks. Many proposals have been made for the development of a dock area between Tilbury and the Royal Victoria and Albert Docks, and in connection therewith for the construction of a great dock road from Tilbury to the Tower.

In so far as the development of the docks is concerned, this again is outside the scope of our inquiry, but the entrance to London from the Royal Victoria and Albert Docks is certainly a problem affecting the central area. Many schemes have been put forward for drastically dealing with the S-shaped mouth of the Lea. To be penny wise is to be pound foolish here. There must be a direct road from the Silvertown dock area to East India Dock Road. Once this connection has been made, direct access to London is provided along Commercial Road. But a vast traffic passes along Cable Street and St. George's Road, and it is to relieve these two streets of warehouses that further improvements have been proposed. Among others, it has been suggested that Fenchurch Street Station and the dock railway be scrapped, and that in place thereof there be constructed a great traffic road. The widening of Cable Street has been considered, and proposals have been made for the entire reconstruction of St. George's Road.

In considering the relative advantages of these different schemes, we are perhaps apt to forget that a controlling factor in the distribution and collection of goods to and from the docks is the position of the warehouses. We must remember that by far the greatest bulk of the goods brought into the London Docks is transferred therefrom by barges to warehouses situated on various parts of the river and by rail to various towns in England, and that, so far as London is concerned, the economic delivery and collection of goods is as much a question of having conveniently situated warehouses as it is of having accessible roads.

London's ships and docks have been brought up to date in advance of her warehouses, and as tonnage increases, it is doubtful if an altered use ought not to be made of the small upper river warehouses and of the smaller docks. It seems rather ridiculous to think that merchandise delivered at the Port of London by titanic steamers down river should be transmitted by barge or wagon to the old up-river warehouses, many of which are worn out, out of date, and only accessible by narrow and congested roads. Combined with a dock road improvement scheme there is the problem of warehouses and smaller docks. The solution of the question would seem to depend very largely upon the erection of more warehouses and cold stores of the most modern type in the immediate vicinity of the latest docks. From thence goods could be transferred by road or rail direct to the retail store. If the question were approached on some such broadened lines, it might be found that the problem of widening and improving Cable Street and St. George's Street would need to be undertaken quite differently. It might be that the parallel roads, Cable Street and St. George's Street, would be better dispensed with, and instead there be constructed direct right-angle approaches to Commercial Road.

Even to enumerate all the belated, disjointed, obstructive, neglected and impoverished areas of London which are crying out for improvement would fill the pages of many volumes. One can only refer to the more important, and of these, those relating to the embellishment and beautification of the river are perhaps the most striking. In an industrial age, and when the discovery of rapid locomotion had quite upset the mental balance of the nation, hideous railway bridges were allowed to span the river, obstructing traffic by water and completely obliterating every river view. The need for central terminals has completely collapsed with the coming of the tube railways, with a separation of suburban from trunk systems and with the introduction of the rapid taxi-cab. No improvements in Central London are more urgently needed than those affecting the Thames bridges and the river. A proposal to construct a south-side embankment is elsewhere dealt with, as also is that for removing altogether from the north side Cannon Street and Charing Cross stations. The construction of a new Charing Cross vehicular bridge is an undertaking that we may reasonably expect to be brought about at a comparatively early date, and its two approaches are so situated in their relation to important traffic centres that they will afford magnificent opportunities for improvements of a minor kind. The different proposals that have already been made for dealing with the intricacies of this problem, both from the engineering and architectural aspects, are very numerous, and are too well known to need describing here. Briefly, it may be stated that they fall under two categories—those which like Westminster Bridge, as it were, spring from the Embankment, and those which like Waterloo take the level of the Strand. Whatever may be said for the directness of the low-level proposal, there is no doubt a high-level bridge would be more dignified and would offer opportunities for fine approaches and new building sites altogether impossible in the case of the bridge that would be approached off a hump in the Embankment and a down-hill approach along Northumberland Avenue.

Very well known also are proposals for improving that unmanageable triangle Hyde Park Corner, with its malformations, its uncontrollable crossings, its straggling islands and its scattered trees. But Hyde Park Corner is merely one of the incidental details that make up London of last century, sorely cut about in later days. It is inadvisable to improve street corners by a repeated application of the spokeshave and to decorate open spaces by sowing them with plane-trees as if they were grass seed to be cast wherever there was a bare spot of clay. Yet these are the methods that have been resorted to in order to keep Hyde Park Corner what may vulgarly be described as a going concern.

Since Burton designed the entrances to Hyde Park and the beautiful Constitutional Hill Arch, Hyde Park Corner has gradually been spoiled.

Of road improvements, none is more urgently needed than that involving the construction of a relief road to Cheapside. A new thoroughfare from St. Martin's-le-Grand to Moorgate Street, and so on to Liverpool Street, would be the means of creating sites for immense blocks of offices that are so urgently needed in the City. This would indeed be a commercial venture of a very safe kind.

Marylebone Road must of necessity have direct access to the proposed Western Avenue, and Pentonville Road must be the commencement of a new avenue eastward.

But a word on road-widening generally, the most important of every kind of improvement that has exercised the minds of authorities since the County Council took the problems of Central London in hand. The road widening of business thoroughfares means rebuilding to an enhanced scale. The scale of London needs increasing if the business of its vastly increased population is conveniently to be transacted. Since the construction of Kingsway 80 feet seems to have come to be considered the right width for a main thoroughfare, but unfortunately this is also the height set for the main cornice. Streets of this proportion are neither narrow nor wide; they are simply nondescript and uninteresting. Holborn and Oxford Street should be as wide as Whitehall; by a drastic order they should be widened on the south side. They should be increased to 150 feet. One trembles even at the thought of the cost and inconvenience that would be incurred were such an order insisted upon. Yet nothing less will suffice if we are to do justice to posterity, who will criticize our temerity in the light of the opportunities for rebuilding that we now enjoy. In the ancient cities of Greco-Roman Asia Minor the foot pavements of the main streets were sheltered under immense arcades. In some of our shopping streets this might be attempted in London. Such a street could well be constructed between Bond Street and Regent Street as a continuation of Grafton Street, or why not rebuild the north side of Piccadilly with an arcade 20 feet wide and 30 feet high?

And finally, a word on slum clearance and flat building. It has not yet been shown that it is expedient to remove all the residential population from the central area, or if expedient, that it would be possible to do so. There are the interstices between the big thoroughfares to be filled in, and whilst there are workshops, garages, inoffensive factories and warehouses which will always require to be packed in behind the more imposing blocks that flank main streets, there should still be room for blocks of three-story flats for the working-class population that works and desires to live in town.

These three-story buildings might be built around enclosed squares, measuring say 150 feet across. Entrances to tenements would be from this courtyard, which would be laid out as a garden adorned with flowers, and from which the splash of a fountain would be music in the hot summer weather.

We have said that London is for the most part worn out and decayed, but that rebuilding is constantly proceeding. There are times when this constant process of rebuilding is accelerated and when rebuilding assumes the proportions of schemes of reconstruction. We are on the threshold of such a time just now. The hundred-year leases that followed Waterloo are expiring, and we are at the termination of a World War. Never since the Great Fire has so unique an opportunity occurred for carrying out schemes of reconstruction on a colossal scale. Let us see that we seize our opportunities, and accept our responsibilities, in a way worthy of so great an occasion. London can no longer be regarded as a place where may be perpetrated indiscriminate building adventure. It must no longer be the vestment of millions upon which may be sewn patches of any material and in any kind of colour. No longer must it typify the clashing of interests and the irresolution of masses. Our duty to posterity is to weld these together and make London an harmonious whole.

THE PORT OF LONDON

THE VISCOUNT DEVONPORT, P.C.

CHAPTER X

THE PORT OF LONDON

THE origin of London has not been penetrated by the historian. One of the oldest, Geoffrey of Monmouth, ascribed the founding of the city to Brutus, who called it New Troy, but the earliest authentic record is that of Tacitus, who, writing in A.D. 61, described London as a place "copia negotiatorum et commeatuum maxime celebre."

Its position 60 miles inland at the head of navigation of a deep tidal river gave to it commanding advantages as a centre of distribution.

To the end of the eighteenth century its shipping trade was carried on either at moorings in the stream by the aid of barges and lighters or at wharves or quays constructed on the riverside.

At that period the legal quays and sufferance wharves where dutiable goods might be unloaded were filled to overflowing. There were no enclosed docks with warehouses where valuable cargoes might be stored in security.

The only existing docks at this time were the Howland Dock at Rotherhithe, constructed in 1694, and the Brunswick Dock at Blackwall, which dated from 1790. These, of small capacity and limited scope, were used for fitting out vessels and had no facilities for dealing with cargo.

Losses by theft and damage became so increasingly serious, both to merchants and to the Revenue, that at length public opinion was aroused in the City of London, and a scheme was promoted and the money guaranteed by the leading merchants for constructing enclosed docks where these disabilities would be overcome. As a result a Bill was passed by Parliament in 1799 authorizing the construction of the West India Docks, the first of the modern dock system as we have it to-day. Pitt and his Cabinet were present on the occasion of the laying of the foundation stone in 1800, and the docks were completed and opened to shipping in 1802.

So successful was this new venture that what to-day we should describe as a "boom" in dock creating enterprises ensued, and further dock schemes in the Port were promoted and sanctioned by Parliament at short intervals, viz.:

1800	London Dock
1801	Surrey Dock
1803	East India Dock
1810	Commercial Dock (Surrey)
1825	St. Katharine Dock
1850	Royal Victoria Dock
1864	Millwall Dock
1875	Royal Albert Dock
1882	Tilbury Dock

The era of prosperity with these various new undertakings reached its zenith in the latter half of the last century, and the fat days were followed by extremely lean ones. For some years a growing dissatisfaction with the administration of the dock systems of the Port by private companies became manifest. Consequently, Parliament in 1900 appointed a Royal Commission to investigate and report upon the condition of the Port generally and the measures necessary for its betterment. The Commission reported in favour of unification and control of all these private undertakings by a public authority. In 1908 a Government Bill giving effect to the Royal Commission's recommendations was introduced by Mr. Lloyd George, then President of the Board of Trade, with whom I was associated as Parliamentary Secretary, creating the Port of London Authority "for the purpose of administering, preserving and improving the Port." It was received with general approbation and became law that year.

The Port of London Authority consists of the Chairman, Vice-Chairman, ten Members appointed by certain Public Departments and Bodies, seventeen Members elected by payers of dues and other Port interests, and one by wharfingers. The Members of the Authority retire every three years, but are eligible for reappointment or re-election.

DREDGING A WATERWAY FOR A NEW DOCK.

A CUNARD LINER IN THE DOCKS.

To face p. 156

THE PORT OF LONDON

The docks transferred to the Authority are shown in the following table, with the areas, including land acquired since :

Dock.	Area in Acres.			Miles below London Bridge by Water to Entrances.
	Water.	Land.	Total.	
St. Katharine	10	13	23	½
London..	35	65	100	1½
Surrey Commercial	164	216	380	3½
Millwall	35	196	231	3½
West India	92	149	241	6¼
East India	31	37	68	6½
Royal Victoria	93	183	276	7
Royal Albert	87	737	824	10½
Tilbury	89	545	634	26

The aggregate length of quay of these is over 30 miles, exclusive of the riverside accommodation.

Early in 1911 the Authority adopted a comprehensive programme of Port improvements, appropriated into three categories, viz. :

(1) A primary or urgent programme, embracing works necessary to be carried out without delay in order to give much needed increase of accommodation.

(2) A secondary programme of such works deemed to be necessary to follow the first programme.

(3) A third or contingent programme ready to meet the development of passenger and other traffic anticipated as the result of the improvements comprised in the first and second programmes.

Following the adoption of the primary programme the various works were commenced, the most important being a new dock south of the Royal Albert Dock.

Its water area is 65 acres, its length of quay 2½ miles, with jetties to accelerate the discharge of vessels with cargo for the quays and for overside delivery.

The entrance lock is 800 feet long (capable of being extended to 910 feet by the aid of a floating caisson), 100 feet wide, depth of water on the sill 45 feet below T.H.W., with a dry dock 750 feet long and 100 feet wide. A short waterway connects this new dock with the Albert and Victoria Docks. The war delayed the construction of the works, which under normal conditions would have been completed in 1916. The new dock will be opened in the summer of 1921.

Valuable improvements have been made in the London Docks by which nine additional berths have been provided, the north quay widened, the crane equipment modernized and pumping machinery installed to afford a maximum depth of 25 feet 6 inches.

Parliamentary powers have been obtained for further extensions of this system, which by reason of its proximity to the City is much in request for vessels of moderate size.

The East India Import Dock, when the Authority entered into possession, was almost out of use owing to insufficient depth of water, inadequate equipment and the restrictive dimensions of the passage giving access to it. This has now been widened to 80 feet, an effective pumping plant installed to increase the depth of water to 28 feet, new quays and sheds constructed, crane equipment and railway communication provided, with the result that since completion this dock is now always full of shipping and accommodates vessels up to 9,500 tons.

The West India Dock system, although the oldest, has still a great future, and is being modernized, as its utility is likewise restricted by the insufficient size of the entrances for the class of vessels which it is capable of accommodating. The improvement scheme comprises a large turning basin at the east end of the three main docks, with a new entrance lock 650 feet long, 80 feet wide and 41 feet below T.H.W. By a connecting passage the Millwall Dock will be joined to this system, in both of which vessels of 20,000 tons will be then able to berth.

The South Dock will be equipped for grain discharge either into existing granaries or into a projected 40,000-ton silo.

Considerable developments in the form of new quays, sheds and modern equipment have already been effected.

At the Victoria and Albert Docks, of which the new dock already described forms a part, other important works have been completed, viz.:

The depth of water has been increased to a level of 2 feet 6 inches above T.H.W.

A NEW DOCK NEARING COMPLETION.

A BUSY SCENE IN THE DOCKS.

To face p 158

The Western Dry Dock has been enlarged to 575 feet in length and 80 feet in width, and heavy lift cranes provided for ship-repairing purposes.

The crane equipment for dealing with cargo has been augmented by the addition of forty-three electric cranes.

At the whole of the Authority's dry docks an equipment of heavy lift cranes and compressed-air plant has been installed, making them available for the most extensive repairing operations.

Sheds of a floor area of 350,000 square feet have been constructed on the south side of the Royal Victoria Dock, with new roads and improved railway facilities.

A cold store with insulated sorting floor has been constructed on the north side of the Royal Albert Dock, with capacity for 500,000 carcasses, equipped with the most modern mechanical appliances for their conveyance.

A further addition to the Authority's cold storage has been made at Smithfield Market by the erection, in 1914, of a new building with a capacity of 78,000 carcasses.

The total cold storage facilities of the Authority are adequate for a million and a half carcasses.

Tilbury Docks have been enlarged by the addition of 600 lineal yards of quay and 17 acres of water area, giving increased accommodation for the largest class of ships using the Port.

In the river at Tilbury an ocean wharf, consisting of a two-story jetty, has been constructed, 1,000 feet in length and capable of further extension, with a depth alongside of 30 feet at L.W.O.S.T. This will provide a facility for steamers of the largest tonnage to load and discharge without entering the enclosed docks.

Deepening of the river channels by the Authority's dredging fleet, acquired at a cost of £400,000, is in constant progress.

The Authority's administrative staff, now scattered over a number of City offices, will be housed in Trinity Square in a building of adequate capacity for present and prospective requirements, now approaching completion.

For the rehousing of those—principally dock workers—displaced by dock improvements, a "garden city" development has been carried out near the Royal Albert Dock and two hundred houses erected; land is held in reserve for the building of further houses as and when required.

LONDON OF THE FUTURE

The expenditure on Port developments totals about £7,000,000, and other improvements included in the secondary programme already sanctioned, and in some cases commenced, will account for at least £4,000,000 more.

The Authority may justly claim that substantial progress has been made in the task of making good the accumulated arrears occasioned by the long period of stagnation prior to its advent.

In 1872 the value of London's oversea imports and exports was £177,000,000. Prior to the war this had risen to £412,000,000.

About forty millions of tons net register of shipping pass annually to and from the Port, one-eighth of the total tonnage of the United Kingdom.

The reasons for this pre-eminence are happily expressed in the *Report of the Royal Commission on the Port of London* (1900) in the following paragraph :

> Our inquiry into the conditions of the Port of London has convinced us of its splendid natural advantages. Among these are the geographical position of the Port ; the magnitude, wealth and energy of the population behind it ; the fine approach from the sea ; the river tides, strong enough to transport traffic easily to all parts, yet not so violent as to make navigation difficult ; and land along the shores of a character suitable for dock construction and all commercial purposes.

There can be no finality in the progressiveness of a port so paramount as London. The policy must always be to keep well abreast—indeed, ahead—of requirements. Experience teaches that improvements in facilities bring increased trade and prosperity. So long as there is no faltering in recognition of this fact, the future of London as the greatest port of the Empire will be continuously assured.

THE EAST END

THE RT. REV. H. L. PAGET (as Bishop of Stepney)

CHAPTER XI

THE EAST END

I

THE London Society has bidden me write a paper on the Future of East London. I am not an archæologist, nor an historian. I have no convinced opinion on housing or town-planning. I am rather the victim of conflicting impressions than the proprietor of settled schemes, less mastering than mastered. Nevertheless, in a haphazard way I have come to know East London pretty well: enough perhaps to excuse, if not to justify, me in writing about it.

But the phrase "East London" covers a large area—too large for comprehensive treatment. It must be narrowed down; but it is not easy to say how. East London is a very different thing from the suburban districts northward and westward, which have come into being by the building over of country districts out towards Ealing or Tottenham. There is more history behind it, more romance attaching to it, than belongs to regions such as those. Long before it came to be what it is now, it was the home of great industries, of large prosperity, of extraordinarily skilful work and of just pride in it. A great part of it, perhaps the most important and interesting part of it, is riverside; and the Thames, too little seen as things are at present, has helped to shape its history. A little to the north and following pretty closely the course of the river runs the Commercial Road, surely a fine and imposing name; and north again of that is the Road—Whitechapel, Mile End, Bow, for so it is called at successive stages—which, parting from it at Aldgate and diverging to the north-east, crosses the Lea and goes on into Essex. North again, Roman Road, Old Ford, Straight Ford carry the mind back to a yet earlier history; but they perhaps lie rather apart from the special area with which I should wish to deal. We must never forget the line of the river; for the river has been dominant in the history of the past, and will be, I believe, the controlling influence in schemes for the future. Even now it is said that the change of air that comes with the flowing and ebbing tide is one of the things that save East London from the unhealthiness, which otherwise would visit an area where housing and other conditions are so bad.

Let us think, then, chiefly of the region that lies between the Mile End Road and the river—and let us remember that it is a part of London that has a special fascination for right-minded people. Walter Besant, some thirty years ago, writes, almost in the spirit of a discoverer, of its interest and charm. Mr. Pett Ridge describes himself, I believe, as a devotee of London east of Aldgate; and one meets now and again unexpected people who own that they prefer wandering in those parts to wandering anywhere else. You cannot brush such preferences aside with the remark that there is no accounting for tastes. There is clearly something in East London appealing, alluring, which gives it an advantage over the far-flung roads and avenues of the western suburbs. For it is urbs, not suburbs. A great piece of it is called (most delightful of names) the "Tower Hamlets," and its western part is almost one with the City herself; and indeed there are parts of East London where the fame of the past still lifts its head on high. To begin with the west. The finest perhaps of all the classical churches in London is the Parish Church of Spitalfields. It marks the piety, the generosity, the aspiration of the great fraternity of Weavers, just as the long low windows in Bethnal Green remind us of the loom; nor is it a mere memorial of past welfare, for it was as recently as 1916 that Mr. George Dorée, prince of velvet weavers, died, on whose loom part of King Edward's coronation splendour was wrought. A whole line of really magnificent churches, St. George's, Limehouse, Poplar, fine stone, fine work, encircling gardens, face you one after another as you go east, and a little to the north lies Stepney, where Sir Henry Colet had his country house, and his fine garden walk, and where his son, John Colet, Dean of St. Paul's and founder of the school, was born. Blackwall, again, farther south and on the river, must have been a wonderful place when, early in the last century, the line-of-battle ships might have been seen in building; and where, tradition said, the wives of the shipwrights scorned to use any coin less than a golden sovereign for tasting butter with. A curious relic of an old enthusiasm survived till 1886 (it may still survive) in the annual excursion of the Fairlop boat—a huge brake with a full ship's rigging, which bore its crew of block and pulley makers to Epping Forest and brought them back towards midnight, all exhilaration, and was galloped along the Road, swaying amid a fine display of fireworks.

Bromley-by-Bow once had a Royal Palace, and fine houses still stand in the Bow Road and on Stepney Green; there are fine houses on the pier at Wapping, and the old Harbour Master's House in Narrow Street, Limehouse, with its wide bow-windows and its balconies and its private access to the river, is like a bit of Venice; and the river itself, when at last you get a fair look at it, is a marvel of beauty. See it, as I once saw it from some high buildings in Blackwall, all burnished bronze with two or three sailing barges floating quiet on its surface. Watch the sunset from Blackwall Pier, or look from the southern angle of the Isle of Dogs across the tulip beds and the splendour of the river to the glories of Greenwich Hospital, and you will agree that this is the very last place in the whole world that should have been allowed to become monotonous, dull, or down at heel. It is a place to live in, to be happy in, to be proud of. In other parts of London, more towards the centre, are neighbourhoods derelict because fashion has forsaken them: they have their own sort of desolation. Their big houses have become the inconvenient homes of five or six families apiece. Their squares are dreary solitudes. A pleasantly designed fanlight or balcony or verandah calls your attention to what the house may have looked like in its better days. But it is not the flight of fashion that has helped to make East London what it is. Something more vital, more honourable than fashion has moved away. The silent wharf, the empty dock, the broken frame of the old weaver's loom, speak of work and industry well done, well paid, worth doing, pleasurable and pleasure giving. These are gone: the wanderer in East London is apt to encounter the ghosts of men and women very unlike the crowds that throng it in the present day.

It is hard to say exactly what has happened. We are told of shipwrights who in difficult and precarious times were obstinate and unbending; they hardly seem to have understood how uncertain was the hold of London on the wonderful art; how suddenly iron might usurp the place of wood. We can fancy vexatious and autocratic rules of pilotage and harbour due that must have tried the temper and clipped the gains of ship captains bound for home. Swifter mechanism may have displaced (it never replaced) the really exquisite products of the weaver's loom. Pride in work, pleasure in work, fellowship in work seemed to leave us. Here, as elsewhere, people no longer cared to live where they worked or to watch with almost affectionate supervision the processes of an industry which they themselves had built up. We gradually became companies, and where companies come companionship seems to retire: for companies are seldom company. The spiritual needs of the district were misunderstood or disregarded. Partly by removals from other districts, partly by growth of population, our numbers increased, and houses were built anyhow, anywhere for us to live in. Last of all, by gradual and most persistent invasion East London became the abiding place of hosts and hosts of aliens from every nation under heaven; foreign in speech and habits, inscrutable, unassimilated, and numerous enough to capture utterly and make their own the districts in which they are settled. "Why," said a distinguished Italian to me, as we stood in Wentworth Street, "this is a veritable Oriental bazaar!" Words fail to express the width, the penetrating depth of the influence of this incursion on the life of East London. The stranger will notice at once the unbroken lines of shops bearing foreign names, the Hebrew posters, the theatre with its Hebrew announcements of the plays that are acted there. Many of the public elementary schools are Jewish through and through, and close on days of Jewish observance. Parishes of fifteen or twenty thousand souls have an alien population of 80 or 90 per cent. The great churches of Whitechapel and Spitalfields stand in the midst of districts where at least three-quarters of the people are aliens. I would not attempt here to judge our invaders; they have obvious good points, they have very obvious defects. But their presence in enormous and increasing numbers complicates beyond measure any forecast as to the future of East London. They have to be reckoned with, and a person by no means timid has confessed to a real though vague sense of terror in the midst of a great crowd, utterly un-English in the very heart of England.

Nor must we forget a foreign element of another kind. Ever

since I can remember, as far back as 1881, the Oriental was a familiar figure in the East India Road. A string of lithe and loose-limbed Indians, ready to sell you an inlaid walking-stick; or a group of Chinamen in native dress; or a big and coal-black Nubian would meet you; and you would wonder where he was going and what he would make of London streets on a Sunday afternoon; for it was on Sundays that you saw most of them. And there were always stories of "opium dens" down Limehouse way where they smoked and gambled and slept. But now more of them have come, and they look as though some had settled down and meant to stay. There are streets in Limehouse wholly given up to them, and they are spreading into High Street, Poplar, and even into East India Road. Strange Chinese shops are opened, and notices in Chinese character are displayed. There is a China Town, on a small but not insignificant scale, adding its own problems to the complications of East London life. Small wonder that the student of human nature finds a field of study east of Aldgate Pump!

II

It is hard indeed to forecast the lines on which a scheme for the improvement of East London might be framed. Those who love it are jealous for it with the same sort of jealousy which might be felt for a town of ancient memories or a beautiful building that has been mishandled. East London deserves to be restored, it ought not to be destroyed. It merits separate treatment; it should not be made just like anywhere else. Certainly the hardship, the cruelty of anything like sudden or widespread displacement and unhousing must be kept in mind and avoided at any cost. The fear of this discounts and qualifies at every stage any ambitious and comprehensive scheme. No one knows how bitterly wholesale disturbance is resented, and how those whom we wish to benefit often ask to be let alone. The sense that any home is better than none is not a mere sentiment: it is a piece of bitter experience for those whom "improvements" have sent away to look in vain for lodgment. But the reconstruction of this part of London is long overdue. It must be done, and it is to be hoped that it will be done in a way that will recognize and accept the suggestions and indications that come from the character, yes, even from the traditions of the place itself. Parts of reconstructed London are dismal, monotonous beyond description. No one wants the East London of his affections to be made like them.

Begin, then, with the river. Work up to it, down to it. Fix heart and eyes on it. Never forget it, or lose sight of it for long. A scheme was afoot before the war for recovering about eight acres of its bank for a tiny park and recreation ground, and the immense possibilities of such a proposal were seen at once. But surely there is scope for more than this. The Victoria Embankment above Blackfriars Bridge is good in its way. But it belongs, all the same, to a timorous and unimaginative age. It is still cold, formal, stiff, unfriendly. We ought to be able to do better than that. Let us begin by grudging every yard of that fine fringe which is shabbily, unworthily used. We must acquire of it all that we can. There is no need to interfere with the docks, the shipping. They are of the river, just as good as it is. But away with all that needlessly conceals it or bars the way to it! We are not like the poor suburbs which have nothing to guide, to inspire the plans on which they are laid out. That has been done for us, as it has been from the very first, by the course of a great stream. Herodotus calls the rich alluvial soil of the Delta "the gift of the river," and many a fair city might bear the same name. It is there, it is what it is, because the river was there before it. It would be a shame indeed to throw away the infinite advantage the river gives us. Only treat it friendly. Rivers are content to bear the burden of our traffic: but I think that so far as their banks go they like to be played with. We want no stiff promenade, no imitative fortification, no frowning heads or hard bronze wreaths. There must be gardens, things to divert the elders and to amuse the young. Why not a big riverside market, such as might relieve the crowd and congestion of our market streets elsewhere and give life and colour and human interest to the recovered bank?

And then, for this is an easy thing, keep hold of and, where need be, regain every scrap of open space in the neighbourhood; and bear them in mind and work them into every plan which you contemplate. They are precious things; far too precious to be unused or—and this is very important—surrounded by mere warehouses. Build, when it comes to building, with reference to them. Everybody knows that all over London a house in "the square" is more attractive than a house in the street, and quite the pleasantest houses in Stepney would be those, neither too high nor too low, convenient and well designed, that look out into the square. And save us from monotony. I would as soon live in a hexagonal cell as in one of the homogeneous tenements or " flats " which various building trusts have erected. We have, I believe, discarded for ever the multi-floor, skyscraping form of " artisans' dwellings." Everyone, from some point of view or another, is found condemning them. We may have indeed to guard against unnecessary displacement—that has been already said. But the gain of lodging the same old number of people on the same old number of square feet would be dearly bought if it implied the same old models, so strangely unhome-like, so proved unwholesome, so dreary for the children!

Nor let us have our houses all of one size. The smallest must be well built, comfortable, fitted with modern labour-saving conveniences. Whatever we do, let us take counsel with the wives and mothers; they are our best advisers in things like these; for they know by bitter, weary, heart-breaking experience what they want. Let us all have hot water and electric light. But let us have larger houses as well as smaller ones. For some of us will get on better than others; and we do not want them to go away simply because they have become prosperous. We had rather they stopped with us. They might easily become our leaders in local affairs, the right men for the Borough Council, for L.C.C., even for Parliament. We do not want our homes or our lives dwarfed by enormous mansions, but we should be all the better were we saved the monotony of a uniform standard; if the outward and almost inevitable tokens of moderate and (probably) well merited success gave us a bit of encouragement. There is a great deal to be said for a district that presents this sort of variety, so long as nobody is horribly rich and no one miserably poor. It is perhaps the sort of place in which the spirit of fellowship and brotherly kindness is on the whole most likely to thrive. We want to avoid the too emphatic distinction between rich and poor neighbourhoods—there has been too much of it in the past; and London as a whole is too like one of those big houses where the servants' quarters are rigorously separated from the rest of the house. We all know the swing-door which is the line of demarcation, with the staircases carpeted on the one side, not carpeted on the other side of it: a house on one side, a barracks on the other!

III

But what of our work? Many, of course, will still follow the industries of the riverside; and the Port of London will want them. But dock labour must be considered by those who are capable of dealing with it. It must be saved from its fatal and heart-breaking uncertainties. It must be "decasualized," as far as ever it can. We wish with all our hearts success and increase to the businesses, the factories and workshops where good work is done, and good wages are paid, and people are fairly and honourably treated. But too much, it seems, of the industry of East London lies away from all this. It consists of thousands of minor employments—of work let and sublet again and again, of work that is often done at the home of the worker, hard to standardize, to regulate, to inspect. It seems to carry little honour, little pleasure with it, it is hard and monotonous, it is still ill paid. Someone must do it: must make the cheap clothing, and the cheap boots, and the cardboard boxes, and the fur and feather trimming, and the umbrellas and the cigarettes. But here perhaps more than anywhere else the complicated business of the minimum wage must be worked out fair and square. Here the steps that secure it must be taken firmly; and for those to whom we are indebted for such thankless work we must take extra pains to provide the healthy homes, the hours of leisure which may help to make their labour at least less intolerable.

It is vain, I suppose, to hope to recapture and win back some of the ancient industries which, like the silk of Spitalfields, gave the place the pride and joy of work done better there than anywhere else; but I own that I should like to see this part of East London famous for something that could hardly be got elsewhere! We are amongst the most quick-witted people in the world. Canon Barnett tested and proved our appreciation for the best in art. Real critics have praised again and again our music and our singing. We have more in us than people suppose. Hand workmanship (not that generally associated with fancy bazaars) still beats the best that machinery can produce, and the world is coming to understand it. We have no wish, indeed, to be led down the blind alleys of amateurism or to have industries fostered that will come to naught. But many people are weary of the products of mere mechanism, and there may yet be a demand for that which hands and hands alone can fashion. "Garden cities" have already been able to attract important industries, and have become the homes of really excellent craftsmanship, and why should it not be so with our reconstructed East London? There is a golden spot in Whitechapel, occupied by a foundry which since the sixteenth century has gone on casting bells which are still amongst the best in the world. Is it like the snow under the hedges, waiting, as country people say, "for more to come"? It is difficult to love East London and not to wish that it might become celebrated, as of old, for something fine of which it held the secret and the skill.

It may well be that in thinking of all this we are merely dreamers, asking for that which is found nowhere else, which the laws of modern development forbid. Some people think we might become a sort of extension of the City. Why should Leadenhall Street break off so short and suddenly at Aldgate, or Eastcheap seem to come to an end of itself at Tower Hill? Why not carry the dignity and splendour of it farther east? It might seem the most natural thing in the world to enlarge by a mile or two that privileged region where land is so costly that the great office buildings stand nine stories high and you must be in a good way of business to have so much as your name on a plate or a topmost window blind. A bigger "City" does not seem impossible. But surely there would be a just outcry against so wholesale an eviction as this would involve. You must not drive people perforce away from the place in which they prefer to dwell. Deportation has its limits; and perhaps a little bit of experience entitles me to say that it is not sheer bliss to live even in excellent air some miles out of London when the privilege is secured at the cost of a journey by train or tram, which is, as things are, the most tiring part of the day's work! I am always inclined to ask the rapturous advocates of "easy" transit to underrate their transports a little, and to test the convenience of their methods at six o'clock in a Chingford train or an East Ham tramcar. It would be a cruelty to many of us to rob us of a domicile within reasonable distance of our work. As things are, we are surely badly served. The tube railways seem to have forgotten us altogether; we have, indeed, the District Railway: but travel by it at the time when we are leaving off work, and you will face the discomforts of overcrowding in their severest form. There are, of course, the main suburban lines, but we cannot waste our time catching trains: we want the train that catches us! And no part of London can get on without us.

Well, then, make a suburb, a residential neighbourhood of it. But what does that mean? It is easy to imagine the place being simply spoiled. So it would be, if great blocks of "model" buildings were thrust upon it, or if it were to lose all trace of character by the construction of rows of mongrel-architecture houses such as we know only too well in other parts of reconstructed London. Why not have in mind from the first, and work out little by little as time goes on, a far more attractive and inspiring scheme? Here is an area of moderate size and with fairly definite boundaries. Westward the City seems to look the other way; eastward the Lea reminds us that beyond it lies another county. The district has possessed a certain unity in the past and had a character of its own. The river—we turn to it again and again—does more than suggest; it claims a special and imaginative dealing with a neighbourhood fortunate in lying on its northern strand. Do nothing suddenly, use no hard and cruel haste, but work from the first with a definite scheme in mind. Determine to make this part of London a place to be happy in, a place to be quietly proud of. Let it have its own completeness, its moderate self-sufficiency. I am no town-planner, but I have seen enough of towns at home and abroad to suggest the sort of place I have in mind. The present open spaces, made the very most of, would almost (not quite) suffice for beauty and for breathing-room; but we must have more buildings devoted to public comfort and common use, for rest and recreation and the pleasure of meeting one another. We want a rare good concert hall and a fine theatre; we want clubs and gymnasia. We might have public halls, such as are provided in some of the big towns in America, where people whose homes are small ones might meet for their private social gatherings, wedding parties and the like. These halls should be under the care of the municipal authorities, who might also provide plants and decorations suiting the occasion for which they were engaged. We want the river bank, wherever we can get it, accessible and attractive as only the bank of a noble river can be.

THE EAST END

IV

Have I shirked; have I left to the last a difficult matter? Plato, I think, somewhere in the *Republic*, seems to postpone and procrastinate with regard to a point that puzzled him. I have been trying to write of the future of East London, and all along I have left myself pursued by a question which sooner or later is bound to arise. What about the alien? You are thinking, planning, building; but after all, who is it for? Some of the districts in this area have an alien population outnumbering ten times over the people of our own race. They occupy at once every house they can secure. Quick-witted, indefatigable, alert, they slip into our places, they take our houses, they sometimes seem to get our work.

Certainly I have no hostility for the alien as such. I am sure it is wrong to judge and condemn them *en masse*, or to sum up under some hasty and scornful verdict their infinite variety. I can do no more than point to what seems to me the real seriousness of allowing a great piece of London like this, the natural home of thousands and thousands of our hardest workers, to be taken from them, driven out as they are by the constant invasion of people of other races. We could assimilate, as it were, a certain number; as it is, they seem more likely to "assimilate" us. It is one thing to offer a friendly welcome, it is another to find yourself fairly overwhelmed!

It is possible, of course, that the pacification and reconstruction of Europe may allure some of them to their own homes. We are thankful to believe that in the past they have found in England a justice and a kindness which were denied to them in other lands. We sympathize with them in their sufferings, and we admire the patience and courage with which those sufferings have been borne. But I hope I am not wrong in claiming East London for the Londoner, and thinking chiefly of the needs and difficulties of our own people.

SOME THOUGHTS ON THE DEVELOPMENT OF LONDON

RAYMOND UNWIN, F.R.I.B.A.

CHAPTER XII

SOME THOUGHTS ON THE DEVELOPMENT OF LONDON

LONDON is a wonderful phenomenon: from small beginnings it has continued for centuries to spread over areas ever growing wider, and to include a steadily increasing population, until to-day it represents the greatest accumulation of people ever gathered together in one town. This city is so vast, its growth has been so continuous, that we have formed the habit of regarding its development rather as a phenomenon of nature to be accepted and submitted to, than as a work of man to be guided and controlled for the benefit of its inhabitants. Cities and towns grow because of the great pleasure which men derive from associated life and because of the great profit which they secure from associated work. Working and living alone, or with only a few companions, a limit is soon reached of what men can do and of the variety of life which they can enjoy; but when large numbers are living and working together there is hardly any limit to that which they can accomplish; and, though the scope of their life, both in interest and enjoyment, may perhaps reach its limit at an earlier stage in the growth of numbers, it is at least vastly increased as compared with that possible for small, isolated groups. Hence it is that men the world over crowd together in cities. On account of this tendency certain conditions usually arise. There is congestion in the centre and keen competition for the occupancy of the most favourable positions, with the result that the price of land is enhanced, and, too often, there follows a degree of overcrowding, with its concomitant disease and misery, that goes far to deprive large sections of the population of those very advantages to attain which the city has come into existence. Too frequently men have allowed themselves to be enslaved to those conditions which they themselves have created. Efficiency of work and the convenience and pleasure of life they allow to be hampered or destroyed as a result of their crowding together for the purpose of securing the benefits of associated life. The inconveniences and the untold evils springing from congested slum life have been accepted as if these were some law of divine ordinance before which men were helpless.

The first thought that I wish to suggest is that the conditions of town life are those of man's own making; that he can alter them and regulate them, and that there are no unalterable laws producing the evils which he accepts. All he needs to do is to regard the city as a great human activity, needing to be guided like any other. The fact is, the growth of towns has become a scramble, and reminds one of a crowd at the ticket office that has not learnt to form a queue. Citizens must learn the queue habit, learn to regulate the tendencies which spring from the desire of many people to live near the centre of the city, and to control the use of the coveted sites there situated in the interests of the whole community. This is very important in reference to London at the present time, for the city is on the verge of great developments. It has been spared some of the worst evils of overcrowding which have invaded cities like New York and Berlin, where the people are packed together in tall tenement dwellings planned with insufficient light and air, but so substantially built, and so costly, that their removal will be a matter of the greatest difficulty. Fortunately, in London the tendency to decentralize has come in time. Even before the war London had ceased to absorb its natural increase of population. The wide area generally known as Greater London was an exporter of population; during the last decade for which figures are available some 200,000 people forming part of the natural increase of the population of the metropolis went to live beyond the bounds of Greater London as measured by the police area. Moreover, the exodus from the central to the outer parts was so great that the population in many of the central areas was actually less in number than in the previous decade. This is evidence of a very marked movement of population taking place in this great city. In addition to this more permanent movement, the daily movement of the population, as shown by the number of journeys per head, has been increasing very rapidly.

SOME THOUGHTS ON DEVELOPMENT

One of the results of the war, which has for five years arrested the normal development of means of transport, while not arresting but possibly stimulating the travelling activities of the people, has been to produce a great congestion in all the means of transport. The people have been going out from the City to live, to such an extent that now they can hardly get into the City to work. This difficulty as to passenger transport is a somewhat serious problem which needs to be fairly faced. For it comes as a last reinforcement to the defeated army of arguments against the decentralizing of dwellings, and if we are not on our guard may result in giving to the tenement dwelling a new lease of life in London.

With the decentralization of the dwellings of the people there has been concurrently going on a concentration of business and the consolidation of industry into fewer and larger units. Mass production of many of the products on which we depend has been growing, and with it has come a call for larger industrial areas and better organization of the facilities for transport of raw materials and finished products. Ready interchange of goods and services between the main industries and those subsidiary industries which minister to their requirements is increasingly necessary. It is becoming more and more evident that industries scattered about in the heart of a great city, to and from which all goods must be carted through the streets, owing to their want of access to either water or railway carriage, cannot be run under modern conditions with sufficient economy to compete with great industrial enterprises which are properly laid out, in direct contact with the main means of transport and near to other allied industrial concerns. Hence we see the development of definite industrial areas; and in the neighbourhood of London we find that the greater part of the level land lying along the banks of the River Thames, from the City down as far as Tilbury, is already occupied, or about to be occupied, by great industrial enterprises which will make use of the river and the railways for transport purposes. Similar development is noticeable also along the main railway lines.

There is therefore a tendency to concentrate industries in relation to one another and the means of transport, and to decentralize them in relation to the city itself. Now we, as citizens of London, can take one of two courses: either we can allow these great movements to go forward haphazard, leaving each individual merchant to elbow his way into an advantageous office or warehouse in the centre, each individual manufacturer to seek out unaided some available spot on which to locate his industry, each individual tenant to scramble for the best tenement he can find in an overcrowded city; or, on the other hand, we can henceforth regard the development of our city as we should regard any other great enterprise, as one needing to be organized and directed towards producing the best results for the whole. No one would think of suggesting that the infantry, cavalry, artillery, medical and sanitary corps composing an army should be allowed, when forming a camp, to scramble for the sites on which to pitch their tents and depots; nor in the great factories which had to be created during the war was it the custom to allow the chiefs of the different sections to choose sites and put up buildings where and how they thought best for their own purposes. In both these classes of large enterprise the importance is generally realized of working to some comprehensive plan, of apportioning the ground in an orderly manner to give the utmost convenience and advantage for all sections, and above all to contribute to the most efficient and effective use of the whole to achieve the purpose in hand, in the one case to provide the most effective fighting unit, and in the other to create the most efficient organization for production. Mistakes are no doubt made in such matters, but in laying out a factory, the natural flow of the processes, beginning with the delivery of the raw material and leading up to the dispatch of the finished product, is at least considered; the location of the different buildings to facilitate this flow with the minimum of transport and waste of time and labour; the placing of the offices to secure efficient oversight, of the workshops to facilitate repairs where most likely to be required, of the change rooms and canteens to minister most efficiently to the needs of the workers, are all based on careful study and planning. Estimates are made beforehand of the number of workers in each building, diagrams are drawn indicating graphically the density of employment in the different parts of the area, and the length of walk from these parts to the canteens, factory gates or train halts, and the whole arrangement and development of the works is laid out to secure, first, the main end in view, efficient production; second, the convenience and welfare of those engaged in the work.

TWO VIEWS IN THE HAMPSTEAD GARDEN SUBURB. (BARRY PARKER AND RAYMOND UNWIN, ARCHITECTS.)

(Showing how Londoners of the Future might be housed.)

To face p. 180.

SOME THOUGHTS ON DEVELOPMENT

The time has come to realize that the same kind of comprehensive organization and planning must be applied to the growth of a city. We need to look at the city and its activities as a whole, to envisage its aims and purposes, and learn to control its development and provide a fitting environment for the millions of individuals whose activities contribute to the realization of those purposes, and whose well-being it is one of the chief functions of the city to secure.

London itself is so immense and complex that it is difficult in the first instance to get a comprehensive view of it; nevertheless, it is extremely necessary at this time. It will only be possible here to touch on a few of the great problems which are raised by the most preliminary consideration of its development.

First, as to the size of London. I venture to suggest that London as a single aggregation of population is already far too large; that no advantages to the inhabitants of London which can result from its further increase could outweigh the disadvantages; and that we should look to the early arresting of such growth, and even to the possible diminution of the number of people already occupying the area of London itself. It may be, however, that we have not yet reached, in certain directions, the limit of efficiency due to concentration; particularly may this be so in reference to commerce and business of various kinds. The central area devoted to business may therefore continue to grow. Moreover, the industrial development along the banks of the Thames may call for additional industrial population. How, then, is it possible to prevent the area of residential London continuing to spread? It has been found in other countries that it is quite possible to set a limit to the size of a city; many have been ringed with fortifications outside which it has been necessary to preserve a belt of ground unbuilt upon for protective purposes. The city has grown up to the limit of this fortified line, but beyond it this open zone has had to be respected, and any further extension has perforce been by means of detached suburbs outside that range. What can be done to secure safety from the danger of very occasional armed attack can also be done to secure any other advantage sufficiently desired by the inhabitants. It is high time that a green belt were preserved around London to protect its inhabitants from disease, by providing fresh air, fresh fruit and vegetables, space for recreation and contact with and knowledge of nature. How is this to be secured? Probably by the development of satellite towns, largely self-supporting, having their own industries, garden cities, and perhaps also by detached dormitory suburbs. The tendency for industries to concentrate outside London along the river's bank and by the railways will greatly assist the development of such satellite towns. As far as possible the industries should be decentralized, as this would reduce the traffic problem by enabling the workers to live near their employment. Any increase of transit difficulties which might result from the suggested development of dormitory towns for those employed in the commercial centre could be compensated for by the reduction of the enormous volume of unnecessary transport which now blocks our roads and lines. There are two ways of meeting transport difficulties. One is to provide additional transport and new facilities, and the other is to reduce the waste of transport, and thus economize in the use of existing facilities. There is a very wide field for the latter method. Mr. Gattie's scheme for the centralized distribution of all London's goods traffic has failed to secure the support of the Committee appointed to investigate it. Perhaps the project has suffered from its own immensity; but there remains very much force in the arguments derived from the useless waste and the needless congestion of traffic in London. I may instance Covent Garden Market. It is one of the greatest single markets of the world, and yet every ton of produce which reaches it or leaves it must be carted through many miles of the busiest London streets, for Covent Garden has no direct contact either with railway or with water transport. A list of other markets and of many factories might easily be made which would indicate a total volume of heavy cartage in and about the streets of London, which, if saved by better location of markets, factories, warehouses, etc., would materially ease the congestion of the streets and lighten the wear and tear of their surfaces. In this connection much may be learnt from such a city as Frankfort, which before the war was developing a great industrial area on its eastern outskirts. This was served by miles of new wharves to accommodate the Rhine-borne merchandise, with sites laid out for factories and warehouses, all provided with direct access to the river and to the complete railway system serving the city. Much also might be learnt from Seattle and other American cities, studies of which have been made for the purpose of increasing the efficiency of their industries and of the handling of their imports and exports.

In connection with passenger transport also there are many questions calling for careful study in this great city. In three or four of the most important cities of the world, where such studies have been made, the conclusion generally accepted is, I believe, that the best results cannot be secured when passenger traffic is dealt with at a number of great terminal stations on the outskirts of the central area of the city. In the competition that was held for the planning and improvement of Berlin, the linking up of its railways and the creation of a central station or group of stations for the interchange of passenger traffic was a main feature in several of the successful schemes. In New York, even on the crowded isle of Manhattan, central stations have been created. A wide study of the problems of transit in Chicago has resulted in the conviction that some linking up of the terminal stations is required. Somewhat similar results could be quoted from other cities. It is questionable whether the terminals in our city of London are now best adapted for their purpose; whether it is most useful that the vast areas of sidings and shunting grounds should be occupying such an extensive part of London's most coveted sites; whether the problem of London transit could not better be met by some underground linking of these main lines which would allow some, at any rate, of the trains to run through London, starting on the distant outskirts, picking up their passengers in the centre and passing thence to their destination. This would permit much of the marshalling of the trains to be carried on outside the city. Such a course may or may not be practicable, but the experience of other great cities would suggest that it is well deserving of careful study. It may be that, as a result of changes now about to take place in the organization of London's traffic, there may some day arise on the site that is now occupied by Covent Garden Market a great central station similar in size, and I hope equal in beauty, to some of those recently built in America.

In considering the decentralization of population and the general growth of a city, we should remember that distance is more effectively measured by minutes than by miles, and that what each citizen who must work in the commercial or administrative centre requires is that he shall live 20, 30 or 40 minutes from his work, and that provided he can do this, it is of less importance to him, whether the distance is 5, 10 or 20 miles. Hence it is instructive to map out residential areas and colour them to indicate the time-distance from the centre. If this is done, it will be found that satellite cities may frequently be nearer to the centre than vast suburban areas. Much may be done, as we may learn from other countries, to reduce the time distance by co-ordinating our different means of transport. Hitherto these have been run too much in competition—the main lines with the tube railways, the tube railways with the trams and the trams with the omnibuses. Efficiency will be found in co-ordinating all these services so that they minister the one to the other and all to the passengers' needs, and in carefully organizing for interchange between them to be as rapid and as convenient as possible. We are only beginning in London to provide for such interchange at all. Golder's Green, with its yard in which omnibuses take up the passengers set down at the terminus by the tube railway, is a crude example: how crude, those who stand in the rain and wind in the open yard waiting for their particular omnibus, or wait at no small risk in the middle of the Finchley Road to catch a passing tram, may realize if they will compare with it one of the interchange stations in Boston, where the passengers alight from their suburban train on a platform at the other side of which the street cars draw up. They have only to step out of the train, cross the platform and enter the tram, under cover, at the cost of a few seconds of time. It is clear that we have not, in London, nearly reached the limits of convenient transport; and it is probable that the development of satellite cities with the proper arrangement of rapid transit from the centre direct to these points, so far from increasing the present congestion of transport to and from the suburbs, would relieve that congestion by sorting the passengers and leaving only those to occupy the tubes and trams who were not journeying the longer distances.

When considering London's needs for improved railway facilities, we must not overlook the great revival of road transport which has taken place, and the equally urgent need that routes for the arterial roads, perhaps ere long to be required to serve a ring of satellite towns developing around this great central city, should be preserved, and should be adequate in width and character to deal with the various kinds of road transit. It may be that

TWO VIEWS IN THE HAMPSTEAD GARDEN SUBURB. (BARRY PARKER AND RAYMOND UNWIN, ARCHITECTS.)

(Showing the way Londoners of the Future might be housed.)

To face p 184

the tram will give place to the motor-bus and the motor-car; but experience of other cities where roads exist of adequate width to provide a separate track where trams can run at high speed, interfering with other traffic to the minimum extent, suggests that the comparative value of the two kinds of transport cannot properly be judged until roads suitable for tramways are available for them. The tram in the middle of a crowded carriage-way, where every passenger who boards or leaves a car is in great danger of accident from passing traffic, and where every other vehicle using the road must constantly cross and recross the tram tracks, is a very different proposition from the high-speed tram running quietly along a strip of turf, with safe paved spaces for passengers to alight upon, and able to run without fear of a collision from one crossing place to the next. In any case, whether required for high-speed trams or high-speed motor-cars, it is clearly wise that ample width should be reserved along the routes where it may be foreseen that arterial roads will be required to meet the future needs of London and its satellite towns.

The fact that London, the largest of cities, has been able to grow to its present size with such comparatively imperfect development and co-ordination of means of transit, and yet to accommodate its people mainly in self-contained cottage homes—that it has in fact escaped the general adoption of the tall tenement dwelling—would seem to disprove any necessity for that type of housing.

The advantages in health and pleasure and in the general amenity of life which are secured by a more open development of the residential areas are so pronounced that even if, to secure them, we must ere long fix a lower limit of population to some of our great cities, this would probably be no disadvantage in itself, and would in any case be a very cheap price to pay for the great advantages gained. It is known that a rapidly reducing return in efficiency results from overcrowding houses upon land, and this is especially pronounced on the economic side at the present time, when the cost of street works is relatively so much higher than the cost of the extra land required.

The following figures speak for themselves; they compare an example of crowded development with one of open development, based on the average price of urban land which is being acquired for housing purposes by the local authorities, and the pre-war and present average costs of road-making and other works of development in urban housing schemes.

	1914.		1919.	
Cost of land per acre	£212		£212	
Complete cost of roads and sewers per yard lin. ..	Ordinary, £5 8s. 0d. Narrow, £3 0s. 0d.		Ordinary, £11 6s. 0d. Narrow, £6 10s. 3d.	
	Open.	Crowded.	Open.	Crowded.
No. of houses to the acre..	12	21·3	12	21·3
Area of plot in square yards	346	164	346	164
Total cost of plot for land and roads	£42 18s. 0d.	£38 1s. 2½d.	£70 16s. 1d.	£68 15s. 4d.
Cost of plot per square yard	2s. 5¾d.	4s. 7¾d.	4s. 1d.	8s. 4·1d.
Extra *per yard* due to increased density	—	2s. 2d.	—	4s. 3·1d.
Rent per week to give 5½ per cent. return on cost .	10·89d.	9·66d.	1s. 6·07d.	1s. 5·45d.
Extra rent per week for larger plot with reduced density	1·23d.	—	0·52d.	—

It is clear also that this type of development, which affords so much greater opportunities for home-life, and particularly for child-life, and gives a lower death-rate and a lower sickness-rate for nearly all the chief diseases, can be combined with the main social, educational and cultural opportunities which spring from city life. It is not possible to fix any exact limit of population necessary to secure the maximum of such opportunities, but many of the cities which in the past have afforded the greatest opportunities in these respects have been small in numbers compared with our large cities; and it is probable that beyond a hundred, or at most two hundred thousand population, mere size can add but little to the benefits which may be enjoyed by a population within the numbers named.

The open type of development, with gardens attached to most of the dwellings, whilst reducing to some extent the need for playgrounds and open spaces, by no means allows these to be dispensed with; and we have in this country much need for the provision of playgrounds and playing-fields in towns which have grown up with little provision for these. In America much more has been done to meet this need than in this country. For the built-up portions of American cities the standard that has generally been adopted as the desirable one is that there should be a playground for young children within half a mile of every dwelling, and a larger recreation ground for older boys and girls within about a mile. In addition many American cities are reserving large areas for parks, pleasure grounds and wild open spaces in the immediate neighbourhood of the cities, so that as the towns expand these areas will in perpetuity remain open. Very large sums, running in the case of some cities into millions of pounds, have been spent in clearing built-on areas and creating necessary open spaces and playgrounds. In the case of London such provision of open space should be made as rapidly as possible in the central area; but perhaps it is still more urgent on the outskirts, because it is at present so much easier and more economical there than it will be later to reserve sufficient area of suitable ground to form the play and pleasure grounds for this great population. It is one of the most valuable features of the map prepared during the war by the London Society that some indication is given of the best grounds for such reservations. Frequently flat land in the neighbourhood of streams, not specially good for building purposes, will form excellent recreation grounds; while high points difficult of access may be invaluable for pleasure and holiday resorts. If the vast population of London is to have reasonable access to open spaces in natural condition, such areas should as quickly as possible be reserved, and to a generous extent, to form a green belt about the present London.

One of the most pressing problems in connection with the development of London is the creation of some unity of control, with a general staff to think out and plan the policy for this great city, and to secure that the broad lines of development shall all be laid down; to determine the best positions for the new satellite towns or dormitory suburbs, the best areas for industrial development, and those which should be reserved for belts of open space, for intensive agricultural use, accommodation land, and so forth. What a few years ago would have been regarded as large towns are already being planned as housing schemes by local authorities around London; and it is most important that all who are concerned with the development of this great city should combine to lay down the main lines of such development. It is not necessary that such a central authority should control all the details of the vast area. We have yet to learn in regard to municipal as in regard to Imperial matters that unity of command in connection with the main lines of policy, and main dispositions which affect the whole, can and should be combined with the utmost freedom of local control and local initiative in those matters which affect primarily the different localities; and that a much more healthy municipal government will result by giving to the different localities the utmost autonomy in regard to their local affairs that is compatible with a general direction on those matters which equally concern the whole city.

There remains one other point to which I would refer. We have been discussing the development of the city of London as if the whole of its site and the area surrounding it were at the disposal of the city and could be used without difficulty for whatever purpose the interests of the city should demand. It is this point of view that I have wished to emphasize, because I believe that the time has come when it is the one which must be taken; for the proper development of London cannot be brought about while the individual owners of small or large patches of ground retain the right to use that ground for whatever purposes they think best, having regard only to their own interest. We must recognize that the high value of land in and around the great city is, like the other conditions which have been referred to, the direct result of the coming together of many people, and of the advantages of one sort or another which may be derived from this associated life. For a population to allow themselves to be enslaved by those conditions, and prevented by the very value of the advantages which their association creates, from enjoying those advantages to the full, would be both futile and foolish. How, then, is the free disposition of land to serve the best interests of the public to be secured without entailing ruinous expense on the public purse? The first step is to recognize that the value of land is due to the advantages to be derived from settling upon it, to the opportunities which it affords. Moreover, that anything which increases those advantages or opportunities, which improves the efficiency of industry, increases the profits of commerce or the pleasures of life in the city, will certainly increase the total amount of the value of the sites which must be occupied to enjoy

DUKE'S MEADOWS, CHISWICK, TO BE PRESERVED AS PLAYING FIELDS FOR THE FUTURE BY THE CHISWICK DISTRICT COUNCIL.

STRAND-ON-GREEN, CHISWICK.

these opportunities. Hence all the improvements or controls which we sum up in the term Town Planning, as applied to the organization and the laying out of the development of a great city, do not destroy but increase the sum total of land values. They do not destroy the total, but they may alter materially the apportionment of such values to the different individual sites. For example, if around the present London there were reserved a belt of open space a mile wide, upon which no buildings could ever be erected, it is clear that this land would cease to have any value for building purposes; its value would be limited to whatever it might be worth for intensive culture, for letting as recreation grounds, accommodation land, orchards and so forth. But as London would continue to require as many additional buildings each year as it would have required apart from this provision, the next belt of land outside that reserved mile would, as a matter of fact, acquire additional building value, and its value would on the whole be increased by at least as much as the value of the open belt had been reduced. There would be a new distribution of values, but unless the whole project were a great mistake and did not add to the total amenity and value of life in the city, there would be no destruction. Moreover, if the whole of the land around the city were in one ownership, it would not matter to that owner which piece of land acquired a building value and which merely retained its agricultural or open-space value. The matter of interest to such an owner would be that the land should be so developed that the total value of the whole would be as high as possible. As that total value represents in fact the sum of the efficiency and pleasure of the associated life of the city, it is equally to the advantage of the city itself that that total should be high and should be increased.

How, then, are we to meet this problem of redistribution? It is evident that nothing need be destroyed, that the total value may, indeed, by wise action be increased. This is a problem urgently needing solution. Many different methods of dealing with it have been suggested. At the Garden City at Letchworth, Mr. Howard purchased the whole of the area of the city and sufficient additional land to form an agricultural belt round it. As the town has grown the land has increased in value. Some of it has been reserved for business purposes, some set aside for factory areas, some for cottage building. Already the value of that reserved for factory buildings is considerably higher than that reserved for cottage building; and it has been shown that land upon which shops and business buildings may be built has a much higher value than that upon which dwellings or even factories only are allowed to be erected. The Garden City Company make the regulations defining the factory areas, the business areas and the residential areas, with a view to the best development of the town, and they do not need to consider their policy in reference to its effect on the value of this bit of land or that bit of land: what they need to consider is the securing of the greatest total value, and this they know will result from securing that development of the area which will give the greatest efficiency and the greatest pleasure of life.

The simplest solution of the problem obviously would be for every city to own its site and a sufficient area of land around its site, as at Letchworth; but there are great difficulties in the way of this solution. Land around our towns has acquired a special speculative value, each owner hopefully anticipating that his particular plot will be one of those upon which buildings will soon be required. Hence if the whole area were purchased on such speculative prices, and any check to the development of the individual town took place, there might be considerable loss to the municipality. If the whole of the land of the country were dealt with in this way, probably the cities whose growth exceeded expectation would compensate for those where the growth was less than was anticipated.

There are, however, alternative methods of dealing with this matter. The plan adopted in dealing with the reduction of the number of public-houses affords a precedent. We have seen that the removal of building value from land required for open space has the effect of increasing the value of the next available building ground. A somewhat similar result was anticipated from the closing of a number of public-houses; it was assumed that those that were left would acquire additional trade and profit thereby, and they were required to contribute to the compensation of those deprived of their business. A somewhat similar arrangement has been adopted, apparently with great success, in some American cities. In the city of Kansas, for example, all improvements such as we have been considering, the creation of parks, boulevards, playgrounds, etc., have for many years been paid for by assessing the greater part of the cost of these improvements upon the sites which have derived direct benefit from them. At first there was naturally some opposition on the part of the owners of those sites, who were sceptical as to the improvement in the value of their land being equal to the assessment; but the last accounts available suggest that the owners have been convinced by actual results that the arrangement is in fact fair. The method of assessment is rather interesting. The City Corporation decide the proportion of the total cost which should be borne by the whole city and the proportion which should be assessed upon the particular sites deriving benefit. The apportionment of the total sum required to the individual sites, however, is left to the expert representatives of the owners themselves. The latest particulars available showed that 83 per cent. of the cost of the improvements, amounting to 11,000,000 dollars, had been assessed on those sites, and only 17 per cent. had been charged to the general city rates. The results have proved that the value of the sites which have been assessed for improvement has, in fact, increased, as compared with the sites not so assessed, by an amount which is decidedly in excess of the amount of the assessment. In other words, those who have paid a special contribution on account of benefit have in fact received more benefit than the amount of their contribution; thus confirming the view that where improvements are wisely made, not only does the value of the ground increase by the amount that the improvement costs, but that it will be likely to increase somewhat more than this. Very remarkable figures are also given as to the increase of land values in the residential areas in New York which were opened up by the underground railway, figures which show that the cost of the railway itself might have been paid out of this increase. So convincing have these figures proved that the City of New York has decided that in the case of any extension of such railways, part of the cost shall be paid by an assessment on the increased land values due to such extension. It is not intended to suggest that either the special assessment practised in Kansas or the municipalization of land would be the best solution for the problem as we find it in London. I do, however, strongly urge that the time has come when this matter should be carefully examined. I further suggest that it may be taken as proved that wise Town Planning regulations, while they will alter the apportionment of land values, will cause more increase than reduction of them; therefore it should be possible to devise a fair system under which town planning improvements could be carried out without injustice to the landowners, but without being hampered by the one-sided policy of compensating the individual in all cases where his land is deprived of value and making him a gratuitous and undeserved present in all cases where the value of his land is improved, which represents very much our present system. We must recognize that this unwise course is a serious obstacle to the proper development of towns, and to the proper apportionment of the different areas to those uses which they may best serve in the interests of the whole community, and as wise citizens we must find a means to change it.

THE HOUSING OF LONDON

W. R. DAVIDGE, F.S.I.

N

CHAPTER XIII

THE HOUSING OF LONDON

THE Housing of London! No one can say in his heart of hearts that London is satisfactorily housed. Charming homes there are, it is true, whether in the West End square or in the distant suburb, but none of us can shut our eyes to the miles on miles of depressing streets that lie between and make up London—not necessarily squalid, but monotonous and uninspiring to the uttermost degree.

Comparatively few Londoners live in houses of which they can be reasonably proud, and only a proportion in homes with which they can be reasonably satisfied.

The difficulty of finding a suitable home is one that presses upon all classes of the community. The joys of house-hunting have with all of us at some time or another been reduced to disillusionment and disappointment in the house that is found. The ideal only too often vanishes in the actual. We know exactly the house we desire, but the houses that are empty or likely to be empty all fall short in so many ways. There are frequently only to be found mouldering, mournful premises which even the enthusiasm of the house agent cannot disguise.

If this is so with the houses of the comparatively well-to-do, with the working-class home it has in the past been next to impossible to exercise any choice in the quality or even in the location of the home.

With the greater proportion of the population, even with increased wages, the family means are strictly limited, and in many cases the ideal of even a separate house is far beyond the attainable. Under such circumstances the conditions overpower all ideal of the home as a place of which the housewife can be proud and to which the children can in after years look back with affection.

LONDON OF THE FUTURE

The census returns for Greater London show that 77·2 per cent. of the population live in premises with six rooms or less; hence the problem of housing the people has been in the past almost exclusively a question of housing the working classes.

In the London of the future all classes must be provided for and houses must be available to suit all tastes, both as to location and accommodation. The houses must be in the right place, with the right surroundings and of the right size and design.

GROWTH OF POPULATION.

The growth of population of Greater London has been steady and consistent throughout the century. It is true that the population of the administrative County of London is not increasing, but this is only indicative of the tendency of the population to spread further afield. Even the limits of the Metropolitan Police District have long since been passed in the growth of the metropolis.

London's workers come in from almost anywhere within a radius of 50 miles. From High Wycombe and from Southend, from Guildford and from Brighton come the daily streams of workers, so that London's effective population is far above the $7\frac{1}{4}$ millions recorded by the last census as living within the metropolitan area.

The length of a man's purse, however, governs the length of his daily pilgrimage, and these comparatively long journeys are at present only for the relatively well-to-do. It is not altogether a question of distance, but of time taken in transit; often, in fact, one can reach Brighton in less time than it takes to reach some second-rate suburb.

TRANSIT.

The *daily fare* is the first governing factor, and it will be remembered how much the cheap workmen's fares on the Great Eastern Railway have contributed to the building of such places as Tottenham and Walthamstow, now a vast neighbourhood of small houses.

The railway companies and omnibus companies can do much to spread the people and to secure their satisfactory location. The relative cost of railway travel or bus fare will always be an important first consideration (Diagram No. 1).

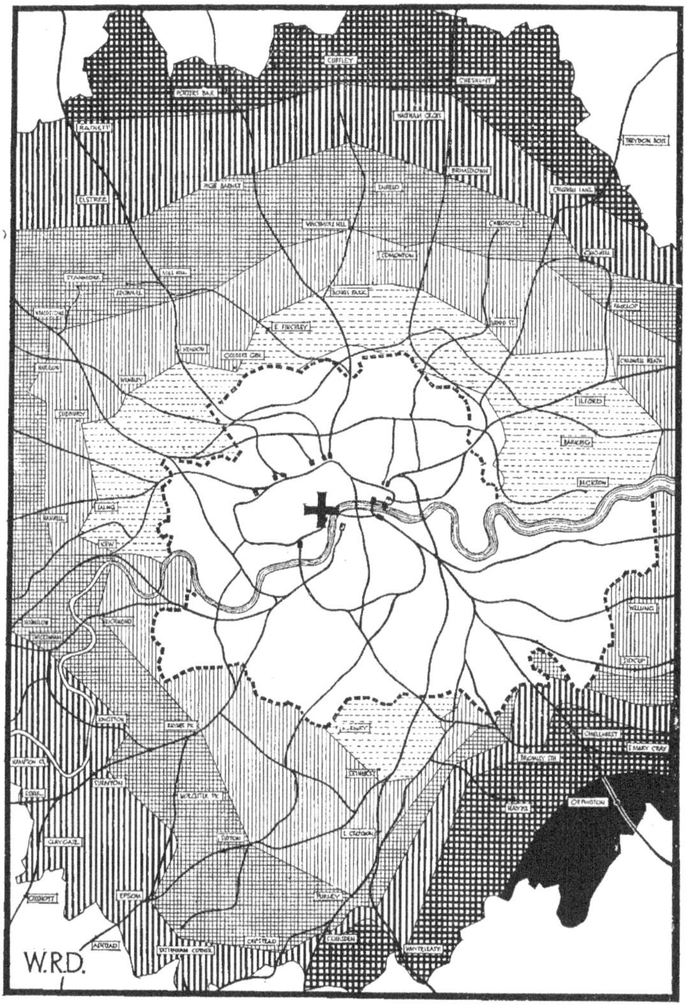

RELATIVE COST OF RAILWAY TRAVEL IN GREATER LONDON: COMPARISON OF SEASON TICKET RATES.

(Diagram No. 1 by W. R. Davidge, F.S.I.)

To face p. 196.

HOUSING

With the revival of cheap fares, quick trains and the provision of better houses in the outer areas, much could be done towards a better standard of life for the mass of the people.

If, for instance, the railway companies introduced cheap return fares and made it a general rule that trains should not stop until 10 miles out of London, an enormous impetus would be given to the development of the area benefiting by the new facilities for travelling. Such places as Hither Green, Purley and Golder's Green have sprung up within an incredibly short space of time, owing to the joint efforts of the landowners and the railway companies.

Good travelling is, indeed, the key to good housing. The one is a necessary corollary to the other, and each without the other falls short of the ideal.

There are still considerable districts in Greater London not fully served by railway, and the diagram attached shows the extent of such areas more than one mile from a railway station (No. 2).

LOCATION.

The proper placing of the community centres round a great central community like London is not altogether a matter of fortuitous chance, and should not be left solely to the enterprise of an individual or a railway company. Some guiding authority there must be to bring all these important agencies into co-operation for the common good. The first essential is a plan ; at present, only too often any new development in a district tends to rob it of some of its natural charm or to depreciate the residences already there ; the second essential is that no one shall be allowed to design a house unless he knows how to do it in such a way as to add to, or at least not to spoil, the beauty of the neighbourhood.

DENSITY OF POPULATION.

The accompanying diagram (No. 3) gives a broad indication of the relative densities of population per acre, from which it will be seen that the heaviest figure per acre is provided by Shoreditch.

The Ministry of Health has wisely laid down that a maximum of twelve houses per acre is the utmost that should be allowed in the future housing schemes in urban areas, or eight houses per acre in rural areas.

Twelve houses per acre is equivalent to a population of from fifty to sixty persons per acre. It will be seen how great an improvement this is on existing conditions from the following figures:

Shoreditch (Ware Street area)	..	333 persons per acre
St. George's in the East ..	..	307 " " "
Spitalfields East	..	275 " " "
Mile End West	..	267 " " "
St. James, Finsbury ..	..	233 " " "

OUTWARD MOVEMENT OF POPULATION.

Already, however, with the displacement of dwelling-houses by offices, factories and other industrial buildings, together with the improvement of means of communication, there is apparent a diminution of population, starting from the centre and gradually working outwards.

The population of the City and Holborn began to decline in 1861; then came the turn of the adjoining areas of Finsbury, Shoreditch, St. Marylebone and Westminster, which have steadily declined since 1871. St. Pancras and Chelsea began to drop off in 1891, followed by Bermondsey in 1901 and Southwark and Stepney in 1911. Islington and Kensington have also begun to lose their population, and even in 1911, in twenty out of the twenty-nine metropolitan boroughs the population showed a decrease as compared with ten years before.

PRESENT-DAY CONDITIONS.

It does not, however, follow that the diminution of population leaves more living space for the inhabitants who remain. Of the thirteen central boroughs named above, no less than ten show in the period 1901 to 1911 an increased proportion of inhabitants living in tenements of one to four rooms.

At the date of the last census, 758,786 persons in the County of London were living in conditions of overcrowding, i.e. in excess of two persons per room.

So far as the County of London is concerned, the sort of accommodation the population secures is shown by the following table:

GREATER LONDON: AREAS SHADED ARE MORE THAN ONE MILE FROM A RAILWAY STATION.

(Diagram No. 9 by W. R. Davidge, F.S.I.)

To face p. 198.

HOUSING

5·9	per cent. of the total	population	live	in	1	room	tenements
14·9	,,	,,	,,	,,	2	,,	,,
19·9	,,	,,	,,	,,	3	,,	,,
17·4	,,	,,	,,	,,	4	,,	,,
10·7	,,	,,	,,	,,	5	,,	,,
8·4	,,	,,	,,	,,	6	,,	,,
16·9	,,	,,	,,	,,	7	,,	and upwards
5·9	,,	,,	,,	,,	Institutions, etc.		
100·0 per cent.							

It will be seen from the above table that 58·1 per cent. of the total population live in four rooms or less, and 77·2 per cent. of the total population live in six rooms or less.

The larger houses are in many cases let as flats or occupied by more than one family, and in many cases whole neighbourhoods average two or three families per house.

Housing in the past has been provided almost entirely by private enterprise, and the municipal housing provided by the local authorities, even taking into consideration the valuable work of the London County Council, has only succeeded in the last twenty-five years in providing accommodation for 70,000 people, or approximately 1 per cent. of the whole population of London.

PROPORTION OF EMPTY HOUSES.

The percentage of empties in London County Council dwellings is instructive, as an indication of the present shortage.

In March 1911	it was	7·11	per cent.
1912	,,	5·96	,,
1913	,,	2·57	,,
1914	,,	1·25	,,
1915	,,	0·95	,,
1916	,,	0·48	,,
1917	,,	0·33	,,
1918	,,	0·23	,,

It will be noted that there is a drop from 1¼ per cent. to ¼ per cent. during the war. This means that at the present time there are practically no empty tenements or houses of the small type. Such "empties" as there are consist almost entirely of derelict property, mostly the larger houses which have outgrown their usefulness.

In the central areas the last thirty years have seen a steadily growing tendency to concentration in tall block dwellings or palatial hotels or flats, while simultaneously in all the suburbs there has been a steady creeping paralysis of two-story villadom, mile after mile of brick and mortar slowly eating up the country-side.

THE FRINGES OF LONDON.

Diagram No. 4 shows in light hatching the growth of a century.

All round the patchwork pattern which is London, the fringes are for ever unfinished; for ever are the threads being woven which will end in covering up all the natural beauty of the country-side.

The suggestion has been made not once but many times during the past three centuries that this crazy pattern of town building should be stopped and a broad border of green park lands should surround the community.

Given adequate transit facilities, there is no special reason why a new start should not be made in a new direction and new towns spring up all around, but separated from the built-up area by a belt of open country.

We are then faced with the alternatives, either to continue building on to the outer fringe of London, adding house to house, or to commence afresh at new centres some distance out and there create a number of self-contained garden colonies or communities.

Transit has been vastly improved in many directions, but it cannot be said to have kept pace with the spread of the population. Tube railways daily grow more congested, and the struggle for a place on a motor-omnibus is more acute than ever it was in the days when the horse vehicle was the only conveyance.

The evils of town life have been emphasized time and time again, ever since the overcrowding which first began to make itself felt in the days of Elizabeth.

The far-seeing Princess and her Statesmen were so appalled at the prospect of London's growth and overcrowding that a statute was actually promulgated enacting that an open space of three miles should be maintained all round the city on which no building whatever should be allowed, and even outside this limit no cottage was to be erected unless it was surrounded with at least four acres of land. These requirements were long observed, both under Elizabeth and James I.

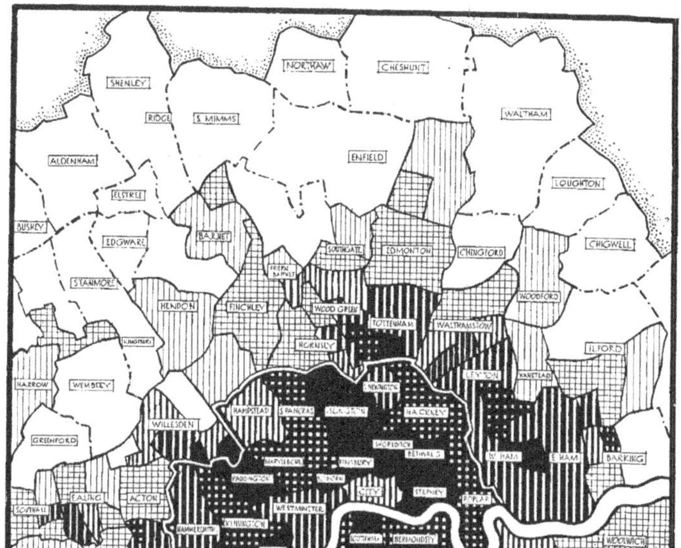

DENSITY OF POPULATION IN GREATER LONDON.

(*Diagram No. 3 by W. R. Davidge, F.S.I.*)

To face p. 200

The turmoils of the Civil War and the growth of private enterprise, however, brought these wise provisions eventually to nothing, and the growth of London's population has gone on unchecked in increasing proportions.

The accompanying table gives an indication of the way in which the population has grown and is growing (Diagram No. 5).

No less than 150,000 houses were built in Greater London during the ten years preceding the war, and it is obvious that, however they are provided and whoever pays for them, at least 300,000 new houses will have to be supplied for London during the next twenty years.

How and where these houses are to be provided will depend upon a number of factors, of which probably the most important is the means of transit between work and home.

The existing main roads, which were adequate a century ago for a community of one million souls, have now to serve the needs of over seven millions. Except for small improvements, the main roads remain the same as they were a hundred years ago; in places they have actually been narrowed since the days of the turnpikes, and the costly work of rounding off corners and widening bottlenecks can do little to make their carrying power equal to the demands of modern times.

The existing railways and tube railways have been in only too many cases planned with a view to the immediate prospects of dividends, and without regard to the wider needs of the future.

The speculating builder has done his best to supply the need for houses as and when it arose, and every new improvement in transit or train service has been followed by a growth of bricks and mortar.

THE POSSIBILITIES OF OWNERSHIP.

One of the greatest aids to contented citizenship is the extension of the possibilities of ownership, and especially of the spirit of partnership in the general prosperity of the community.

Under the Small Dwellings Acquisition Act as now amended, it is possible for a working man to buy the house in which he lives up to a value of £800 with the aid of a loan from the local authority.

For those who prefer the principle of co-partnership, it is possible to form a Public Utility Society, and with the aid of the State, through the medium of the Public Works Loan Board, to obtain an advance of 75 per cent. of the cost of building and developing an estate.

In Greater London there is room for every form of housing enterprise, except such as in time past has taken the form of exacting the highest possible rent for the worst possible houses, but it is essential in the public interest that the problem should be considered in relation to transit, food supply, recreation and other facilities, and that all such enterprises should be co-ordinated by some authority with the widest possible vision.

THE LONDON STREET.

Fifty years ago Dickens wrote, in describing Bob Sawyer's quarters: "There is a repose about Lant Street, in the Borough, which sheds a gentle melancholy upon the soul."

The same thing might be said of nearly every street in suburban London; most are monotonous, if not melancholy.

To the artist there is a great charm in London's sunsets, but to most of us the interest of the street is not in the architecture but in the people.

Only in the houses of the well-to-do, and then only occasionally, has the architect been called in to guide the design, and as a consequence our suburban streets have acquired a monotony and repetition which is the reverse of attractive. However useful or desirable a bay window might be, it appals one when repeated a hundred times in a hundred similar houses in a hundred similar streets. London's suburbs are a byword. Architects have been employed in some instances, it is true, but probably not in 5 per cent. of London's houses. You can tell the difference anywhere between the architect's house and the builder's stock design, but how many appreciate the change that might be wrought by the simple insistence on the employment of a qualified architect in the design of even the most matter-of-fact houses in the most matter-of-fact street?

Even a building line with properly designed breaks and well set back from the road may be made a thing of beauty and not a mere line of bricks. Present-day London owes much to the foresight of the legislators of a hundred and fifty years ago, who

HOUSE-TOPS AT SHADWELL.

A STREET STILL EXISTING NOT FAR FROM GOLDER'S GREEN.

(Showing how many Londoners are still housed.)

To face p 202.

insisted on such roads as the Euston Road and other turnpike roads being laid out 150 feet wide between the buildings.

If London is to be better, her new buildings must be better built, and must be designed and built by men who have been trained to appreciate that subtle distinction between the comely and the commonplace.

CAUSES OF PRESENT SYSTEM OF DEVELOPMENT.

Before discussing how such transformation may best be accomplished, let us first investigate the causes which have brought about the present methods of development. These may be summed up as:

(1) The leasehold system of London;
(2) The lack of transit facilities;
(3) The lack of co-ordination in municipal government—

the latter of which has resulted in an almost complete absence of any provision for town planning or new routes and a complete lack of civic ideals.

The leasehold system has many advocates, and there can be no doubt that many of the West End squares would never have been provided had it not been for the provision of these amenities by far-sighted landowners, who saw in their provision, what experience has since proved, that such open spaces not only considerably add to the value of their property, but also afford one of the readiest means of maintaining the character and value of the district.

The "falling in" of the leases of a large estate at approximately the same date also affords, in the case of what are now the central districts of London, an opportunity for reconstruction on a broad and comprehensive plan.

Such results, however, are only attainable at rare intervals, and in the long years when the lease is beginning to run out there often ensues a period of depression, dilapidation and neglect which throws an appearance of blight over a whole neighbourhood. Such instances will rise to mind in all directions, and however useful the system may be in exceptional cases, it is undoubtedly true that leasehold tenure leads in only too many cases to under-leases and sub-leases and so on, by which, at each process, the speculator can squeeze up the ground rent to his own profit, with the result that an economic rent can only be obtained by overcrowding buildings and sub-tenants.

The difficulties of transit have already been touched upon as a primary cause of London's unsatisfactory housing, and it must be obvious to all who have studied the housing problem of London, in common with all large cities, that no matter how excellently the houses may be built, no matter how healthy their location, they will be of little use in solving the housing problem unless there is ready and rapid means of access to the industrial centres of the town.

Transit by air has not yet come into practical service, and until such time as it does we must rely upon improved main roads and train services. It will be obvious, however, that much can be done in the improvement of existing services to encourage the development of the outlying and the detached suburb, and the speeding up of all such means of transit is an all-important first consideration in the proper development of London and London's housing.

The lack of co-ordination of municipal government is evident in all directions, especially in the areas immediately outside the county boundary. Here are to be found entirely different codes of building by-laws, different ideas as to overcrowding, as to sanitation, and even as to ordinary rules of construction.

Rates in such a case are grossly unequal, and under present circumstances it passes the wit of man to devise a workable and satisfactory scheme of equalization.

While such conditions prevail it is obviously difficult to expect any complete co-ordination of proposals with respect to town planning and arterial roads, or even a general plan of development, and London has yet to wait a little longer for the realization of this first essential, that LONDON is one community.

COTTAGE *v.* FLAT.

The need, so far as Greater London is concerned, is undoubtedly for the small self-contained house, such as can only be built where land is comparatively cheap, that is, not in the centre of London, but on the outskirts.

The need for block dwellings arises only in comparatively few

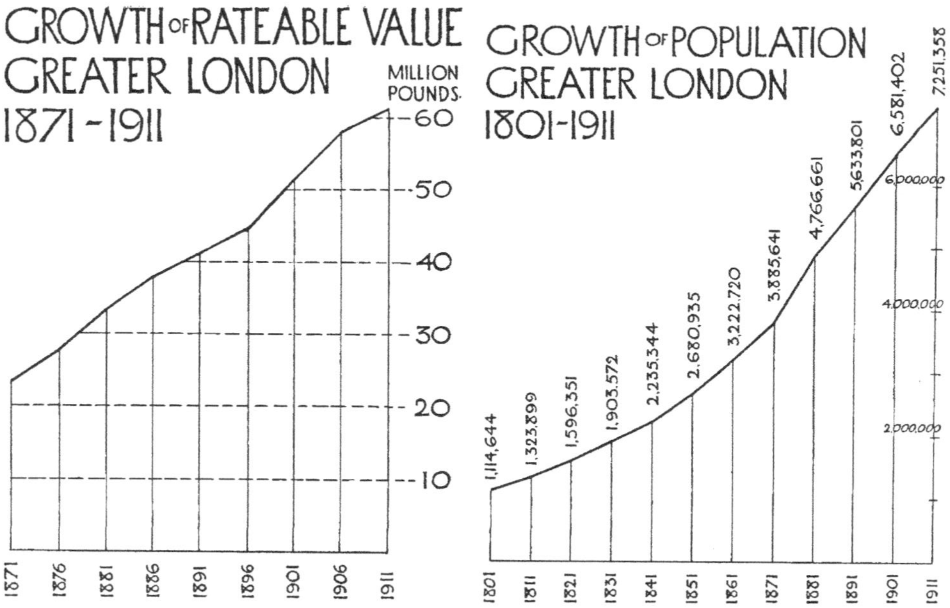

(*Diagram No. 5 by W. R. Davidge, F.S.I.*)

To face p. 204.

instances where it is essential to house the workers in the heart of London. Even in these cases it may be well argued that cheaper rents and healthier conditions in the suburbs more than outweigh the slight saving of time effected by living in a crowded tenement. In the one case, the whole family live perforce in crowded conditions, with scanty and cramped accommodation and at high rents, in order that the bread-winner may be near his work.

The only positions where block tenements can reasonably be considered are in the rare cases where it is necessary to house workers on a particular spot of limited area. Such cases may arise in the immediate neighbourhood of the docks or in close proximity of the railway termini, but such block tenements should be discouraged as far as possible.

The general adoption of the eight-hour day is a new and very important factor in the distribution of population. Previously, certain classes of labourers—for instance, dockers—who might have to begin work at any hour, working perhaps four hours one day and twenty-four hours the next, had perforce to live within a few hundred yards of their work. This is no longer necessary to anything like the same extent, and one of the stages in town planning is the bringing home to the mass of the people that they can live farther away from their work.

THE PRESSURE OF LOCAL RATES.

From the diagram (No. 6) of the incidence of local rates it will be seen that in almost every case the rates are highest where small property abounds and people are poorest.

Even where there are contributions from the Rates Equalization Fund, the discrepancy in the incidence of rates still exists. The main item responsible for this increased burden is education, which in the poorer neighbourhoods presses very heavily on the harassed ratepayer. Added to this, the increased rates for sanitary and other services form a heavy demand on the local community.

So pronounced is this tendency that it is in many cases true to say that every additional workman's house means an addition to the rates; hence the fight put up by many of the outlying local authorities against the building of additional workmen's houses within their area.

The pressure of rates has the effect of directly increasing the rent, though even with increased rents the unfortunate owner of small property is no better off, and the tenants themselves show their resentment by the way in which they treat the property.

This vicious circle may in part be due to our system of rating, but, whatever the system, the remedy, it is clear, lies in the broadening of the rating area. At present the area of Greater London is cut up into considerably over a hundred separate rating authorities, and the burden of rates is consequently heaviest where it can least be borne.

In the crowded districts of the east of the County of London, where the amenities of life are least, the rates are invariably the heaviest, and even here it is only the existence of factories and other valuable property which keeps the rates from going higher still. To build a new colony of small working-class houses in one of the outer suburbs is thus not always welcome to the local authority.

The area of Greater London is wealthy enough to bear its own burdens, and the real weakness lies in the want of co-ordination between its innumerable local authorities. Each loyally strives to keep its own area intact within a cast-iron compartment, and refuses to recognize that it is but part of a larger whole and responsible for its share of the common weal.

The diagram (No. 5) of the growth of rateable value gives some indication of the increased total of property value in London.

Although the rateable value has trebled during the past forty years, the increased public services have more than absorbed the increase.

NECESSITY FOR AN IMPROVED STANDARD—A HIGHER CONCEPTION OF HOUSING.

During the past few years men's ideas have broadened, and what was good enough ten years ago will not be good enough in the immediate future.

Until quite recently the minimum size for a living room in London County Council dwellings was 12 feet by 12 feet, or 144 square feet, and generally not more than two bedrooms were provided.

Now the Government requirements for the State Housing Schemes are for the living-room 180 square feet, i.e. 12 feet by

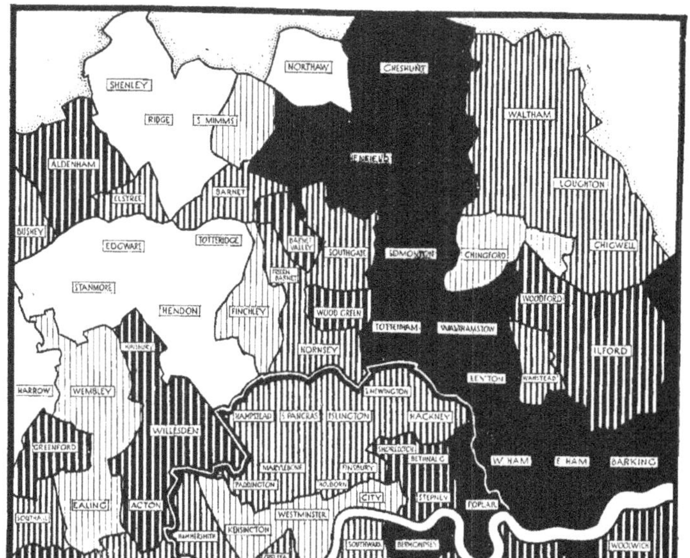

APPROXIMATE COMPARISON OF RATES LEVIED IN GREATER LONDON.

(Diagram No. 6 by W. R. Davidge, F.S.I.)

To face p 206

15 feet, a parlour of 120 square feet, with at least three bedrooms and a bath-room.

LONDON'S PLAYGROUNDS.

The question of playgrounds in Central London is a difficult one, and in recent years has only been partially solved by the opening of old burial-grounds for this purpose.

In the open country, of which there is still much within a short distance of London, land is still both cheap and plentiful, and the playground can in some cases be as wide as the hills themselves.

There are many disappearing beauty spots, but all Londoners will strain every nerve to preserve those broad expanses of heath and upland, of dell and down, which are still to be found on the Surrey hills or in the highlands of Buckinghamshire and Hertfordshire, where London's dormitories are already extending.

These health-giving expanses must for ever be preserved for the community as a whole. The cost of their preservation is as nothing to the terrible cost of letting them slip from our hands.

The needs of the community as a whole must come first, but the community, after all, is but the sum of the separate units, and the primary end and aim of communal government is the protection and well-being of the individual.

External security is the duty of the State. Security of health and happiness should be the duty of the city. Only too often in the past the sanitary authorities have carried out even the essential health services in a more or less niggardly spirit, and the few amenities that have been provided have been subservient to the need for keeping down the rates.

THE ESSENTIALS OF THE HOME.

The essentials so far as a home and its location are concerned are:

That the house should be the right size, not too small, so that the family is overcrowded, not too big, so that the mother is overworked, and not too dear for the family income.

(*a*) *In the right location.*

Accessible to the town.—Not too far for the workman to go to his work, not too far from the shops, the church and the picture palace, and not too far from the school.

Accessible to the country.—Not too far to the allotment, not too far from the parks and the hills of the open country, and not too far from the children's playground.

(*b*) *Of sound construction.*—Weather-proof, warm in winter, cool in summer.

(*c*) *Sanitary.*—No harbour for the microbe in wall or roof or floor. No refuse matters or decomposition tolerated to remain.

(*d*) *Pleasant* in design and surroundings.

The home must accord with the wishes of its inmates; it must be easy to maintain and easy to work; its accommodation must provide for all reasonable needs, and its surroundings must provide for all reasonable aspirations.

Last, but not least, it must be reached in all reasonable comfort within a reasonable time.

Broadly speaking, however, the essential requirements of every home are:

(1) At least three bedrooms.

(2) A bathroom and lavatory.

(3) A living-room, scullery and larder, and generally speaking a "parlour."

There is nothing startlingly fresh in this statement of accommodation; it has long been regarded as the minimum to be provided by any speculating builder who sets out to gauge the public needs.

A different standard of measurement is, however, essential. In the past the speculating builder has provided a house which has sold well, and having sold one, he was prepared to build a hundred more just like it. If one street was a success, he would build a dozen more just the same. The public have but rarely had the opportunity of choice between living in one of the dozens of suburbs built on this pattern or of living in a garden suburb, where each house is designed by an architect for the particular position and surroundings.

When the public has had such an opportunity it has invariably declared its delight with the innovation, and slowly but surely the modern British citizen is realizing that those long, dreary streets of Suburbia are not a necessity. He always knew they were not beautiful; he now finds that they are not economical or satisfying.

The future of our towns lies with the architect.

Constant thought and skilful guidance are needed. Too often in the past the opening out of new thoroughfares has been prevented again and again by comparatively unimportant buildings standing across the only route possible for the new artery.

The development map of The London Society is destined to become an invaluable guide to the London of the future. During my comparatively short term of office as Housing Commissioner at the London Housing Board, every new housing site submitted was set down on the Society's map and carefully considered in relation to the proposed arterial roads and general scheme of development, and this is but one example of the steadily growing value of the work of The London Society.

Important above all else is that every house built, whether in Inner London or in the outer suburbs, shall fall into its place in a general plan of development.

THE GOVERNMENT OF LONDON

W. E. RILEY, F.R.I.B.A.

CHAPTER XIV

THE GOVERNMENT OF LONDON

THE complex machinery instituted in the past for the government of London requires some description, in order that those interested in its simplification may appreciate the difficulties which surround this important question. A general outline of the services and the powers under which they are administered will therefore be necessary as a preliminary introduction to the subject.

The Administrative County of London comprises the City of London and 28 metropolitan boroughs. In 1911, the population was given as 4,521,685, the area at 116·95 square miles. "Water London" is that area supplied by the Metropolitan Water Board with water, and embraces portions of five counties: Kent, Essex, Surrey, Herts and Middlesex. "Greater London" and "Police London" are practically the same areas, extending to a radius of 15 miles from Charing Cross, the latter term applying to the area patrolled by the Metropolitan and City Police. Before the war the population was given as about 7¼ millions. The Port of London extends from Havengore Creek to Teddington. There are fifteen authorities having independent and (in several services) collateral powers, embraced in twelve classes of service; the foremost and most comprehensive powers are those with which the County Council is charged. In that body there are 137 members, of whom 118 are elected by the ratepayers triennially, 19 are aldermen selected by the councillors for a term of six years. A chairman, vice-chairman, and deputy chairman are elected annually in March.

The Council is represented by 51 of its members on nine outside authorities, amongst which are the Metropolitan Water Board (14), Port of London Authority (4), etc.

The City of London has 206 common councillors elected annually and 26 aldermen directly elected for life. The City is presided over by the Lord Mayor, who is elected annually.

The 28 boroughs are governed by Councils of from 30 to 60 members (the City of Westminster and the Royal Borough of Kensington are embraced in the 28); the elections take place triennially. Aldermen to the number of one-sixth the councillors are co-opted for six years, and each borough is presided over by a mayor.

These several authorities control the majority of the services with which the London Society is chiefly concerned. How they are all elected is largely a matter of enacted procedure, which was brought into being in 1888. The franchise is now so enormously increased and the representation so modified by the enrolment of women voters and their presence in the County Council, that the details would require much space to make clear. Those interested in these important proceedings had better read up the most recent legal routine rather than depend on a summary. Suffice it to say that it is akin to Parliamentary procedure, but its vital importance to ratepayers is strangely overlooked by those who have to abide by the actions of the elected and meet the liabilities they incur in their period of representation; so apathetic, indeed, are the voters that at the two earliest County Council elections less than 50 per cent. of the electors voted, and in subsequent contests this percentage has only been slightly increased. At five borough council elections prior to 1913, only once did the voting reach 50 per cent., and the average of the five was only 47 per cent.

One of the most important of the questions dealt with by the governing bodies is that of finance. There are two classes of estimates put forward annually to meet the liabilities and the operations with which they are charged; they may be broadly indicated as (*a*) capital expenditure and (*b*) expenditure on rate and revenue account (usually called maintenance). The first of these is submitted to Parliament as a Money Bill by the London County Council, on which the borrowings of each financial year are based; the second head of expenditure has to be met out of the rates. The word "maintenance" is not very concise; in the Imperial Service, for instance, it is applied to votes for maintaining services, e.g.

"repairs and maintenance of buildings," and when so used has a special meaning easily understood, such as is implied by the "good tenantable condition" of an ordinary dwelling-house. In municipal affairs it means much more.

The London County Council is the sanctioning authority for loans to the Metropolitan Borough Councils, boards of guardians, metropolitan asylums, district managers, etc.; the last published return gives these loans as over 15 millions. This does not represent the total indebtedness of these authorities, as they can borrow from other sources. The total net debt of the Council and the other authorities was over £114,000,000 when the last return was made in 1913, and it is quite certain to be now much more; but there is a primary security for over 50 per cent. of the loans raised for carrying out undertakings of a revenue-producing character.

The twelve principal services allotted to the various authorities may be summarized as follows:

1. Health.
2. Protective.
3. Amenities.
4. Traffic.
5. Financial.
6. Care and control of the defective.
7. Regulative.
8. Administration of Justice.
9. Education.
10. Domestic.
11. Public assistance.
12. Constitutional machinery.

No. 1 embraces main drainage, sanitary by-laws, infectious diseases, housing (clearance schemes), housing of the working classes, water supply, infectious sickness and about twenty other services, and there are eight authorities charged with the responsibility in connection with their administration; the four principal authorities are the County Council, the City Corporation, the Metropolitan Borough Councils and the Metropolitan Water Board. As examples of the refinements of control, the County Council has the power to make by-laws regulating the construction of drains and other means of communicating drainage to the sewers; these by-laws are administered by the Metropolitan Borough Councils; but an appeal lies to the Council against any order of a sanitary authority in respect of these by-laws. The main drainage has been reviewed at different periods by the County Council, and a comprehensive scheme dealing with it has been put in hand: the total length of the sewers in the main drainage system is about 370 miles, draining an area of 149 square miles, embracing a population, according to the 1911 census, of over 5⅓ millions. This colossal work has cost the Council over 5½ millions sterling.

The service which at the moment takes a prominent position under heading No. 1 is the housing of the working classes. The London County Council, the Metropolitan Borough Councils and the City Corporation are empowered to deal with certain phases of this question. Parts I, II and III of the Act of 1890, amended in 1894, 1900, 1903, 1909, formed the instrument under which a considerable amount of housing was provided up to the outbreak of the war. The Act was again amended in 1919.

Part I places upon the County Council the responsibility of dealing with unhealthy areas after sanction by the Local Government Board (now the Ministry of Health); the initiation of such a scheme lies with the Medical Officers of Health, whose attention could be drawn to the existence of unhealthy areas by two Justices of the Peace or twelve ratepayers.

Part II empowers the London County Council and the Metropolitan Borough Councils either conjointly or separately to deal with small unhealthy areas. The procedure is similar to that described for Part I, but an official representation by the Medical Officer of Health is not necessary.

The Local Government Board, up to the time of its absorption in the Ministry of Health, could require or dispense with the necessity of providing accommodation for working class persons displaced by the clearance of unhealthy areas.

Soon after the conclusion of hostilities in the recent war the Housing and Town Planning Acts were re-cast, and two very important Acts passed in 1919.

The salient features of this legislation are as follows:

(1) Every local authority within the meaning of Part HI of the Housing Act, 1890, is placed under obligation to consider the needs of its area with respect to the provision of working-class houses, and to submit a scheme to the Ministry of Health within three months from the passing of the Act. The Ministry may

DUCANE ROAD, OLD OAK ESTATE. (W. E. RILEY, ARCHITECT.)

WEST END OF TOWER GARDEN, WHITE HART LANE ESTATE.

(Two examples of L.C.C. cottage housing schemes.)

To face p 216.

extend or amend the scheme, which must then be carried out by the local authority (Sections 1 and 2).

A scheme must specify:

(*a*) The number and nature of the houses to be provided.
(*b*) The quantity of land to be acquired.
(*c*) The average number of houses per acre.
(*d*) The time within which the scheme is to be carried out.

(2) It provides powers for the Ministry of Health and county councils to act in default of any local authority who may neglect to carry out its powers and obligations (Sections 3 to 6).

(3) It empowers the Ministry to recoup, out of moneys provided by Parliament, part of the losses incurred by local authorities in carrying out housing and rehousing schemes (Section 7).

(4) It empowers County Councils to borrow money for eighty years, instead of thirty years as provided by the Local Government Act, 1888, to meet expenses incurred in housing employees or buying land therefor (Section 8).

(5) It provides that in the case of insanitary property acquired under Parts I and II of the Act of 1890 the purchase money shall represent the value of the land as a site cleared of buildings (Section 9).

(6) It empowers local authorities in carrying out housing schemes under Part III not only to acquire lands, but also to acquire buildings thereon, and to utilize and develop such buildings for housing purposes, and to acquire land for leasing purposes in order that such land may be developed for housing or general building purposes (Section 12).

(7) It empowers local authorities to acquire land by agreement under Parts I and II in anticipation of the sanction of the Ministry of Health (Section 13).

(8) It extends powers of local authorities in dealing with land acquired for housing purposes so as to permit of the provision of roads and open spaces and the sale and exchange of land and the sale or lease of houses (Section 15).

(9) It empowers local authorities (including County Councils) to promote the formation of, or assist, public utility societies, whose objects include the provision of working-class houses, and it

empowers the Ministry of Health to assist financially such societies and housing trusts (Sections 18–20).

(10) It provides for loans by local authorities to private persons for the improvement of housing accommodation (Section 22).

(11) It provides for the relaxation of building by-laws (Section 24).

(12) It provides power to authorize the conversion of a house into several tenements (Section 27).

(13) It empowers local authorities to require working-class houses to be repaired and made reasonably fit for human habitation (Section 28).

(14) It amends the provisions of the Town Planning Act, 1909 (Section 42), and requires every borough or urban district containing on January 1, 1923, a population of more than twenty thousand to prepare and submit to the Ministry within three years from that date, a town planning scheme in respect of all undeveloped land (Section 46).

(15) It increased from £400 to £800 the value of houses which may be purchased under the Small Dwellings Acquisition Act, 1899, and increases from 80 to 85 per cent. the limitation on the amount which may be advanced (Section 49).

The salient features of the second Act of 1919 put on the County Council and the Corporation of London in the City the responsibility attached to the "local authority" (Section 11). They may be summarized as follows:

(1) Provides that payments may be made to persons or bodies of persons constructing houses which:

(*a*) Comply with the conditions prescribed by the Ministry.
(*b*) Are certified to be complete in a proper workmanlike manner.
(*c*) Are commenced and completed within twelve months from the passing of the Acts (December 23, 1919), or such further period not exceeding four months as the Ministry may allow.
A proportionate reduction shall be made in respect of houses not completed within twelve months, if the Minister allows.

(2) The aggregate grants shall not exceed £15,000,000, and

THE MILLBANK ESTATE. (W. E. RILEY, ARCHITECT.)

THE BOURNE ESTATE. (W. E. RILEY, ARCHITECT.)

(Two examples of L.C.C. Block Dwellings.)

To face p. 218

grants shall not be made in respect of houses erected by local authorities in respect of which payment may be made under the Housing Act, 1919.

(3) Where it appears to a local authority that the provision of dwelling accommodation may be delayed through deficiency of labour or materials, arising out of employment of labour or materials in the construction of works or buildings (other than those authorized by an Act of Parliament), and that the construction of those works or buildings is of less public importance than the provision of dwelling accommodation, the authority may prohibit the construction of such works or buildings, subject to conditions prescribed by the Ministry. Appeal is provided to a tribunal of five persons appointed by the Minister.

(4) If any person after December 23, 1919, without the permission of the local authority, demolishes in whole or part, or uses otherwise than as a dwelling-house, any house which at that date was reasonably fit or reasonably capable without reconstruction of being rendered fit for human habitation, he shall be liable to a fine of £100 or three months' imprisonment. An appeal to the Minister is provided.

(5) The Act empowers a local authority to borrow money by the issue of bonds for housing purposes.

(6) If a local authority or an authorized association desires to acquire land for development of a garden city, or for a town planning scheme, the Minister may acquire such land on behalf of such authority or association and vest it in them.

(7) The County Council may require district surveyors in London to perform such duties, and will pay them such remuneration, as it may think fit.

(8) Duration of the Act shall be two years from December 23, 1919.

Up to the passing of the Town Planning Act, 1909, and subsequent to that period, the provision made in Part III of the Housing Act had been regarded as a voluntary service. The recent Acts since the war (especially the two of 1919) have removed this question from the voluntary category. The whole of the housing in London, provided under Parts I, II and III, up to the declaration of war, carried out by the County Council, gave accommodation officially recognized for 58,870 persons. A substantial portion of this was in respect of Part III, and the writer was responsible for the design and execution of about 88 per cent. of this work. Since the armistice, and under the Act of 1919, he designed and let contracts for an addition of over nine hundred houses, now in the course of construction.

The second great group of services in London were referred to as "protective services." They include fire brigade, theatres, music-halls, cinematograph halls, and about eighteen others of a minor kind. The City Corporation carries out in the City ten of these services, and the Lord Chamberlain—and, in certain cases, the Home Secretary—licenses a number of theatres and other premises for the purpose of entertainment. These buildings amount to sixty-eight, and they are as follows :

THEATRES LICENSED BY THE LORD CHAMBERLAIN.

Adelphi.
Alexandra.
Ambassadors'.
Apollo.
Brixton.
Comedy.
Cripplegate Institute.
Criterion.
Dalston.
Daly's.
Duke of York's.
Elephant and Castle.
Gaiety.
Garrick.
Globe.
Haymarket.
His Majesty's.
Kennington.
Kingsway.
London Opera House.
Lyceum.
Lyric.
Middlesex.
New.
Palace, Bow.
Pavilion.
Playhouse.
Prince's.
Prince of Wales's.
Queen's.
Rotherhithe Town Hall.
Royalty.
St. George's Hall.
St. James's.
St. Martin's.
Savoy.
Scala.
Shaftesbury.
Strand.
Vaudeville.
Wyndham's.

OTHER PREMISES LICENSED BY THE LORD CHAMBERLAIN FOR STAGE PLAYS.

Alhambra.
Bedford Palace.
Camberwell Theatre and Picture House.
Camberwell Palace.
Camden Hippodrome.
Canterbury.
Coliseum.
Collins's.
Empire.
Empress, Brixton.
Finsbury Park Empire.
Hackney Empire.
Islington Empire.
King George's Hall.
London Hippodrome.
London Music Hall.
London Pavilion.
Metropolitan.
Palace.
Palladium.
Poplar Hippodrome.
Queen's Palace, Poplar.
Rotherhithe Hippodrome.
Royal Victoria Hall.
Shoreditch Olympia.
South London Palace.
Victoria Palace.

The means of escape and protection against fire in both new and old places of entertainment are dealt with under the Metropolis Management Act of 1878. The responsibility for dealing with this service rests with the London County Council and was inherited from the Metropolitan Board. In the early exercise of this control, buildings built prior to 1878 could only be dealt with under the Act if the defects required to be remedied were such as could be remedied at a moderate expenditure, but it has been found in practice that the managers of theatres have generally been quite willing to bring such places of entertainment up to a reasonable standard of safety. The maintenance of the means of escape of these buildings is also subject to the surveillance of the County Council, and such work is carried out under the direction of the Chief Officer of the Fire Brigade.

There are two theatres which enjoy certain privileges and are called patent theatres, deriving their grants directly from the Crown. Thus three classifications are recognized, viz. :

(1) Patent theatres.
(2) Those licensed by the Lord Chamberlain.
(3) Those licensed by the County Council.

The applications for these licences have to be made on or before October 1st in each year, and the County Council has referred to the Theatres and Music Halls Committee the duty of investigating these applications and submitting recommendations to the Council in its capacity as licensing authority.

Music-halls are dealt with under the Local Government Act of 1888, by which the power exercised by the justices in this connection was transferred to the County Council, and the Council has, by standing orders passed in 1896, fixed November as the month in which the Council will consider granting licences for music and dancing. The passing of the Cinematograph Act in 1909 extended the responsibilities in regard to means of escape in the case of fire. In London the licensing authority is the County Council, excepting in the cases of theatres under the jurisdiction of the Lord Chamberlain, when licences must be obtained from him. Up to 1913 there were 680 places licensed for music and dancing, stage plays and cinematographs within the county.

FIRE BRIGADE.

The laws for protecting London against fire have existed for centuries, but control gradually became centred in the Metropolitan Board of Works, and has since been transferred to the County Council. The arrangement arrived at was authorized by the Metropolitan Fire Brigade Act of 1865. It is now called the London Fire Brigade, and is under the command of the Chief Officer. The cost of this service is met partly out of the rates, partly by the fire insurance companies and partly by the Government. Fire stations are of three classes, namely, full stations, sub-stations and street stations; but the latter classification is, as far as possible, being dispensed with. There were within the county, when the last return was made in 1913, 96 land stations and 3 river stations, together with a repairing depot. Sixteen stations were equipped with motors, 67 with horses, 2 sub-stations without horses and 11 street stations. The writer has, during the past twenty years, built a large number of new and remodelled many old stations. The organization of each full station and sub-station is centred in the watch-room, which is in telephonic communication not only with the exchanges but also with the fire-alarms in the streets. The fire-alarm system has been found of very great service, but is often inconsiderately used by mischievous and irresponsible people.

The third important service is that dealing with public and other amenities. These are parks (with bands), gymnasiums, advertisement regulation, museums, historical houses and small holdings.

PARKS.

The Metropolitan Management Act, 1856, extended to the Metropolitan Board of Works the authority to apply to Parliament for providing parks, etc. The acquisition in 1857 of the ground on which Finsbury Park was formed provided the basis of the system. The park was laid out in 1863.

More active steps were taken on the passing of the Gardens in Towns Protection Act in 1863, and in 1866 the Metropolitan Commons Act was passed as the result of a serious attack on the preservation of the commons. The open spaces which came under the control of the Metropolitan Board of Works as a result were Blackheath, the Hackney Commons, Clapham Common, Streatham

THE BATHING LAKE, TOOTING.

THE LAKE, TOOTING COMMON.

(Recreation for Londoners of the present and future under the care of the L.C.C.)

To face p. 222.

Common, Borstall Heath and Tooting Bec Common. Epping Forest was placed under the control of the City Corporation.

Hampstead Heath was not acquired until 1871.

It is estimated that in the Metropolitan Police District 12,000 acres of common land have been put under local management.

The Open Spaces Act of 1887 extended the powers, and the important areas of Wormwood Scrubs, Highbury Fields, Clissold Park, Ravenscourt Park and Parliament Hill were acquired under this Act. Victoria, Battersea and Kennington Parks and Bethnal Green Gardens were placed under the control of the Metropolitan Board of Works through the vote for their maintenance being defeated in Parliament; this led to these parks being transferred in 1887.

At the time the London County Council was created there were 40 such places transferred to them, having an acreage of 2,656.

Since then various powers have been conferred upon the Council which have resulted in raising the number of open spaces to 118, with a total area of about 5,100 acres.

Within the county, Brockwell Park, Wandsworth Park, Avery Hill, Eltham Park, Hilly Fields, Borstall Heath, Ladywell recreation grounds, Golder's Hill, Waterlow Park and Springfield Park have been acquired. Outside the county, Hainault Forest and Marble Hill. In addition to these the County Council has taken over a large number of disused churchyards, squares and small gardens—mainly in the East of London, preserving them as open spaces, where they were much needed.

The production of music by bands and the regulation of games are within the authority of the County Council for these parks and open spaces controlled by them; they have contributed considerable sums towards the cost of providing 53 parks and open spaces maintained by the Metropolitan Borough Councils. The total number of places maintained by the City Corporation and the Metropolitan Borough Councils is 189, having an aggregate area of about 327 acres.

MUSEUMS.

Another service which is an amenity of great importance to the public is the management of museums. Museums are within the jurisdiction of the Government, London County Council, City

Corporation and the Metropolitan Borough Councils, but it is only in recent years that the County Council has undertaken work in this connection. Horniman's Museum and Library was presented by Mr. F. T. Horniman through his son, Mr. S. J. Horniman. The museum is divided into two departments, ethnology and zoology. Geffrye Museum was acquired in 1911, and has been put to use as a furniture museum, and may be regarded as an effort to improve the facilities of the craftsmen in the district, many of whom are engaged in the cabinet-making industry.

The principal work of this kind, which has been carried on so successfully in recent years, has been the preservation of and recording the particulars of buildings of historical and architectural interest; this important work is also carried out by the City Corporation, and since 1912 a systematic survey of some portions of London has been undertaken: it was, however, interrupted by the war, and the publication of the buildings surveyed was suspended.

The provision of public libraries is governed by the Acts of 1892 and 1901. In the County of London these powers are administered by the Metropolitan Borough Councils. The City Corporation is the authority under the Acts in the City of London.

It was by the Public Libraries Act, 1901, that the Museums and Gymnasiums Act of 1891 was extended to London.

TRAFFIC.

Another great service in London is that connected with traffic; the power of acquiring existing tramway lines devolved upon the County Council in 1911, and various powers have since that time been acquired to construct new lines and work the services. The Metropolitan Borough Councils have the power of veto on tramway undertakings in their various areas.

The large generating station at Greenwich was built for the Council by the writer in two halves, the first being opened in 1906 and the second in 1911. It is one of the largest buildings of its kind in the world. Its normal capacity will, when fully equipped with turbines, be equal to 52,000 k.w. A great central depot for repairs and a number of car sheds and sub-stations have also been erected by the Council.

GOVERNMENT

BRIDGES.

The Thames bridges within the county, except railway bridges and those within the boundary of the City, are in the custody of the London County Council; several of them were originally toll-bridges, but were purchased in 1877 by the Metropolitan Board of Works; this defunct authority also built the Victoria, Chelsea and Albert Embankments. As an example of the refinements of control, it may be noted that the roadways and footways of the Victoria Embankment, as well as those of all the Council's bridges across the Thames, are under its control, but the footways only of the Albert and Chelsea Embankments; the Grosvenor Road Embankment (from Millbank to Chelsea) was constructed by H.M. Commissioner of Works about 1850. Westminster Bridge was also built by H.M. Government, but these structures were transferred to the Metropolitan Board of Works, and have thus come within the custody of the London County Council.

IMPROVEMENTS.

The great work of street improvements, when they are of more than local importance, is generally carried out by the London County Council, and is usually authorized by special Acts of Parliament.

The Metropolitan Borough Councils carry out local improvements generally under Michael Angelo Taylor's Act, a Metropolitan Paving Act of 1817. The City Corporation carry out within the City most of the street improvements on authority conferred by special legislation.

In some of these cases the London County Council contributes, but not in all.

CARE AND CONTROL OF THE MENTALLY DEFECTIVE.

The care of lunatics is a service which is carried out by the London County Council, the City Corporation and the Metropolitan Asylums Board, the latter authority taking care of the harmless insane. There are ten asylums controlled by the London County Council, one by the City Corporation, and seven by the Metropolitan Asylums Board.

REGULATIVE SERVICES.

The great regulative services are: construction of buildings, town planning, formation and naming of streets, street signs, etc.

Laws regulating the construction of buildings have been in existence since 1604, but the most notable legislation was after the Great Fire, when an Act was passed in 1667 "for rebuilding the City of London."

The Act under which buildings are now constructed was that passed in 1894; this has been considerably amended, notably in 1905 in regard to the provision of means of escape from existing buildings, and 1908, allowing greater cubical extent, and still more drastically in 1909, dealing with skeleton steel and reinforced concrete construction, the regulations for which came into force in November 1911. The London County Council is the authority for administering these Acts in the county: certain sections do not apply in the City, and the City Corporation have retained to them the power of dealing with dangerous structures.

There are certain sections in these Acts which enable the Council to impose the condition that land in front of any building which may be advanced in front of what is known as the "general line" must be surrendered and thrown into the street; by this means improvements are frequently made. A most notable instance can be seen in the case of Euston Road, which is gradually being widened to 100 feet throughout.

For the formation of streets rules are enacted, and from the inauguration of the Council to the year 1913 about 240 miles of new streets had been sanctioned. The regulation of lamps and signs and the abolition of sky-signs is also dealt with. The naming and the numbering of all new streets and the initiation of town planning schemes under the Town Planning Act of 1909 were placed upon the Council. It is estimated that 12,600 acres of land still remain uncovered within the county. An immense volume of work is involved in dealing with this important question. In the twenty-four years ending 1913 nearly 650,000 buildings were dealt with as new buildings or were altered and added to.

EDUCATION.

Perhaps the greatest additional responsibility which has ever been thrown upon one already heavily charged body was the affiliation of education with the other work of the County Council. From 1870, when the Education Act was passed, until 1903, the care of education in London was carried on by the London School Board. Since that time it has been within the responsibility of the County Council. There are still what are called "non-provided" schools, which are managed as voluntary schools, but on these there must be four foundation managers, together with two others, one representing the County Council and the other representing the Council of the Metropolitan Borough in which the school is situated. In every "provided" school the number of managers and the manner in which the schools should be grouped is fixed by the Council of each borough, which appoints two-thirds and the County Council one-third; women in the proportion of not less than one-third of the whole body of managers must be included.

There are about 585 elementary schools of the "provided" class and about 364 of the "non-provided" schools, besides central schools, of which there are 49; also 85 open-air playground classes.

Provision is also made for teaching the blind, the deaf, and those who in other respects are defective, at special schools. This authority is given by the Elementary Education (Defective and Epileptic Children) Act, 1899, but is a voluntary provision.

In 1913 there already existed 96 special schools for mentally defective children and 36 day and 3 hospital special schools for physically defective and invalid children.

The qualification for admission is the state of mind, between imbecile and merely dull or backward. Those qualified as physically defective are to be certified as physically "incapable of receiving proper benefit from the instruction in the ordinary public elementary schools."

Special art teachers give instruction to the physically defective children, and some of the pupils have attained some success in this work.

INDUSTRIAL SCHOOLS.

Authority to maintain industrial schools is conferred on the London County Council by the Children Act of 1908, but schools of this class were established under an Act of 1866. The children received in these schools are generally under fourteen years of age; they are schools of a preventive character, and take care of those who are in danger of criminal contamination. There are ten such institutions—nine are of a residential character and one is a day industrial school.

By the Act of 1902–3 the London County Council is empowered, after taking the necessary steps, to supply or aid education other than elementary education, and in 1904 that body was definitely empowered to undertake higher education. At that time there were 88 public secondary schools which were not conducted for private profit, but the Council has found it expedient to establish 22 secondary schools; the fees charged in these 22 schools vary from £3 to £30 a year.

Probably the most drastic change in regard to elementary education was that taken in March 1912, when the following resolution was passed by the London County Council:

> That the Education Commitee do forthwith prepare and submit a scheme for the approval of the Council and the Board of Education, which will within a period of fifteen years from March 31, 1912 (by means of an annual programme for building new schools and enlarging or structurally improving existing schools) provide for reducing to 40 in the case of senior departments, and 48 in the case of infant departments, the accommodation of all class-rooms (in public elementary schools, etc.).

This arrangement involved a pre-war expenditure of about £4,500,000 and continued pressure to give effect to it extending over fifteen years in five triennia. Work which practically aecomplished the undertaking of the first triennium was carried out, but the concentration of effort in other directions due to the war after 1915 suspended this gigantic undertaking, and since that time agitation has begun for the purpose of further reducing the minimum number which may be taught in one class. Formerly it was sixty, then it suddenly became forty and may become much less; in any case, the resolution of March 1912 will require a stupendous sum to give effect to it now, and it would be interesting to know to what extent the voters in 1919 understood this question or the liability it involved on the future finance of the county.

During the war many of the smart writers dealing with the sayings of the rank and file of our Army wrote down a kind of English attributed to those brave men which would have to be translated to become intelligible to a great many of their fellow-creatures who are supposed to understand the English tongue, and still no one seemed to appreciate the absurdity of the situation, as every soldier had been through the educational programme. The writer knew, in his youth, a poor country peasant who fought at the Battle of Waterloo, and the veteran could certainly not write; but his power of relating his experience was classical if compared with the crudities with which the Tower Hamlets conscript of 1918 chronicled his ideas, according to modern literary men. Was it a series of literary pictures of the type of some of those canvases which graced the walls at Burlington House in 1919–20 or was it a sample of the results of the gospel of education, in the effort to raise the standard of citizenship which has been laboured at by those representatives who have made the law with so much zeal, and the results of which have been administered with such sacrifice of time and energy? Moreover, education costs 8s. 6d. per head more in London than the average of Birmingham, Liverpool, Manchester, Sheffield, Leeds and Bristol!

NEEDS OF THE FUTURE.

I do not propose to further detail the kind of service which is voluntarily carried out by the ædiles of London; it would have been well to have had access to a recent census before making any suggestions for the future or comparing the effect on this great county of the government of the past decade, and it is much to be deplored that immediately after the war election a census was not made, whereby we could doubtless have better estimated the value of many of our theories as to what was the most urgent want. We had, during the war, squandered huge sums of money, built war factories all over the country, and in some cases endeavoured to accommodate the workers employed in them. Moreover, the country was teeming with Colonials and allies, and we were finding them shelter, so that a sudden cry for more houses arose, and has since become the most pressing demand of the country; but I venture to think the real problem of normality is not known with the certainty that a census would have assisted to provide.

We are too much given to panic on the one hand or procrastination on the other to intelligibly foresee or solve any great social question.

The welter into which municipal government has drifted will be appreciated by those who think out the effect of so much conflicting authority in London administration, as outlined in the foregoing pages, and which has for better or worse been conferred on the several bodies charged with the direction of affairs.

The City of London enjoys an unbroken heritage of a powerful governing body, backed by numerous Acts of Parliament, Royal Charters, etc., which provided ample powers to make control effective; but it was not until 1899 that the London Government Act attempted to create great authorities in London, and it was expressly stated that it was not intended to touch the City of London. The result of that legislation is the continued existence of 28 municipal boroughs plus the Corporation of London. The London County Council had preceded this legislation by eleven years, yet the abolition of the vestries and the creation of these 28 boroughs modelled on the City precedent of mayor, co-opted aldermen and elected councillors, was a great reform. The experiment has attained its majority, but there is hardly one writer on the subject of municipal government in recent years who has not urged the necessity of still further reform. The School Board has indeed ceased to exist, and its duties have been transferred to the London County Council, with numerous other services at intervals. Education was added to the authority of that body by the Education Act of 1903. One can readily recall the forcibly expressed opinions of a vast number of those who thought it should have been left in the hands of an independent authority. Those advocates of autonomy appeared to fear that the burden of education would become unmanageable if added to the already stupendous duties of the Council, and there is no doubt it greatly changed the character of its control of other services, and not in every case with the happiest result; but the disaster of the war came at a time when every effort of social advancement, especially where in the experimental stage, was badly hit by the revolutionary nature of the progress of this "great overturn," and it will require many years of wise and restrained work to place such questions in the advantageous position of pre-war days.

The occasion calls for the greatest wisdom and experience which is available, and perhaps the opportunity for making a really efficient change of system will never present itself again with such obvious justification. The doubt that there is enough talent to efficiently govern this huge mechanism is often expressed. Unlike the representatives at St. Stephen's, it should be borne in mind that the services are unremunerated in cash; that they are exacting can hardly be questioned; that they require a high standard of general knowledge is equally obvious. Moreover, it is clear that they want extended experience and marked ability to clearly distinguish between representative policy and that which is purely departmental and administrative.

It would not be an extreme view to say that the average man requires fully three years to get even an elementary knowledge of the important public work which has been adumbrated in the foregoing pages, yet we find not only the ratepayers but an "enlightened Press" striving hard to effect as great a change as possible at each election. It would be greatly to the public advantage that those who make this kind of work their interest, provided they really work at the duties they are returned to do, should be gratefully sent back to serve as long as they are competent to act. The voters have hardly any voice in the selection of those for whom they exercise their choice: the candidates are selected by a caucus, and the option left to the voter in practice is either to vote for the selected candidate, his opponent, or abstention.

Recent returns show that in the County Council there is an average of over sixty committees and sub-committees sitting each week; some of these deal with an immense volume of work at each sitting, and it is a full occupation for earnest representatives to properly attend to it, yet they have to submit themselves to a considerable outlay and frequently an acrimonious triennial contest—to what end? Simply to be allowed to give unstinted zeal and unlimited energy gratis for the benefit of others, who show appreciation by every alternate one failing to be sufficiently interested to vote.

A word here is not misplaced in inviting a thought for the officials who spend their lives in a never-ending strain to make good government possible and give effect to the policy which is evolved by the machinery devised to govern; they are invariably considered fair targets for the Press and the public, and not infrequently are tried almost beyond endurance by those who are sent in this aimless way to direct their efforts. This is a silent service which does its duties economically and with efficiency, and is seldom heard of outside the circumscribed area of operations: yet anyone who dares to say a word of appreciation is classed as a bureaucrat.

LONDON OF THE FUTURE

A criticism which ends at destruction is useless, and yet the remedy is more difficult than is generally understood. If London is extended to what is known as Greater London, some great change becomes inevitable. To be practicable it must end in the delegation of detail to local authorities and the establishment of a great co-ordinating central body with parliamentary duties.

It would be well, if it were possible, to banish what are generally understood as politics from these local services, and the green university man without experience is not of signal service in this machine. Municipal service will never reach an ideal condition if it is simply regarded as the stepping-stone to St. Stephen's; it requires a better and more consistent effort than results from fleeting ambition.

Simplification and good organization are essential, and the solution of the problem will probably be found in paying for the services of the mayor and other experienced ædiles and the giving of more power to highly trained officials, who may thus find it worth while to devote their lives to the one aim of rendering efficient municipal work.

THE PARKS AND OPEN SPACES OF LONDON

DAVID BARCLAY NIVEN, F.R.I.B.A.

CHAPTER XV

THE PARKS AND OPEN SPACES OF LONDON

IMPORTANCE OF FRESH AIR IN LIFE OF THE NATION.

DURING recent years we have had many opportunities to admire the clear-eyed, straight-limbed men who, from beyond the seas, came to take their part in the great crusade, and we know that wholesome open-air life has much to do with the upbringing of such hardy offshoots of a virile stock.

THE PROPORTION OF TOWN BRED TO COUNTRY BRED.

Recent statistics have given us an insight into the results of city upbringing. We are told that in one of our towns 540 men from a potential battalion had to fall out before a gun was shouldered or a shot fired, and that only 460 were found to be fit for military service out of an average 1,000 men. In London the disproportion would be even greater, were it not for the steady inflow of healthy stock from the provinces. Life in cities, cramped houses, lack of green fields and pure air, as surely produce casualties as do the hazards of war. Everything possible, therefore, should be done to ameliorate conditions (avowedly bad) which are actually worse than they appear.

THE IMPORTANCE OF LONDON SETTING AN EXAMPLE TO OTHER CITIES.

The population of London is equal to the combined white population of Australia, New Zealand and South Africa, and it must be mànifest that the best which is or can be provided in the way of open spaces or parks for recreation is not too much for the well-being of its inhabitants or for the upbringing of the generations to come.

LONDON'S EXISTING OPEN SPACES.

At first sight London seems to be relatively well provided with parks and open spaces, numbering as they do no fewer than two thousand. These may be classified as follows :

(*a*) *Public Open Spaces.*—Under the control of, first, the Crown; second, the Government; and third, the local authorities.

(*b*) *Permanently Open Spaces.*—Not necessarily accessible to the public, such as Palace gardens, reservoir areas, allotments, parks, cemeteries.

(*c*) *Private Recreation Grounds.*—Comprising golf links and other club lands.

In addition, there is the Thames with its bridges, banks and gardens; streams like the Lea and the Wandle, with their fields and meadows, and the Canals, many miles in total length.

OPEN SPACES BADLY DISTRIBUTED.

Invaluable as all these spaces may be, they are badly distributed—many of them are not available to the public, others are difficult of access—and must be greatly added to and co-ordinated before we shall be in possession of a park system adequate to the needs of the present or the expectations of the future.

It is of prime importance that the community should, without unnecessary delay, secure a communal centre in the form of a really good civic park to each of the twenty-eight or more boroughs comprised within its boundaries, and control a continuous open zone right round London, besides having ample playing-fields for growing youths within easy reach of all the important residential districts, and a generous provision of supervised gardens (open-air play centres) for the little children as near as possible to their dwellings.

THE DEVELOPMENT PLAN OF GREATER LONDON.

This has recently been published by The London Society, and shows for the first time an eminently practical proposal for linking these spaces together, by parkways, water-ways and by tree-shaded boulevards, into a well ordered scheme, such as is essential to the well-being and continued health of the people.

THE LAKE, KENWOOD.

HAMPSTEAD HEATH FROM THE AIR.

(The preservation of Kenwood for the future is the natural complement to the efforts made in the past to preserve Hampstead Heath.)

To face p. 236.

PARKS AND OPEN SPACES

THE PARKS.

Civic Centres.—One would like to picture the more important of the parks as civic centres. We have such a centre in Hyde Park, and there are other parks pertaining to this character; but few have just such qualities as are likely to arouse that civic pride which should belong not only to London itself, but in lesser degree to each of its boroughs. Of the existing parks, some are merely odd-shaped open spaces which, by accident, have been left unbuilt upon, often difficult of access, frequently more or less derelict, in many of which can still be found tracks and accidental features reminiscent of the fields from which they sprang. Few are fully developed; consequently we fail to get from them the pleasure which we might expect or to make use of them as we should.

An Ideal.—In central parks of a civic character there should be opportunity for social intercourse and recreation, ample space for playing-fields, tennis lawns, running tracks, bowling greens and even swimming pools. It should be permissible to walk about freely, to sit on the turf or drift through a summer's day, for in our ideal all parks and other spaces would be inter-related—linked up—an unbroken system. In many cases these links can only take the form of tree-planted streets or boulevards. The boulevard as a public resort, of ample width, gay with constant movement, refreshing in its verdure, having handsome buildings and numerous cafés, has so far been practically unknown. In Paris, for a length of 20 miles, the great encircling boulevard is 140 feet in width—four miles of it are no less than 240 feet wide—while the Champs-Elysée is even more—275 feet. These widths are not necessitated by traffic conditions, but are adopted from a desire to emphasize the importance of the thoroughfares and to render them stately and beautiful. The results obtained fully justify the area sacrificed, the boulevards being in reality not only trunkways of travel but noble residential regions set in a continuous parkway.

Scientific Planting.—Within the parks themselves there should be more planting of flowering trees and shrubs, not individual specimens, but great masses of sweet-smelling bloom. Travellers tell us of the festival in Japan at cherry-blossom time; our climate is not dissimilar, and from various causes the atmosphere is becoming ever purer: surely, then, we might emulate such encouragement of tree-growth. In our parks there might be a series of beauty spots like the Rhododendron Vale at Kew, filled with a succession of flowering shrubs and trees, almonds or laburnums, sweet-smelling lilac or cherry trees, with rhododendrons and azaleas or even crab-apple or maple trees, and, in addition, there should be masses of climbing roses, clematis and wistaria, so that each month would have its special concentration of blossom. All these, properly disposed, with view-points and vantage grounds, and every feature which a man of taste would wish to include in his own demesne, might be collectively enjoyed by an enlightened democracy: thus would the beauty of London be increased in a very simple manner and the pleasure of its people greatly enhanced.

Open-air Cafés.—In the greater parks and other suitable places a reasonable number of open-air cafés might very well be permitted. The war has caused many changes in our habits; multitudes have seen something of the life of other lands. We have been brought into contact with vast numbers of colonials and many thousands of refugees, all of whom have helped to spread a liking for the conditions which prevail in other lands.

During the war the Y.M.C.A. canteens proved themselves to be an admirable substitute for the public-house. At the front, millions appreciated their wholesomeness, and many would welcome the permanent establishment of something similar throughout the land. The country is ready to support a great movement to this end. The war has given the opportunity to try the system on a large scale; it has been proved in a searching test, and the time has come for its home application. Conducted in a proper manner, with good food and drink, with perhaps pleasant music, and all at reasonable prices, these hostelries would be popular places of refreshment and recreation, necessary and helpful to the life of a well-ordered and contented community. London more and more is becoming a holiday centre, and the greater its attractiveness, quite apart from the advantages to the citizens, the greater will be the return.

BOULEVARDS AND PARKWAYS.

Immediately external to some of the central parks there are miles of roads, such as Piccadilly, Knightsbridge and Bayswater, which might immediately be doubled in apparent width and increased

DE BEAUVOIR SQUARE, KINGSLAND ROAD, HACKNEY.

ST. MATTHEW'S CHURCHYARD, BETHNAL GREEN.

To face p. 238.

infinitely in importance and attractiveness by pushing back the high, prison-like railings, so as to leave an outer strip of ground for development as a boulevard garden. Piccadilly would then vie with Princes Street in Edinburgh, and Bayswater would partake of the character of the Champs-Elysée, and this without costly acquisition, but merely by making better use of what we already possess. Here would be provided promenades for the people, broad paths between well-kept lawns with beautiful flowers against the background of existing trees. All should be fully open to the public, and well-lighted after nightfall to ensure their being not only respected but protected by the people for themselves.

Provision of Fine Sites for Memorials.—There also would be found desirable locations for regimental or other memorials, set to terminate the vistas down important streets. Such memorials, to the perennial youth of a Right-loving people, should certainly not in any sense be funereal, but should partake more of the nature of garden adornments. Cut in Portland stone, an allegorical altar, a magnificently chiselled vase or a rostral column would soon acquire some of the weathered charm of the sculptured pedestal which sustains our only beautiful equestrian monument, and would be a welcome contrast to the statues of frock-coated statesmen in bronze or marble which have so often brought the art of the sculptor into disrepute.

SQUARES AND OPEN SPACES.

The garden square is peculiarly a London feature. It is to be found not only in Bloomsbury and the West End, but elsewhere. These gardens originally were private property, railed off and reserved for the enjoyment of an exclusive class. Some years ago the L.C.C. made a determined attempt to have certain of them thrown open to the public, only to find they were in advance of the times. Since then much has happened: societies like The London Society have come into being, and although the owners of many of the squares had reserved rights to build over them at will, all recent attempts have been successfully resisted and public opinion is not likely again to permit this; but the matter should never again be one of dubiety, nor should it be left to the vigilance of any organization to warn the public against threatened encroachment. The permanence of all such open areas should be legally assured, and a policy adopted, so that the future use of each space may be considered in relation to the needs of the community.

During the war some of the squares were thrown open to the wounded, a privilege they greatly appreciated, but every class should have access to many of them. In certain cases the whole character of the neighbourhoods in which they are situated has changed. The following are examples: *Russell Square*, which is now a centre of boarding-houses and hotels; *Hanover Square*, in a district purely devoted to business, and *Leicester Square*, surrounded by places of public resort. In such cases the treatment of the squares themselves should be radically altered.

In the vicinity of Russell Square there is an increasing number of people of limited means temporarily or permanently resident. During the past years these have comprised nurses, convalescent soldiers, anxious relatives, colonials, refugees, often with time hanging heavily, and who, in the heat of a London summer, found the streets fatiguing, in most cases treeless, without seats or resting places, and with the shady greenness of the square out of reach, surrounded by unclimbable railings, and seldom entered by the privileged few who have keys. Again, take the case of Hanover Square. This is now in the centre of a large business district in which there are multitudes of workers—some of them delicate girls, toiling long hours in nerve-straining workrooms—to whom the cool green square is forbidden ground; in this case especially tantalizing, as it is rare indeed to see a living soul within its locked enclosure.

Surely the time is ripe to communalize such areas: to remove the prison-like railings and to treat each square with its encircling streets as a public place, with ample provision of seats, wide paths, well-kept grass, flowers and shady trees, open for ever to the use and enjoyment of all the people.

Smaller Open Spaces.—London, as the Mother City of millions, owes to itself the provision and maintenance in the most useful form of as much open space as possible; not only parks, parkways, boulevards and squares, but a multitude of quiet, homely gardens or resting places. Manifestly, it is impossible to provide large parks everywhere. In certain semi-suburban districts where there are neglected corner sites and odd pieces of land—remainders unbuilt upon because too expensive for the speculator—these, with ingenuity, could very well be planted and prepared as playing-grounds for little children and resting places for their elders. Business enterprise, seeking pecuniary return, has shown us that even derelict land can be made attractive and remunerative: the wonderful scenic aspect of the exhibitions, the clever planning, the architectural value of even slight and temporary buildings, suggest innumerable methods of doing this, and in older districts, where there are no remaining pieces of land and where houses aggregate forty or more to the acre, an enlightened public should now demand that a certain number of the houses be demolished and a definite minimum of garden playground be provided for the well-being of growing children, it being recognized that the streets with their deleterious influence can no longer continue to be the only playground. Such a clearance has already been made in at least one London borough, a district which had become a byword because of the ravages of preventable diseases.

Small Front Gardens.—Again, the tenants of small suburban houses to which there are tiny front gardens do not possess, and cannot individually be expected to have, the implements necessary to keep them in order. Consequently, if these are not to continue to be squalid and neglected as they now are, they must be dealt with collectively and kept in order at the public expense.

Roof Gardens.—In addition to all this, how much better off would many of the inhabitants be if they could make use of their roofs. There are square miles of small dwellings in London each possessing a minimum of back garden, mere yards, into many of which one can peep when passing by train out of and into London. Although mean and inadequate, these are taken full advantage of. Flat roofs are not only applicable to great city buildings, but also to small houses. Already the possibilities are indicated by the success of those constructed over Selfridge's, and in connection with some of the hotels, hospitals and elsewhere. With modern construction there is no reason why urban dwellings should not be covered by good permanent, watertight flat roofs, and there is little reason to doubt that facilities thus furnished would be greatly enjoyed; it would be possible in hot weather to take meals there, and to use the space as a large open-air room, which, properly protected, would be an excellent place for children to play in and to enjoy the fresh air.

Times are changing; flat roofs covered with asphalte are no dearer than pitched roofs, with their complex construction, involving the use of much timber, covering dark and useless lofts, unget-at-able, never cleaned, a harbourage for litter, dirt and germs.

Conditions in London are improving; the impervious paving of streets and courtyards has greatly reduced the humidity of the atmosphere, fogs are less objectionable than formerly and much less frequent. Better methods of smoke consumption prevail; the advent of motor traction has brought with it cleaner streets, and the electrification of railways and many factories has further helped to purify the air.

If, therefore, in addition to playing-fields and public gardens (which must generally be some distance away) we could have breathing spaces on our roofs, playgrounds over schools, and reere-ation gardens on City buildings, it would be the beginning of a new state of things; and who knows but that London of the future may be as famous for its roof gardens as ancient Babylon was? Then, " able to see the passing clouds, breathe the free air, feel the sunshine and face the four winds of heaven," we might realize the full measure of our release from the domination of enclosing walls and the depression of never-ending streets.

Public Gardeners.—For the maintenance of roadside gardens and many such purposes there might very well be constituted a corps of uniformed gardeners, probably skilled women—something between land girls and women police. These attendants, in their daily itinerary, would prevent wanton damage, would encourage individual effort and exercise a guiding and restraining influence upon the children. They should also mow grass, trim shrubs, nail up straggling creepers and repair broken fences. They might even attend to such little matters as window flower-boxes in districts where there are not even small gardens, and thus help to brighten dull streets. At a nominal charge they could supply pots and guard rails and from time to time replenish earth, furnish plants and seeds, and do all that is possible to encourage simple pleasure in the love of flowers. All this would greatly brighten the way by which the working man goes from his home to his work, and is surely of some importance to his physical state and mental outlook.

The cost of such attentions in some cases might very properly

TWO VIEWS OF THE ROOF GARDEN ABOVE MR. SELFRIDGE'S BUILDING.

To face p 242

be recoverable from the landlords, because of the enhancement in the value of their property and because of the general improvement to the whole neighbourhood.

Allotments.—The success of the allotment system has been one of the surprises of the war, and now that workpeople have more leisure they have the more time to devote to this, but the sporadic efforts of the years of war should be better organized, as, apart from beneficial recreation, the willing labour devoted to the production of food is of great value to the community. There might be an almost continuous belt of allotments round London, not too far from the homes of the people who live on the outskirts; but the pieces of land must be of suitable character, laid out and prepared upon some considered plan. There is no reason why allotments should not be beautiful as well as useful. They should be divided by good paths; the more important of these might be marked by some simple form of pergola; this, covered by rambler roses or wistaria, would afford grateful shade in summer and be pleasant at all seasons.

GREEN ZONE OR PERMANENT OPEN SPACE ROUND LONDON.

But to complete our scheme of parks and open spaces it is necessary that there should be secured for all time an irregular belt of open space round London, including such splendid existing areas as Richmond Park, Banstead Downs, Epping Forest, Hampstead Heath and the nearer commons.

This might be about a quarter of a mile in average width; it would embrace parts of certain streams, the Wandle and the Ravensbourne on the south, and the Crane, Brent, Lea and Roding on the north. This area could extend not only along valleys, but spread out to embrace hill ridges in parts as much as two miles or more into open country. In such reservations we should pass from the formality of town to the simple freedom of meadows, and finally to tilled fields. Through these there would be quiet ways, rustling woods and even hospitable farms; there also would be glades for the children, resting places for their elders, lawns and pavilions for sport, every natural feature preserved and every view-point maintained. Water is a never-failing attraction; valleys and the lower ground which are undesirable for building are often eminently suitable for pleasure treatment. By some of these streams can still be found the "willow herb and many wild flowers: we can walk under oaks and birches, between old thorn-trees—over which trail honeysuckle, bramble and the wild rose—listen to the song birds while wild pigeons coo from the tree-tops." Scenes and country sounds like these and the scent of wild flowers give pleasure to young and old alike. Here citizens in their thousands at every season, on high days and holidays, would enjoy the beauties of nature without costly journeyings or fatiguing disabilities.

Not only would this be a never-failing source of pleasure, but, having regard to its own attractions and in view of the enhanced value of all surrounding land, it might be expected to become of the greatest importance in all schemes for town expansion; contiguous thereto, at the present time, the authorities might very well inaugurate a considerable section of their housing proposals and demonstrate municipal development likely to create a standard to be aimed at in less favoured suburbs.

Here, too, might very properly be found drill grounds and locations for aerodromes and airship stations, which, in convenient relation to arterial roads and to suburban and other railways, must soon be provided for the development of aviation if fullest use is to be made of its potentialities.

Adjoining this great open space there should also be a circumferential boulevard, providing direct communication between the different aerodromes, linking up radial roads and tending greatly to the better distribution of traffic, besides being of military importance. With such improved intercommunication we might hope to see many great institutions and hospitals decentralized and rebuilt in healthful positions, thus freeing congested sites in London greatly needed for other purposes and inaugurating a system of metropolitan hospitals and curative institutions in which there would remain in London itself little more than casualty stations and receiving houses.

The cost of the acquisition of this great green belt round London should not be prohibitive; much of the land can be bought at agricultural prices, while improved values can be calculated upon, for considerable portions to be devoted to building. Nor would it ever be necessary to turn the whole area into non-productive reservations; much of it could still be cultivated. From this

WATERMEADS, MITCHAM.

(The banks of the smaller streams round London are shown as Riverside Reservations on The London Society's Development Plan for London of the Future.)

To face p. 244.

also rent would be derived, but such portions as are once dedicated to be open space should be sterilized from the possibility of encroachment—a great communal estate—secure for all time to the use and enjoyment of the people of London.

THE RIVER THAMES.

Having dealt with the provision and improvement of parks and gardens and the proposed surrounding zone, we may now consider the earliest and by far the most important of our open spaces, viz. the Thames, with its banks, bridges and gardens—a noble waterway of which any city would be proud; this not only drains the soil, but with its recurring tides extracts the polluted and fetid atmosphere from mean streets. Once London's greatest thoroughfare, it is indeed an indestructible asset of never-ending fascination; devoted to commerce below London Bridge, it should have embankments above this on both sides, a fit setting for stately buildings, with gardens, turf and verdure—the waterfront of a noble city.

We are told that Napoleon, when at St. Helena, amused himself by planning improvements in London. He would make, he said, "a grand thoroughfare from St. Paul's to the Thames and wide streets along the river on either side, would build more bridges, and would remove from the vicinity of public buildings the mean structures which disfigure them." Now, after one hundred years, we still need further wide streets and embankments and more bridges—not mere connecting links, but noble structures, amply planned, where, enhanced by the open view, one could linger by the ever-flowing water. As did the countryman who saw London "clothed by the changing seasons, now ringed in green, now shrouded in white; on summer mornings when it lay clearly defined like a finished model, and the sun sparkling on its vanes set the long lines of windows ablaze in the Houses of Parliament and turned the river into a riband of polished steel; or, again, when the cupola of St. Paul's and the Clock Tower at Westminster pierced upwards through a level of fog, as though hung in mid-air, or when mists, shredded by a south wind, swirled and writhed about the roof-tops until the city itself seemed to take fantastic shapes and melt to a substance no more solid than the mists themselves."

The Tributary Streams.—Besides the valley of the Thames there are other large spaces containing tributary streams, such as the Lea and the Wandle, ripe for imaginative development. The River Lea, in parts still wonderfully beautiful, but little bridged, is the dividing line between groups of rapidly growing suburbs, which tend to close in upon it. On the low ground there are numerous factories, and in the near future there will be many more. The whole district is ready for town planning, where should be displayed a happy relationship between villages and their working and recreative areas. Workpeople's cottages would naturally occupy the higher ground, while factories would occupy the lower land with its road, rail and water facilities. Between these would be planned tree-shaded roads, leading pleasantly by flowing water, with recreation fields, allotments and public gardens, a communal entity in its co-ordination.

The Canals.—The canals and their banks and quays, where within London, form quite an important section of its open space, and must be considered in any comprehensive scheme for its beautification. We cannot but suppose that the canal-owners would welcome any proposal to improve the vicinity of their property: a canal in certain cases might become a central feature to a parkway, and the occasional passing of barges—as in Dublin—would only give it added interest. In hot weather children are irresistibly attracted by the cool canals, and in the dog-days one can almost calculate on a succession of letters to the newspapers from people shocked by the needless drowning calamities which there take place; in due course this is followed by a leading article insisting that the time has come for steps to be taken to prevent such fatalities, but as by then the hot weather has been followed by the usual thunderstorm, the agitation dies away. How much better it would be to provide the children with occasional shallow bays in which they could sail their boats—offshoots from the main canal, deepening into bathing pools, in which they might safely be left to follow their bent and disport in cool water to their hearts' content. The vicinity of many of the smaller streams and waterways which flow through London might in parts be made as safe and beautiful as the valley garden at Bournemouth, charming playgrounds for the children, with the living interest of flowing water to lure them from the dangers of the dusty streets.

Some cities have long been popular by reason of their open-air amenities and owing to their having been well laid-out. In London the people may not yet have fully caught the out-of-door spirit, but the throngs which on Sundays and fine afternoons parade in Hyde Park and in every open space give proof of the increasing vogue of such enjoyments. Humanity is very sensitive to its surroundings, therefore not only should good houses be provided for the people in pleasant locations, with plenty of light and air, but if traffic facilities are convenient and ample opportunity is given for recreation and physical development, the town dweller of the future will be a contented citizen, more in harmony with his environment: healthy and fit, an asset of the utmost value in a well-ordered community.

LONDON AS THE HEART OF THE EMPIRE

THE EARL OF MEATH, P.C., K.P.

CHAPTER XVI

LONDON AS THE HEART OF THE EMPIRE

THE Great European War of 1914 to 1919, which was really waged by Germany for the destruction of the British Empire, though ostensibly for other reasons, far from carrying out the designs of its promoters, has ended in adding enormously to its extent and, what is of far greater importance to the citizens of the Empire, in consolidating and strengthening its component parts.

Had it not been for this war, it is doubtful what length of time would have been needed to prepare public opinion within the Empire for the acceptance of an Imperial War, and then Peace, Cabinet, which is now practically a *fait accompli.*

It was the magnificent services rendered by the people of India during the world conflict, which carried their victorious arms into Europe, Africa and Asia, which led to the appointment of a distinguished Indian as Under-Secretary of State for India, with a seat in the House of Lords, and to the extraordinary advances towards self-government made by the British Government and Parliament in the constitution of India and its forms of government.

Before the war, in Africa alone, the British Empire covered some 2½ millions of square miles. When the great conflict ended she had added some 1,200,000 square miles to the above, making a total of 3,700,000 square miles in Africa subject to British Imperial rule. It is impossible to say what will be the net increase in land area of the British Empire when the final account of her territorial assets is presented to the world, for all these matters are still in a condition of flux; for instance, no one knows whether the Empire is to retain any part of her gigantic conquests in Mesopotamia, and if so, how much, or which, and how many, of the Empire conquests in the Pacific are to be retained by the Mother Country, Australia or New Zealand. What is perfectly certain is that the map-makers will shortly have to scrap all their most recent publications and produce entirely new ones, and that all the statistics and information in regard to the British Empire will have to be re-drafted.

Before the war, the population of the British Empire was calculated to amount to over four hundred millions (400,000,000), which was about one-fifth, or 22 per cent., of the inhabitants of the globe, and its extent was reckoned as about 12,000,000 square miles.

These figures will have to be enormously increased. Before the war, the nations outside the British Empire possessing the largest extent of territory were Russia (8,000,000 square miles), United States (3,623,000 square miles), Brazil (3,220,000), and those possessing the largest population outside the British Empire were China (350,000,000), Russia (130,000,000) and the United States (about 100,000,000)—all less than the British Empire, with its population of 400,000,000 and its land area of 12,000,000 square miles.

Now, all these figures will have to be revised, leaving the British Empire without a rival in the world in these respects.

All great political organizations possess a capital, of which they are usually immensely proud, and they endeavour in their respective degrees to improve and beautify and enlarge it, striving to place it beyond the possibility of rival competition in these respects. The only political organization which does not officially possess a capital, though practically it does, is the British Empire.

The object of this essay is to claim that, since the British Empire has received such enormous additions of population, of territory and of consolidation as the result of the war, it is time that London should be officially recognized by the Empire as its capital, so that the whole Empire may take a pride in its beautification and development as the centre of the greatest political organization the world has ever known. I would suggest that with this view the Lord Mayor and Corporation of the City of London and the County Council of London should be empowered to co-opt on their respective governing bodies leading representatives, so long as they reside in London, of the Overseas Dominions, of India and of the Crown Colonies, so that all parts of this great confederation of States which is called the British Empire may feel that they possess a governing interest in the management of their great capital, and that each citizen of the Empire, when he visits London, may feel that this vast city, containing in the area known as "Greater London" 7¼ millions of inhabitants, and its wonderful historical, literary, architectural and scientific traditions, is part and parcel of him or her, and not a strange though interesting city like Paris or Rome.

The time would appear opportune for such a move.

A Bill has just been passed by Parliament entitled the "British Empire Exhibition." The British Government under this Bill have taken a step which I believe to be unique in its history, or in the history of any previous British Government. They have undertaken to guarantee, under conditions, to the extent of £100,000, the expenses of running an Exhibition which is to be held in 1922 for promoting the general economic and commercial interests of the Empire.

This, together with the Government official recognition of the Empire Movement in 1916, demonstrates a somewhat rapid advance towards a realization of the overwhelming importance in world politics of Imperial sentiment, and with such a step as I suggest in regard to the Corporation of the City of London and to the County Council, would, I believe, hasten materially the unification of the British Empire and greatly strengthen the Imperial sentiment throughout the vast dominions of H.M. King George V.

Already the principal self-governing Dominions are establishing themselves in palatial buildings, worthy of the great rising populations they represent, in the most important thoroughfares of London, the last of which is the new home of Canada which is to be erected on the site of Morley's Hotel, Trafalgar Square, beneath the shadow of Nelson, whose life and death made possible the expansion of the Empire to its present wonderful proportions.

The formation of a permanent Imperial Peace Cabinet means that the most eminent statesmen of our great Overseas Dominions will constantly be arriving, residing in and leaving the capital of the Empire. Formerly these distinguished men, as a rule, never visited London, except, perhaps, as private individuals coming back to see the homes in which they and their ancestors were born; now, they will arrive invested with all the authority and glamour of high station and of representative rank. The position within the

Empire at present occupied by India, with its vast population of 300,000,000 and the quickened means of transport, means that thousands of our fellow Indian subjects, including their ancient princes and nobles, will visit the capital of their Empire, and will either be impressed favourably or the reverse by the opinions they will form of London and its inhabitants.

Is it not, therefore, in the interests of the Empire that the capital should rise to the height of its great position, and so order its affairs that these distant citizens of the Empire may return to their several homes proud of their capital and of their position as citizens of the British Empire?

Almost all the capitals of Europe which used to be surrounded by fortifications erected for their protection have destroyed them, and turned them into rings of beauty surrounding the cities, composed of gardens, parks, avenues and parkways joining open spaces together. The American cities, although not possessed of fortifications, have in many cases done the same thing. There is nothing except expense to prevent us in London from copying this example, by making a continuous avenue, broken by parks and gardens, uniting the numerous beautiful open spaces we possess on all sides outside London.

Inside, the Euston Road and its continuations could with little alteration be turned into a beautiful Ring like that at Vienna or Cologne. It should always be remembered that London attracts the refined, the literary, the educated by its antiquity and traditions, and that no greater mistake could be made than to destroy these attractions. No amount of modern embellishments would compensate for the loss of historic houses, streets, alleys, churches and monuments. But if care be taken to lay no unholy hand on the London of historic interest, there are miles and miles of commonplace brick boxes which call themselves houses, the removal of which would be a loss to no man or woman of sense or sensibility. There is ample scope in these squalid and uninteresting streets for the work of the modern and enlightened architect.

As regards open spaces, there are few capitals in the world more plentifully supplied than is London, with its health-giving lungs and oxygen-producing trees and foliage. If the reader will take the trouble to consult the pages of the pre-war annual reports of the Metropolitan Public Garden Association, issued from its

EBURY SQUARE GARDEN, PIMLICO.

(A London Square maintained by the Metropolitan Public Gardens Association at the cost of the Duke of Westminster.)

ST. KATHARINE COLEMAN CHURCHYARD, FENCHURCH STREET, E.C.

(One of the threatened City churchyards.)

To face p 254

office at Denison House, Vauxhall Bridge Road, S.W. 1, it will be seen that in 1883 there were rather over 4,000 acres of public spaces within the area that was afterwards formed into the County of London, for its population at that time of nearly 4 millions, or 1 acre of public space to 950 people; and that twenty years later (1902), whilst the population of the County of London had increased by about 18 per cent. to 4½ millions, the public open spaces had increased in the same period by no less than 50 per cent., to over 6,000 acres, thereby reducing the number of people per acre of public space from 950 to 750.

The provision of open spaces in and around London is largely due:

1. To the generosity of the Crown.
2. To the Corporation of the City of London, which between the years 1873 and 1890 possessed the right to levy a duty of 4d. a ton, for London improvements, on coal brought to London.
3. To the Metropolitan Board of Works before 1889.
4. Since that date to the London County Council.
5. To the Middlesex County Council.
6. To the different Borough and Urban District Councils and Vestries in and around London.
7. To the propaganda work and practical activities since 1883 of the Metropolitan Public Garden Association and of the somewhat older organization, the Commons (and Footpaths) Preservation Society—which, as its name indicates, deals mainly with commons in all parts of the country—and in a lesser degree to the Kyrle Society.

Since 1902 this rate of increase within the County of London has not been maintained, chiefly because the area of land available either for public spaces or for building purposes is a rapidly diminishing quantity and has risen in price. For these and other reasons, the present public open-space area in the County of London, viz. about 6,650 acres, shows only a moderate increase of about 10 per cent. since 1902, but as the population is estimated to have remained stationary at about 4½ millions, the number of people per acre of public space has been further reduced from 750 to about 680.

In the rapidly expanding suburban districts adjacent to the county boundary, which, with London proper, go to form the area known as Greater London (with its 7¼ millions of people), to which the attention both of the Association and of local authorities has been irresistibly drawn, there has been, however, quite an abnormal growth of public spaces since 1902, to meet the needs of the constant influx of population. Moreover, in these suburbs are to be found a number of large Royal parks and other spaces, which Londoners frequent in large numbers, especially at holiday times; e.g. Richmond Park (2,350 acres), Epping Forest (5,375 acres), Wimbledon Common (1,200 acres), Hampton Court and Bushey Parks (1,800 acres), Kew Gardens (288 acres), Alexandra Park (172 acres), etc. Consequently, as regards public spaces, London compares very favourably with other large cities, both at home and abroad. Paris, within the city, has only about 560 acres of public open spaces, which gives the very poor average of 1 acre of public space to 5,300 people. But on the confines are the two large areas known as the Bois de Boulogne and the Bois de Vincennes, together amounting to about 4,500 acres, and if we include them the proportion becomes much improved. Moreover, the gradual conversion of the Paris fortification belt into open spaces should make a material difference. Berlin possesses State and municipal parks and open spaces amounting to nearly 1,300 acres, which provide 1 acre of public space to about 1,600 people. Thus London is well able to hold its own. But, as in other cities, the parks and open spaces in London are very unevenly distributed. Whilst in the borough of Shoreditch there are only 10 acres of public spaces for its 90,000 inhabitants, a neighbouring borough, Hackney, with only double the number of people, possesses sixty times the amount of open space, viz. 618 acres. But these disproportions are rectified to a considerable extent by ease of communication. There is, however, a feature in connection with the open spaces which London possesses which is not to be found, at least to anything like the same extent, in other cities either at home or abroad: I mean the large number of squares and similar enclosures and of disused churchyards which are to be found scattered all over its surface, and which number about 430 and 320 respectively. About 50 of the former class and

CHRISTCHURCH CHURCHYARD, BLACKFRIARS ROAD.

(Much needed in a poor and crowded locality.)

ST. BOTOLPH'S, ALDGATE, CHURCHYARD.

(One of the threatened City churchyards.)

To face p. 256

120 of the latter have been converted into public gardens, chiefly through the instrumentality of the Association, and are most useful sources of enjoyment close to the homes or the work of the people. All these small spaces, whether open to the public or not, form important lungs and air-holes in the midst of houses, the value of which cannot be overestimated, and their trees, flowers, grass and other foliage, which all can see, provide refreshing relief to the tired eye. It is said, with a good deal of truth, that there is scarcely a street in London from which a tree is not visible. These small areas are the envy of our American visitors, who often complain of the absolutely solid manner in which New York and other cities of the U.S.A. have been built up. An American friend wrote to me: "Apparently in England it is not attempted to secure land upon which buildings have been erected; we do this constantly in our country. In Philadelphia we have secured a number of our city spaces through acquiring ground with buildings on it and then razing the buildings. While Central Park (New York), 800 acres, cost 5 million dollars, three small spaces on the east side, covering not quite 10 acres, cost 5¼ million dollars. It will be seen how enormously New York has had to pay in order to get a few small open spaces." This is striking testimony to the supreme importance of these smaller grounds, and the utmost care should be taken to preserve them in connection with any rebuilding schemes. There is some attractive force which London possesses in a greater degree than any other city, and which causes British citizens all over the world to love the Empire's capital above all other cities, and to return to it, whenever opportunity offers, with never-failing joy and delight. It is, I venture to think, its homeliness which is London's greatest attraction. This sense of home is due in no small measure to the numerous small squares and gardens to which I have alluded; to the comparatively narrow but clean and well lighted streets, with their shops and houses not too lofty and easily distinguishable on either side; to the many methods of locomotion, which renders it a simple matter to get from one part to another, and to the distinctive but unobtrusive characteristics of its component parts. All these features tend to prevent that fatigue and monotony which sometimes attaches to other cities which may be of greater grandeur, but which often do not inspire any feelings of affection. Great care should therefore be taken that these price-

less advantages should not be destroyed by reconstruction and re-building. Public convenience should be paramount in any such schemes, and nothing should be done which would tend to displace or to drive away trade and business, upon which the welfare of the capital depends.

In any reconstruction which may be made, let us bear in mind that we should desire to make London a *real home* for the children of the Empire—a home to which they all may desire to return; and that in making it a clean, sweet, sanitary and beautiful home we should do nothing which may destroy or weaken those indescribable qualities associated with home in the mind of every true man and woman—qualities more often to be found in modest surroundings than in the dwellings of the millionaire.

THE SMOKE PLAGUE OF LONDON

The late SIR WILLIAM RICHMOND, K.C.B., R.A.

CHAPTER XVII

THE SMOKE PLAGUE OF LONDON

During the last hundred years England has attained a foremost position in many phases of sanitary science, and in no part of the country has greater progress been made in this direction than in London. The River Thames is carefully protected from pollution, and every streamlet and ditch in the Home Counties is carefully watched to prevent the pollution of drinking water. Effective measures have been devised for dealing with the disposal of sewage, for controlling the spread of infectious diseases and for protecting the worker from the evils of sweated labour or unhealthy conditions of employment. With commendable persistency, too, the authorities responsible for safeguarding the public health have aimed at a high standard of efficiency so far as the purity of our food supplies is concerned. In short, whether he buys or sells, produces, distributes, or merely consumes the products of the industry of others, it has been the constant aim of Parliament to ensure for the individual protection against nuisances and conditions tending to lower vitality or to retard the social and physical development of the community.

In view of such evidences of the recognition of the importance of sanitary science in its wider aspects, it is extraordinary that no whole-hearted effort has been made to deal with the all-important subject of the purity of the air. This is the one matter that touches every town-dweller—high or low, rich or poor, young or old—and yet it has been consistently shelved by a long succession of Governments, each professedly interested in the health of the nation.

Indeed, it is not too much to say that the failure of Parliament to provide for the abatement of preventable air pollution has been a blot upon the annals of public health legislation.

It is true that lime and alkali works have been subjected to stringent conditions imposed to prevent the dissemination of harmful acid fumes. This is as it should be, and it shows that it is not impossible to devise conditions of working, even in the case of highly specialized industries, without crippling trade. It is also true that when contamination of the air arises from insanitary neighbourhoods or from dust-heaps the nuisance is promptly suppressed. Such sources of atmospheric pollution are infinitesimal when compared with the vitiation of the atmosphere by the ceaseless outpourings of smoke, sulphurous fumes and dust from the myriad household chimneys and factory shafts of London.

Day in and day out the pitiless rain of grime continues, but no serious effort has ever been made by the Department of State charged with the duty of protecting the public health to abate the evil since that evil assumed serious proportions.

It cannot be said that no demand has ever been made for the abatement of the coal smoke nuisance, for at intervals during the last seven centuries the voices of reformers or far-seeing visionaries have been raised to demand its abolition.

To appreciate the position and to visualize accurately the series of failures of the nation to free itself from the incubus of this veritable " old man of the sea " it is necessary to study the successive stages in the history of the evil.

As far back as the year 1228 a thoroughfare in the City was known as Sacoles (Sea-Coles) Lane, so that even at that early date there must have been a considerable trade in the commodity. Before Edward I had occupied the throne for a year, the use of coal was prohibited in London as being " prejudicial to human health," and even smiths were compelled to burn wood.

This early and drastic effort failed to prevent the use of coal, and Mr. R. L. Galloway records, in his *History of Coal Mining*, that the " nobles, prelates and others " going to London to attend Parliament were greatly annoyed by the increasing smoke and took the lead in demanding that the use of coal should be prohibited. In consequence of this agitation a Royal Proclamation was issued in 1306 prohibiting artificers from using coal in their furnaces. This was followed in 1307 by a Commission of Oyer and Terminer, which was instructed to "inquire of all such who burnt sea-cole in the City or parts adjoining and to punish them for the first offence with

THE SMOKE PLAGUE: SUNDAY, 11 A.M.

THE SMOKE PLAGUE: MONDAY, 12 NOON.

(Two views in a manufacturing town.)

To face p. 262.

great fines and ransoms, and, upon the second offence, to demolish their furnaces." The early coal smoke abatement crusaders at all events were whole-hearted in their efforts to stop a growing nuisance!

But it was inevitable that the rapid destruction of forests for the smelting of iron and for use as fuel should, notwithstanding all attempts at repression, lead to a correspondingly rapid development of the coal trade. Now and then protests were raised, and in 1578 the Worshipful Company of Brewers undertook in a petition to the Privy Council to use only wood in the breweries near Westminster Palace because the Queen "findeth hersealfe greately greved and anoyed with the taste and smoke of the Sea-Coles."

John Evelyn, in his *Fumifugium*, written in 1670 at the command of Charles I, describes the "infernal Smoak" of London in sentiments, if not in language, to which many sufferers of the present day would whole-heartedly subscribe. He says:

> That Hellish and dismall cloud of sea-coal is not only perpetually imminent over her head, but so universally mixed with the otherwise wholesome and excellent aer, that her inhabitants breathe nothing but an impure and thick Mist, accompanied with a fuliginous and filthy vapour which renders them obnoxious—corrupting the lungs, and disordering the entire habits of the bodies, so that Catharrs, Phthsicks, Coughs and Consumptions rage more in this city than in the whole earth besides.

The next stage in the growth of the nuisance was marked by the invention and development of the steam engine. This speedily led to an enormous increase in the consumption of coal, and was followed in 1819 by the appointment of a Parliamentary Committee charged to inquire how far it was practicable to compel persons using steam engines and furnaces to erect them in a manner less prejudicial to public health and public comfort. The Committee reported that "the nuisance so universally and so justly complained of may at least be considerably diminished, if not altogether removed." In a subsequent report the Committee expressed the view that smoke-preventing appliances existed which could and should be used.

These conclusions have been frequently endorsed during the last hundred years and have never been gainsaid, but for some incomprehensible reason no practical step has yet been taken to give full effect to them. In 1843 a second Select Committee urged the need of legislation to prohibit the production of smoke from furnaces and steam engines. Still a third Committee reported to Parliament in 1845 that "opaque smoke issuing from steam engine chimneys may be so abated as no longer to be a public nuisance."

Seventy-five years passed before the Government could be persuaded again to inquire into the subject, when, in 1914, the Local Government Board appointed a Departmental Committee on Smoke Abatement, under the Chairmanship of Lord Newton. The inquiries of this Committee, interrupted by the late war, have recently been resumed. In the meantime, the Government rested content with the introduction into several statutes, dealing with railways and public health, of provisions giving to various sanitary authorities feeble and totally inadequate powers to deal with smoke nuisances. The exercise of these powers was thwarted by technical difficulties involving proof that the smoke emitted was black in colour or, worse still, involving the necessity of establishing that the furnace or steam engine concerned did not "as far as practicable" consume the smoke generated during the combustion of coal.

It soon became apparent that such powers contained loopholes which, in practice, rendered them almost valueless. Few sanitary authorities even pretended to take any steps whatever to suppress smoke nuisances. Some, seeing the worthless nature of the Government provisions, went to Parliament for special powers applying only to their own areas. Others were discouraged by the difficulties of securing a conviction and by the knowledge that the fines inflicted for an infraction of the law were so paltry as to constitute no deterrent to offenders. Coal was cheap, and it was soon found by the owners of factories that it was easier to pay a rarely imposed fine of five shillings than to trouble their heads about the pall of smoke incessantly emitted from their chimney shafts. Moreover, the officials of many local authorities were gravely handicapped in the performance of their duties by the fact that among the members of the Councils employing them were representatives of the firms who were the worst offenders. They were further discouraged by the apparent absence of public opinion upon the matter. People, indeed, had come to accept, either as a proof of prosperity or as a necessary and unavoidable evil, the continuance of a foul atmosphere.

In these circumstances, factory chimneys belched out smoke

in an ever-increasing volume, and, as London grew, the smoke from the chimneys of private dwelling-houses sensibly added to the prevailing gloom. The London County Council in 1891 succeeded in applying to the Metropolis the smoke abatement provisions which had applied to the rest of the country since the Public Health Act, 1875, was placed upon the Statute Book. But, for the reasons already indicated, these provisions were not enforced and they speedily became a "dead-letter." Winter fogs grew in density and duration. They often lasted for many days, and it was only on rare occasions that London enjoyed a really smokeless day from November to February.

I felt that the time had come to arouse the public to the need for action. The obvious step was to form an independent body, untrammelled by local influences and determined to see that the law of the land, with all its shortcomings, should be obeyed and that it should be strengthened where experience showed that it required amendment. Accordingly, in 1899, the Coal Smoke Abatement Society was formed. Since that date the history of the movement has been the story of this little Society's work.

Our early efforts were met with nothing but indifference or derision, and even well-wishers informed us that attempts to arouse interest in the work were doomed to fail. The law had become a closed book in the case of nearly all metropolitan local authorities, and officials, at first, either ignored our existence or plainly hinted that they regarded our organization as the outcome of the efforts of a few self-advertising "quacks and busybodies." The Society, therefore, had a fourfold mission to perform. It had to arouse the public conscience to the urgent necessity of taking steps to abate the evil of coal smoke from the point of view of the health and comfort of the community; it had to demonstrate to manufacturers that black smoke, so far from being a necessary accompaniment of prosperity, was ocular proof of an avoidable waste of valuable fuel; it had to encourage the inventors and makers of smoke-preventing furnaces, devices, fuels and grates not to accept the past indifference of the Legislature and the supineness of most Local Authorities as conclusive evidence that nothing could be done; and, finally, it had to stimulate local authorities to a sense of the responsibilities they owed to the general public in protecting the atmosphere from unnecessary and unlawful pollution.

It soon became apparent that in its crusade the Society had behind it the overwhelming support of sanitary and engineering experts and also of medical men. Physicians of such world-wide eminence as Sir Thomas Barlow, Sir James Crichton-Browne, Sir Frederick Treves and Sir William Bennett have championed the cause, their views being ably summed up by Sir James Crichton-Browne, who said of coal smoke that

> it injured the health of the people, both directly and indirectly. It was charged with noxious chemical vapours which poisoned the blood, with a grimy compost that blocked up the pores of the skin, with gritty particles that lacerated the mucous membranes, and directly led to illnesses such as anæmia and tuberculosis. The indirect action of smoke in shutting out the beneficent sunlight was equally grievous, because light was the cardinal condition of animal and vegetable life. Anyone who filched away, by creating a pall of smoke, this primary necessary of life was guilty of a grave offence against the community and ought to be mulcted in severe penalties.

It was proved times out of number, by information collected by the Society, that while fogs seriously affect the health, such visitations are far more injurious when heavily laden with soot and dust, and that under such conditions the death-rate is apt to assume alarming proportions. It was also shown from official data furnished by the Meteorological Council that, owing to smoky fogs, London only received about one-third of the amount of sunshine enjoyed in districts not affected by its smoke; it was also established by Sir Napier Shaw that the abolition of coal smoke would cut off 20 per cent. of fogs altogether, besides materially reducing the intensity and duration of all other London fogs.

The smoke of London is distributed over the country-side to a surprising extent. I had experience of this once when staying at Lockinge, near Wantage, 64 miles from town. On an unusually hot summer's day there travelled up with the south-east wind dense clouds of smoke, which finally obscured the rolling downs, the trees and the copses within a small distance from any point of observation. The moment the thick veil reached me I smelt that peculiar stuffy odour of London smoke. A shepherd told me that he and his friends of the hills called that mist "London dirt," and he said that when it passed over the snow in winter-time it left a residuum of black upon it.

It was further established that owing to the deposit of sulphurous acids left behind by the tarry particles of soot and smoke every building and work of art was being fretted away or ruined.

THE SMOKE PLAGUE

The recent appeal of the Dean of Westminster for the vast sum of £250,000 to repair and protect the fabric of the venerable Abbey is a potent reminder of the disastrous results of our wasteful system of crudely burning sulphur-laden coal.

Having collected a mass of uncontrovertible material, the Society set to work to force local authorities to prosecute flagrant offenders. We appointed inspectors whose duty it was to carefully observe factory shafts, in order to ascertain whether any smoke was emitted from them, and, if so, what colour and density the smoke assumed and for what periods it continued. Where the reports showed that an unnecessary amount of harmful smoke was being discharged, a complaint in regard to the offending firm was made to the Borough Council concerned. A few of the Councils—such as those of Westminster, the City, Kensington and Fulham—always received the Society's reports with sympathy. Others had to be goaded into even a faint semblance of activity. The Society found a stanch ally in the London County Council, which, fortunately, is enabled to act in cases where the Borough Council is guilty of a dereliction of duty.

For a long time our effort proved to be an uphill task, but gradually it came to be recognized that the Society had behind it the backing of a powerful public opinion, and, with a few exceptions, the Borough Councils could be relied upon at any rate to protest to the smoke-raisers against a continuance of their nuisances.

Our reports of nuisances averaged from 1,200 to 1,500 per annum until the outbreak of the late war led to the suspension of smoke prosecutions. In the meantime, the Society could claim with pride that a majority of the firms that originally and consistently offended had ceased to do so. An inquiry was addressed by the Society to a number of these firms in order to ascertain whether the means adopted were effective and economical in working. Over 70 varieties of trades, from engineering to candle-making, came within the scope of the inquiry, and the replies were remarkable. Out of 168 manufacturers who replied, only two reported that they did not consider that they had succeeded in their efforts to prevent smoke. Owing to the heavy rise in the price of coal and labour, several of the firms stated that their working and fuel bills had increased, but no less than 70 per cent. of the firms volunteering information definitely claimed that the adoption of modern methods of steam-raising or power production had resulted in considerable economy, coupled with greater efficiency. Some of the firms went so far as to express the view that even if smoke abatement involved increased expense to them, it ought to be enforced in the interests of the general community.

No complaint was made that the suppression of smoke had involved any hardship on trade, and the voluntary testimony of many of the largest firms around the Metropolis conclusively proves that smoke abatement can be fairly insisted upon as a real advantage to the manufacturer.

But it must not be thought that smoke from factory shafts is the only serious cause of atmospheric pollution. The chimneys of private dwelling-houses are also grave offenders, and the smoke they emit is of a peculiarly harmful character, on account of its clinging and tarry nature. Within the Metropolitan Police District there are upwards of 600,000 private houses contributing to the canopy of smoke. If kitcheners could be abolished, the output of grime would be greatly diminished, for the kitchener is a bad offender. The efforts of the Coal Smoke Abatement Society in regard to household chimneys have been necessarily limited by the fact that the law—such as it is—against smoke nuisances does not apply to them; it can only be enforced against railway engines and tugs, and furnaces in factories, hotels and trading concerns generally. Private houses are wholly exempt from control. The Society has therefore encouraged manufacturers to improve the standard of grates and kitcheners, and, under the auspices and with the powerful co-operation of H.M. Office of Works, it has conducted several series of exhaustive tests of grates and fuels. These tests have aroused world-wide interest and have led to the manufacture of better types of grates and other heating appliances.

This source of smoke pollution is, moreover, being materially lessened by the extraordinary expansion in the use of gas fires and cooking stoves. The use of electric apparatus, too, is steadily growing, and efforts are being made to treat coal in such a way as to withdraw from it the bulk of its tarry constituents, which contain valuable oil, motor-spirit, gas, and other by-products, leaving a satisfactory and smokeless domestic fuel of the "coalite" type. These modern developments are factors of enormous import in the great task of cleansing the air.

"BEST" WESTMORELAND SLATES FROM THE ROOF OF CHELSEA HOSPITAL.

NEW AND OLD STONEWORK FROM THE TOWER OF LONDON.

It will thus be seen that much has been already accomplished as a result of the movement that led to the formation of the Coal Smoke Abatement Society, which has certainly deserved well of London, and has more than justified the existence of the organization. But it must not be imagined that the battle has yet been won. There are yearly consumed in London no fewer than 17,000,000 tons of coal, containing, it is estimated, an average of nearly 2 per cent., or 340,000 tons, of sulphur. It is almost certain that something like 200,000 tons of this sulphur must each year be poured out in gaseous form, or in the shape of soot, and when it is remembered that it is from sulphur compounds that the greatest injury results from the smoke nuisance, the appalling gravity of this source of pollution becomes apparent. The researches of the Atmospheric Pollution Committee have shown that the soot-fall in London may reach 76,000 tons per annum. Is it any wonder, then, that smoke fogs still come and that winter sunshine is still deficient, even although in both respects most recent years have shown marked improvement?

Now that the pinch of the financial strain is being felt throughout every grade of society, perhaps some attention will be given to the wanton waste involved by the unnecessary and unwanted smoke plague. The thermal efficiency of the household grate, on the most sanguine computation, rarely reaches 20 per cent. In most cases it is far less. The rest of the heat is literally wasted by our barbarous methods of combustion. According to the data authoritatively submitted to the Royal Commission on Coal Supplies, we must lose at least 4,000,000 tons of coal each year by our foolish methods of generating power and heat. This, at the present price of coal, represents a dead annual loss of £12,000,000—a huge sum to waste upon an unwanted nuisance, and one that, if available for public use, would now relieve the ratepayers of all anxiety in these days of crushing local expenditure. To get rid of smoke, too, would save untold expenditure in the cleansing, washing and renewing of fabrics, works of art, and, indeed, property of every description. It would enable flowers that will not now bloom in sullied air to thrive in our parks and gardens.

There is, then, still much to do. During the long years of war much of the good, wrought with so much effort, was undone. Factories were permitted to use any fuel they cared. They might smoke incessantly with impunity, and many have not yet renewed their former efforts to abate smoke. It is time that the law was again put into operation. It is time, too, that the law was strengthened where it has proved to be inadequate. Many of us are anxiously awaiting the long over-due Government measure on the subject. London suffers not only from the smoke generated in her midst, but also from the motley crowd of factory shafts outside her borders. These pour out smoke which blows over the Metropolis, and in most cases there is no redress. This, too, must be remedied.

It would be futile to look forward to a time when Londoners may feel justified in applying to the Metropolis the proud boast of Augustus in regard to the Imperial City: "He found Rome of brick and left it of marble." But there is no reason why the dust and grime and gloom of London smoke should not give place to sunshine and to a pure air. Those who can give to posterity those priceless gifts will richly deserve, as they will surely receive, the gratitude of future generations.

THE SPIRIT OF LONDON

THE MARQUESS OF CREWE, K.G., P.C., F.S.A.

CHAPTER XVIII

THE SPIRIT OF LONDON

THE foregoing sections of this book on London of the Future represent a civic survey, by competent observers, of the Greater London which is the home of from seven to eight million souls. They describe what actually exists within that vast and teeming area; what might be; and what cannot be from the loss of opportunities that can never recur. The various writers describe the streets in which these millions live and move, the port and the railways by which they are fed and provided, the parks and squares through which they breathe and the smoke that chokes them. These things represent the facts of the present and the hopes of the future; but they all hinge on the London of the past, and cities that have a past must cling to it as closely as they can, without pedantic sacrifice of the well-being of citizens of to-day and of years to come. Just as Edinburgh or Florence possesses a soul denied to Chicago or Johannesburg, with all their human interest and enterprise, so London has its own soul to keep among all projects of material improvement and industrial expansion. And this may well be, even though necessary and desirable changes must obliterate a great deal of the past. We are used to regard the Great Fire of 1666 as an unmixed blessing to London, as having swept away the miserable rookeries where the Plague flourished; but we may be sure that among the thirteen thousand houses that it destroyed there must have been hundreds of beautiful half-timbered structures, like the few that still variegate the oldest streets. It seems strange to read that Aldersgate Street "resembleth an Italian street more than any other in London"; but there were fine old houses there up to 1878. I will say a word about improvements directly, but first it is worth while to consider what can be done to maintain the

London spirit in the simple and obvious way that will appeal to everybody. Landor wrote that "The noble mansion is most distinguished by the beautiful images it retains of beings passed away; and so is the noble mind"; and though we cannot exhibit beautiful portraits of all the great figures of the past, even in our public galleries, something can be done to keep green the memories of those who have lived and worked, have found enjoyment and faced trouble, in the London of past days. Here and there it has been possible to acquire the house in which some great man has lived, to maintain it as far as possible in its original state, and to collect in it personal memorials. This was done, some years ago, with Thomas Carlyle's dwelling, 24 Cheyne Row, where it is hoped that changes of fashion in philosophers and historians will not prevent the visits of as many pilgrims, British and American, as will make it possible to maintain the house; and, more recently, Mr. Cecil Harmsworth, with rare public spirit, has secured No. 17 Gough Square, off Fleet Street, where Johnson wrote *The Vanity of Human Wishes* and presided over the preparation of the Dictionary. In Kensington, in Holland Park Road, is the temple of Classical and Eastern art which was once Lord Leighton's home, and is filled with relics of his work, given to the country by the liberality of his sisters; and far away to the east, in sharp contrast, is the house of John Wesley, in the City Road, next to his chapel and to the graveyard in which he lies, and made sacred to many by the presence of some of his books and other personal relics. There may not have been many opportunities of keeping untouched the residences of great men, and if there have been, few at any rate have been taken. Nobody knows where Shakespeare lived in London, and of Milton's different homes none is left, the last, I believe, having been engulfed in Queen Anne's Mansions. Dryden's house in Greek Street, Soho, is gone, though a tablet marks the site; and even if it becomes possible to obtain the house at Hampstead where Keats lived as a guest and listened to the nightingale, it was considered some years ago that his British and American admirers would do well to concentrate on acquiring the house at Rome in which he died, and which is now devoted to the Keats-Shelley Museum. I am not sure that the abodes of statesmen and other public figures have been so much more piously preserved than those of men of letters as might have seemed probable. Perhaps, in the changed circumstances of to-day, the beautiful villa at Chiswick which witnessed the deaths of Charles Fox and Canning will once more be inhabited by the family of its owner. Arlington Street, the great Ministerial street of the early eighteenth century, has not entirely retained its political traditions, though the remaining great houses on the west side of the street, with the continuing line along the Green Park as far as Lancaster House, combined with what is left in private hands in St. James's Square, Berkeley Square and Mayfair, make up an irregular Faubourg Saint-Germain of the West End. And the survival of Nos. 10 and 11 Downing Street, of the Admiralty House, and of the Speaker's residence in Palace Yard must not be forgotten. But I know of no statesman's house which is specially maintained by private care to carry on a particular political or legal tradition for the public benefit.

Short of the dedication of shrines like these, it is sought to perpetuate personal memories by placing tablets or plaques of association on the actual houses in which famous men or women have lived, and sometimes on houses occupying the same site. For many years the Society of Arts undertook the task, on a rather vague system of selection, and placed some thirty-five tablets on houses and buildings, mostly in Inner London. In 1901 the Society of Arts handed over the duty to the London County Council, and the first ceremony was undertaken by Lord Rosebery, at the house on Campden Hill which was the last home of Lord Macaulay. Since then the Council has thus distinguished forty-five more houses in all, the homes of statesmen, writers, men of science, painters, musicians and actors. Mr. E. V. Lucas, in the last of his delightful London books, *London Revisited*, has talked so fully and so pleasantly of these memorials that nothing is left to be said of them; but those who wish to follow the expression of the London spirit through the course of years may concentrate a moment's attention on three or four of those who have been Londoners above everything, and to whom London owes most.

As regards its material aspect, Sir Christopher Wren, of course, stands alone. If the river were still the main London highway, Sir Christopher's work would not be the most prominent feature, for between Lambeth Palace and the Tower the eye would dwell on the Houses of Parliament, and at all events with unalloyed admiration on the Victoria Tower; it would pass admiringly by

Norman Shaw's fine fortress at Scotland Yard; and it would rest with complete satisfaction on the river front of Somerset House. But everywhere else, eastward, Wren is supreme, and, apart from his mighty dome, people hardly realize how completely the view of London from any elevation depends upon his towers and spires and on a few of those built by his pupils. And, of course, the most famous of all London's lost opportunities is displayed in the great plan for its reconstruction after the Fire, from the cost of which even the cheerful age of the Restoration was bound to shrink.

Sir Christopher was not a Londoner born, for he came from Wiltshire, but he was a Westminster boy, and was distinguished in many intellectual directions as a man of science before he found fame as an architect. It is here, of course, that he is immortal, above all for his work in London; but he was something of an Admirable Crichton in many ways, and did not disdain to represent three constituencies in Parliament. His memory as a great Londoner stands alone in his own sphere; but I pass on to name three great writers, Johnson, Lamb and Dickens, who seem to me, in their very different ways, to have expressed the spirit and genius of London more completely than any others. It is a flattering reflection for the great city that all three, though absolutely unlike, were, as was Sir Christopher Wren, people of the highest probity and of delightful personality. All three enjoyed the devotion of countless friends, and intimacy with any of them was a high privilege. All three, at some time of their lives, knew the deepest depths of trouble and must have been tempted to despair. All three faced fate with the manliest courage, and often with humour whose freshness the passage of years has not abated. Nobody who reads the story of their lives, of which it would be impertinent to repeat even the outlines here, can ignore Dr. Johnson's continual good-humoured, dawdling and disorderly acceptance of poverty, discomfort and bad health, accompanied by "no passion for clean linen"; or Charles Lamb's noble serenity and devotion after his appalling family tragedy of 1796; or the unforgettable tale of Dickens's boyhood and the blacking warehouse near Hungerford Market. With Johnson we live in close contact with many of the brightest figures of the second half of the eighteenth century. Reflected in Boswell's undimmed mirror, and lit up by his unequalled zest for every form of enjoyable life, Gibbon, Garrick, Sir Joshua

Reynolds, Goldsmith, Burke and Thurlow step into the easiest intimacy with our humble selves; and the smaller figures of Bennet Langton, the polite and peaceful gentleman, and of Topham Beauclerk, the ironical dandy, become equally familiar in our circle of acquaintance.

Charles Lamb was a Londoner of Londoners, born in the Temple and a Christ's Hospital boy. In middle life he wrote of "London, whose dirtiest, drab-frequented alley, and her lowest-bowing tradesman, I would not exchange for Skiddaw, Helvellyn and the rest." But his typical London figures are not historical like Johnson's circle, and their charm often depends on the kindly humour and art of their delineator. Some of them, indeed, are real people and sufficiently well known. "Some of the Old Actors" were famous, and some of the "Old Benchers of the Inner Temple," though now only remembered in these pages, did their work and made their fortunes in the sight of all men. But most of the portraits inhabit the borderland between fiction and fact, in the vanished rooms of the South Sea House and the India House, in quiet parlours and second-hand bookshops, some under thinly assumed names, others in real names that have long passed from recollection.

Thus Johnson's London is crowded with real people with real names; Lamb's London is on the debatable ground between fiction and fact; while the inhabitants of Dickens's London are the offspring of pure imagination, but remain as authentically real as the cleanest-cut figures in history. None of the company at The Club or at Mrs. Thrale's exist more vividly than do Sam Weller, Micawber and Mrs. Gamp. Bob Sawyer's *ménage* at Lant Street in the Borough, the Marchioness's care of Dick Swiveller, the flight of Bill Sikes, Mr. Tulkinghorn's chambers, the waterside scenes in *Our Mutual Friend*, the atmosphere of Doctors' Commons, and the dwellers in half a dozen boarding houses are as genuine relics of London eighty years ago as any which can be established in the dullest book of reference.

Here one might well stop with the tale of the giants; but the love of London, fortified by the deeper knowledge of its history acquired through affectionate research, has persisted and still persists among men of lower stature than those. Sir Walter Besant has a place of his own as a not inconsiderable writer of fiction; but his name will live longest as a devotee of London. His boyhood at Stockwell College, when his holidays were given up to excursions in the City, and his days at King's College led up to the two famous London stories, *All Sorts and Conditions of Men* and *Children of Gibeon.* Everybody knows, or ought to know, that the "Palace of Delight" of the first of these stories became the People's Palace in Mile End Road, the outcome of a fund of £75,000, added to the Drapers' Company's gift of £20,000 for the Technical School, which has blossomed into the East London College. Politicians know that they can count on one hand speeches that have averted a hostile division; and novels that have swept away abuses or induced reforms are equally rare. Sir Walter Besant's book can join the select company of *Oliver Twist* and *Bleak House,* of *Uncle Tom's Cabin* and of *It is Never Too Late to Mend.*

Sir Walter Besant died in 1901, and contemporary with many of his later years was a man far less known to the public at large, but his equal as a lover of London, Sir Lawrence Gomme. He was Clerk to the London County Council, and to his credit must be placed the admirable records of Old London which from the first linked up the new municipal creation with the ancient traditions of the county area. The publications of the Council attest this, and I believe that to Sir Lawrence, among many other services, are due a revival of the old name of *Aldwych,* and the happy adaptation of the general term *Kingsway* as the title of a great arterial street.

Lastly, I cannot refrain from mentioning once more the name of Mr. E. V. Lucas, the sympathetic biographer of Charles Lamb, who in his reminders of London traditions and his resuscitation of noble London ghosts combines most of the merits belonging to the writers that I have already cited.

My purpose in this article has been to plead for understanding of the London of the past as a help to knowledge of what is needed for the London of the future. When the rehousing of London is discussed, it is amusing to reflect on the figure of Ben Jonson, with a bricklayer's trowel in one hand and a book in the other—a form of "ca' canny" which the most austere employer ought to condone. When we ponder over the problem of London smoke, it is interesting to be reminded that, in Charles II's reign, John

Evelyn was responsible for a Bill dealing with smoky chimneys, adding that the "nuisance could only be reformed by moving several trades which are the cause of it," though Garden Cities were undreamt of; and that a hundred years later, when Franklin came as Agent to the General Assembly of Pennsylvania, he spoke of London as "one great smoaky house," and complained that the air was full of floating sea-coal soot, so that pure breathing could only be got by riding some miles into the country.

It is the conclusion of the whole matter that in designing great London improvements we ought to revere, and so far as possible to conserve, what is left of the London of the past. To ensure this has been the aim of The London Society since its foundation, and other agencies, such as the London Topographical Society, with its valuable volumes of illustrated records and carefully chosen reproductions, and the London Survey Committee, with their series of important monographs, have contributed excellently to the same object.

It is supremely important also to remember that where funds are limited—and for a long time they will be limited—it is wise to embark on no piecemeal changes which can hamper, or even forbid, improvements on a great scale which our wise forefathers would have welcomed, such as the building of a free and splendid bridge at Charing Cross. In the reorganization of London we cannot stand still, and we ought not to stand still; but we can advance with reverence and see to it that the immemorial spirit of London does not suffer amid the rush and stress of our modern life.

INDEX

INDEX

INDEX

Spotted something that isn't quite right?

Let us know and we'll fix it for future reprints. And as a thank you for your diligence, we'll send you a free Sothis book of your choice.

publisher@sothis.press

This page intentionally left blank

Except of course for that line above. And this one.
And whilst we have your attention, perhaps you'd
like to follow us on Instagram @sothis.press. Go on.

Made in the USA
Monee, IL
08 November 2026

67812155R00208